Finnish Summer Houses

Finnish Summer Houses

JARI & SIRKKALIISA JETSONEN

Princeton Architectural Press, New York

Published by
Princeton Architectural Press
37 East Seventh Street, New York, NY 10003

For a free catalog of books, call 1.800.722.6657.
Visit our website at www.papress.com.

© 2008 Princeton Architectural Press
All rights reserved
Printed and bound in China
11 10 09 08 4 3 2 1 First edition

No part of this book may be used or reproduced in any manner without written permission from the publisher, except in the context of reviews.

Every reasonable attempt has been made to identify owners of copyright. Errors or omissions will be corrected in subsequent editions.

Text: Sirkkaliisa Jetsonen
Photography: Jari Jetsonen
Translation from the Finnish: Gareth Griffiths, Jüri Kokkonen

Editor: Nicola Bednarek
Design: Paul Wagner

Special thanks to: Nettie Aljian, Sara Bader, Dorothy Ball, Janet Behning, Becca Casbon, Penny (Yuen Pik) Chu, Russell Fernandez, Pete Fitzpatrick, Wendy Fuller, Jan Haux, Clare Jacobson, Aileen Kwun, Nancy Eklund Later, Linda Lee, Laurie Manfra, Katharine Myers, Lauren Nelson Packard, Jennifer Thompson, Arnoud Verhaeghe, Joseph Weston, and Deb Wood of Princeton Architectural Press
—Kevin C. Lippert, publisher

Library of Congress Cataloging-in-Publication Data
Jetsonen, Jari, 1958–
Finnish summer houses / Jari and Sirkkaliisa Jetsonen.
    p.   cm.
Includes bibliographical references.
ISBN 978-1-56898-752-1 (alk. paper)
1. Vacation homes—Finland. 2. Cottages—Finland.
I. Jetsonen, Sirkkaliisa. II. Title.
NA7579.F5J48 2008
728.7'2094897—dc22
                        2007037738

Contents

- 8   Acknowledgments
- 9   Foreword
- 10   Introduction
- 18   Map of Area

- 20   **Lasses Villa, 1895** Lars Sonck
- 28   **Villa Pulkanranta, 1900–1901** Eliel Saarinen
- 38   **Villa Oivala, 1924** Oiva Kallio
- 48   **Villa Flora, 1926** Aino Aalto
- 54   **Villa Huttunen, 1937–38** Erkki Huttunen
- 64   **The Blue House (La Maison Bleue), 1938–39** J. S. Sirén
- 72   **Villa Silla, 1947** Kaj Englund
- 80   **Muuratsalo Experimental House, 1952–54** Alvar Aalto
- 92   **Summer Villa, 1955** Bertel Saarnio
- 102   **Villa Skata, 1953–55, 1962–67** Heikki and Mirja Castrén
- 108   **The Pulkkinen Cabin, 1967** Mikko Pulkkinen
- 116   **Lingonsö Holiday Island, 1966–69** Kaija and Heikki Siren
- 124   **Ruusuvuori Cabin and Sauna, 1968** Aarno Ruusuvuori
- 130   **The Ilonen Cabin, 1970** Pirkko and Arvi Ilonen
- 138   **Two Saunas, 1985** Reima and Raili Pietilä
- 144   **Weekend Atelier, 1991–92** Juha Kaakko, Ilkka Laine, Kimmo Liimatainen, and Jari Tirkkonen
- 150   **Villa Sara, 1994** Pekka Pitkänen
- 158   **Summer Cabin, 1991–95** Juhani Pallasmaa
- 164   **Holiday Home, 1996** Kristian Gullichsen
- 172   **Villa Aulikki, 1986–1994, 1995–2003** Erkki Kairamo and Aulikki Jylhä

- 182   **The Architects: Selected Works**
- 190   **Selected Bibliography**
- 192   **Illustration Credits**

Acknowledgments

We are grateful to all those whose generous contributions have made this book possible. Special thanks go to the Greta and William Lehtinen Foundation and the National Council for Architecture for their support of the research and preparation of this book. We are grateful to Nicola Bednarek, our editor at Princeton Architectural Press, for having faith in this project.

We would like to thank the students of the Tulane University School of Architecture, New Orleans, who enthusiastically documented the houses presented in this book and made new measured drawings and scale models. Their work has been particularly invaluable in those cases where the original architect's drawings no longer exist. Big thanks also go to their American teachers, who were with us in Finland during the summers from 2003 to 2006: Professor Pia Sarpaneva, from the University of Arkansas, Professor Scott Wall, from the University of Tennessee, and Professor Bradley Bell, from the University of Texas in Arlington. Many of the students' drawings were lost during Hurricane Katrina in August 2005. Sadly, the material was never recovered, but the remaining drawings have been returned to Finland after many adventures around the States.

The greatest thanks, however, go to the owners of the summer villas, the architects and their relatives who, between 2000 and 2006, allowed us into their private homes to take photographs and who assisted us in finding archival images and illustrations: Jan-Olof Stengård, Martti Saarinen, Tuula Paalimäki of the Finnish Association of Architects, Maila and Hamilkar Aalto, Ari Huttunen, Marko Huttunen, Terike Haapoja, Hannu Siren, Jukka Siren, Leif Englund, Markku Lahti at the Alvar Aalto Museum, Ulla Kapari, Timo Saarnio, Mirja Castrén, Hannele Castrén, Matti Linko, Mikko Pulkkinen, Heikki Siren, Kirsi Aropaltio, Anna Jäämeri-Ruusuvuori, Timo Ruusuvuori, Pirkko and Arvi Ilonen, Raili Pietilä, Kimmo Liimatainen, Ilkka Laine, Juha Kaakko, Jari Tirkkonen, Helena and Pekka Pitkänen, Hannele Jäämeri, Juhani Pallasmaa, Kristian Gullichsen, and Aulikki Jylhä.

We would also like to thank the Alvar Aalto Museum and its staff, Katariina Pakoma, Maija Holma, and Risto Raittila; and the Archive of the Museum of Finnish Architecture and its staff, Timo Keinänen, Petteri Kummala, and Elina Standertskjöld, who all provided generous help with finding drawings and photographs in their archives.

    Sirkkaliisa and Jari Jetsonen
    Helsinki, May 28, 2007

Foreword

The northern way of life is strongly tied to nature and the changing seasons of the year. The short and intensive Scandinavian summer allows people to be more unencumbered than usual. For Finns, the ideal way of spending these months is at one's own cottage and sauna amidst nature, by the shore of a lake. The summer villas that Finnish architects have designed for themselves over the course of the centuries are rooted in the same basic traditions of the Finnish lifestyle. As Alvar Aalto once said, a home must not be a design exhibition. Even when imperfect it should primarily be a safe haven where one can relax and live in accordance with nature.

When designing a summer residence for themselves, architects function as clients and designers at the same time. Their concerns here are not only professional but personal, and the final result may thus come as a surprise to its designer. Nevertheless, the summer houses included in this book mostly resemble their architects. They can be compared to the diaries or unpublished writings of an author or a poet. It is in these works that architects are usually at their most exposed and most sensitive.

Due to the personal nature of these designs, becoming acquainted with and documenting them required more than the usual time, effort, and tact from the authors. Interviewing the owners and measuring, drawing, and photographing the summer villas, Sirkkaliisa and Jari Jetsonen gained deep insight into the nature of the Finnish summer house. Their personal contacts with the owners often developed into deep friendships, bringing additional warmth to the book. Indeed, the photographs, drawings, and texts presented here not only convey the architecture of the buildings and the personality of their inhabitants but also present vignettes of life. Reflected in them are peace and harmony, so typical for life in a Finnish summer house, but values that are ever rarer in a globalizing world. In the words of the Finnish poet Lauri Viita:

Ei pidetä kiirettä, istutaan.	Let's not hurry, let's sit.
Ei hätäillä, annetaan mennä;	Let's not panic, let's take it easy,
ei maata somemmin ainoakaan satelliitti lennä.	no satellite flies sweeter than our planet.

Severi Blomstedt
Director, Museum of Finnish Architecture
Helsinki, August 2007

Introduction

The Tradition of Summer Homes and the Finnish Lifestyle

For some 150 years summer villas have been an important part of the Finnish lifestyle. The first ones were located near towns and cities, while later summer cottages were built in the countryside on the shores of lakes and by the seaside. For a few months of the year, they provide their users with the experience of living near nature. During the early period of the villa culture in the late nineteenth century until the 1930s, the whole family would move to the countryside during the summer months to live, sometimes even to till the land. In the early twentieth century, people traveled to their villas by train, steamboats, or horse-drawn carriages. The spread of automobiles made the summer home more accessible, while decreasing the time spent there. As early as in the 1920s and 1930s houses were marketed as weekend cottages, although it was not until the 1960s, with increased use of private cars, that people were able to spend such short periods at their summer homes.

During the nineteenth century, summer residences were an upper-class pastime. The era's tendency toward romanticism and yearning for a different time or place, or a different culture, found its expression in Italian-influenced villas or Swiss hunting chalets. Toward the close of the century, English villas were forerunners in many respects. Industrial cities engendered villa communities with gardens in their environs as an alternative to cramped and unhygienic conditions. The interiors of these villas provided the opportunity to seek alternatives to the more formal representation of city dwelling. Architects such as M. H. Baillie Scott (1865–1945) and Charles Voysey (1857–1941), a prominent proponent of the arts and crafts movement, among others, began to design space from the inside out and to underscore the importance of light, siting, and healthy living conditions. Their works became examples for Finnish architects, who closely followed English arts and crafts magazines such as the *Studio* and adapted these new design ideals in their own works.

Villa life during that time was marked by a bourgeois lifestyle; servants took care of the daily chores while the villa owners enjoyed leisure activities such as gardening, reading, and peaceful walks. Many artists also had their own summer homes, which provided the opportunity to withdraw to the wilderness from the bustle of the city and to work in peace. Their residences pointed the way for a new national-romantic villa design. From the 1910s onward, owners of summer houses sought a new kind of comfort and homelike atmosphere in their cottages, and numerous villa design competitions were held around this time. The summer cottage culture of the second half of the twentieth century, in turn, marks a more prominent return to nature and conditions that are generally more primitive than in city dwellings. The disappearance of servants and the smaller size of summer homes proceeded apace with the growing number of middle-class owners of summer cottages.

The tradition of the summer home has often included a return to experiencing the pioneer spirit. In the early villas this remained a distant allusion. Beginning in the 1910s, old farmhouses served as an example, and architects sought inspiration in the unassuming crafts of the countryside and the folk spirit. Being close to nature and healthy modes of habitation became important objectives. The folk aspect has remained one of the main undercurrents defining the model of the Finnish summer home today.

In Finland, life is dictated by the seasons; summer holds the promise of leisure time and, in a sense, of liberation from the community—from school or work. People construct dreams for the summer—often a cottage built with their own hands. The summer home still has an important place in Finnish culture. It is there that people spend their leisure time, where they withdraw to calm down and work, and where they can experience a return to nature for a few months every year.

The Summer House, the Experimental House

Many architects who design their own villas or cottages view these buildings not only as summer residences, but as testing grounds for new ideas or the crystallization of concepts and theories. Without the limitations or budget imposed by an outside client, architects can realize their own ideals and objectives. In their summer homes minimalist habitation and the relationship with nature are recurrent themes, but contemporary design projects also leave their mark, and summer houses are sometimes prototypes for the architects' larger projects or reminiscent of earlier work. The summer villas can thus be regarded as experimental houses that provide the opportunity for the architect to study a technical or functional aspect in concrete terms or to develop spatial ideas.

Some of the works presented in this book were built when the architects were still students, while others are syntheses from the course of a long career. Although the architectural trends of different decades are evident, a sense of timelessness that derives from the presence of nature and the simplicity and simplification of building is markedly present in most of the designs. Architectural ideals and everyday life come together in an interesting and fruitful manner. The summer house is important for its designer, and many architects regard it as their most significant work. Lars Sonck once said: "There is only one thing that I do not regret as an architect, and that is my villa."[1] The architect Bertel Saarnio, in turn, called his summer residence his "dream house."[2]

The summer houses are of a highly personal nature, giving a glimpse into the private lives of their designers. They are almost like portraits of the architects and can be read like diary entries. All of the houses in this book are the realizations of dreams, and most of them are still used by the architects or the families of their children.

Vernacular and Mediterranean Inspirations

Many summer homes of the early twentieth century and, perhaps surprisingly, of the 1950s and 1960s look back to classical and vernacular examples. The courtyard, for instance, is an archetypal spatial element that has been popular in summer villas. In keeping with the spirit of the times, there was also a "return" to log construction at the beginning of the century, which lies at the core of the Finnish building heritage. Logs later became established as a popular material for summer cottages.

The villas by Lars Sonck, particularly those designed around the turn of the century, combined elements of the Karelian farmhouse with features of Swiss and Norwegian wood architecture, which were all characterized by their impressive forms as well as ornamental details. The Karelian region of Finland borders Russia to the East, and its folklore, language,

Lars Sonck designed Ainola for the family of composer Jean Sibelius in Tuusula, 1904

Oiva and Kauno S. Kallio, SOK headquarters, Helsinki, 1919–21

Alvar Aalto, Säynätsalo Town Hall, Säynätsalo, 1950–52

and architecture were in the center of the Finns' interest during the nineteenth century, representing a kind of "pure" Finnish culture. Karelian farmhouses have roots in Russian vernacular architecture. They typically have an exposed log structure and decorative details, especially around windows and along the eaves. As all functions of the household were under one roof, the volume of the house was massive and impressive. Both Sonck's small- and large-scale works are dominated by the plasticity and three-dimensionality of grouped volumes, and materials such as timber, brick, and masonry play an important role. Fellow architect J. S. Sirén once described him as the master and succinct dramaturge of grey granite and tarred timber. Sonck skillfully developed the character of his buildings from the landscape in a monumental yet nuanced expression. He designed numerous log houses at the end of the nineteenth and beginning of the twentieth century (the last one in the 1940s), for which his own summer residence, Lasses Villa (1895), served as a prototype. His wooden buildings had a warm, homey atmosphere, and there is a similar monumentality and richness in the summer cottages as in his larger buildings.

The 1920s were marked by Nordic classicism, which interpreted the heritage of Mediterranean architecture and urban culture in a creative manner, applying it to the climate and conditions of the north. Examples were atrium courtyard villas with their intermediary forms of exterior and interior space. Courtyard villas have appeared in different forms throughout the twentieth century. Villa Oivala (1924) by Oiva Kallio, Alvar Aalto's Experimental House at Muuratsalo (1952–54), and Villa Sara (1994) by Pekka Pitkänen present variations of this theme. Drawing both on the classic Mediterranean courtyard and the closed yard of traditional Finnish farmhouses, Villa Oivala is a fine example of how influences were combined. This personal project also reflects Kallio's experiences of various environments during his childhood.

Kallio is known as an architect for banks and insurance companies; he was also influential in reviving the culture of the Finnish sauna bath. The works of Oiva Kallio and his brother Kauno S. Kallio represent a blend of solemnity and practical considerations. A classical undertone is visible throughout their œuvre. The head office of the SOK Cooperative (1919–21) designed by Oiva and Kauno S. Kallio is a building of castle-like solidity. The main series of interior spaces culminates in a glass-roofed exhibition room, whose courtyard mood is enhanced by a design that resembles an outdoor space. The large central hall forms the heart of the building, just as the courtyard is the center of Kallio's summer house.

Alvar Aalto, in turn, varied and adapted his sources of inspiration throughout his career. He experimented with interspersed interior and exterior spaces, interlocking rooms, and variations of enclosure in different contexts and scales. Both the Muuratsalo Experimental House and the Säynätsalo Town Hall (1950–52) enclose in their cores a spatial and mental central point. At Säynätsalo, the central courtyard, raised higher than its surroundings, creates an intimate private mood. The exteriors of both buildings, emphasized with brick walls, are closed and monumental in nature. The use of red brick, one of Aalto's favorite materials in the 1950s, references the urban culture of Siena and Tuscany, and the cradle of the Renaissance, which he admired. Aalto regarded brick as a flexible material that represented both "biological elasticity" and permanence. In the Muuratsalo house, he adapted classical themes and created cultural references that also play a role in the design of the Säynätsalo Town Hall.

The features and principles of vernacular buildings, perfected over the course of centuries, also provided a natural point of departure for the design of summer homes. In the design of Villa Skata (1953–55, 1962–67) by Heikki and Mirja Castrén and the buildings on Lingonsö Holiday Island (1966–69) by Kaija and Heikki Siren, history is not manifest as an isolated selection of formal motifs, but rather in the use of time-proven principles, though with a modern approach.

Herman Gesellius, Armas Lindgren, and Eliel Saarinen, Hvitträsk, Kirkkonummi, Atelier House, 1902–03

Alvar and Aino Aalto, Villa Mairea, Noormarkku, 1938–39

Laiho-Pulkkinen-Raunio Architects, Turku Arts Academy, Turku, 1993–97

Themes of Habitation

A summer house can also be a natural testing ground for different ways of living. Unlike a permanent or year-round home, it is not bound by the same requirements of everyday life. It offers change, a less formal atmosphere, and closer contact with nature. Summer villas provide a release from the bounds of representation, and short-term residence permits more primitive solutions, involving various kinds of minimalist habitation.

Designed by Eliel Saarinen for his parents, Villa Pulkanranta's (1900–1901) focal point is a shared space, a version of the *tupa* or main room of the traditional farmhouse, where the family came together and daily chores were performed. The location of other rooms at different levels offered peace and quiet and organized the Pulkanranta house spatially. Though the villa is the work of a young architect, Saarinen had already designed several works with Herman Gesellius and Armas Lindgren. Their joint Atelier House (1902–03) in Hvitträsk replicates some of the features of Pulkanranta in a more varied way: the spatial multi-layeredness, the gable motifs of the exterior, and the strong roof shapes. In the gable end of his own residential wing Saarinen used a similar shingle siding as on Villa Pulkanranta. And just as in his parents' summer house, the main room at Hvitträsk was a place bringing together members of the household and guests alike.

For female architects themes of habitation and the design of homes have been an important field. Aino Aalto's (neé Marsio) architectural career was much involved with the design of interiors and furniture, especially in connection with her work for the Artek company, founded by Alvar Aalto and Aino Aalto, Maire Gullichsen, and Nils-Gustav Hahl. Aino Aalto's objective was to create comfortable spaces and a domestic atmosphere. She was able to realize these aims both in Villa Flora's (1926) modest earthiness and in Villa Mairea's (1938–39) refined elegance.

Architects started investigating the concept of the minimum dwelling before World War I, and related research benefited both workers' residences and houses for leisure use. During the pioneering stages of modern architecture, the minimum dwelling became a central theme. It was also one that Kaj Englund explicitly studied in his summer home, Villa Silla (1947). Englund's practice focused on residential design, and it was only natural that in his own house he would apply the efficient use of space characteristic of his other projects, while seeking to add nuances to it by opening up changing views and other features. Aarno Ruusuvuori, on the other hand, regarded the minimum dwelling as the reinterpretation of tradition and drew upon vernacular examples for his summer cabin (1968), which resembles a row of storehouses—an entity formed by separate rooms.

In many villas efficient use of space and a wide range of uses are intermixed. Examples include the Weekend Atelier (1991–92) by Juha Kaakko, Ilkka Laine, Kimmo Liimatainen, and Jari Tirkkonen; Juhani Pallasmaa's Summer Cabin (1991–95); and the cottage of Pirkko and Arvi Ilonen (1970). In these houses, most of the activities share a space and only those that require peace or privacy are confined to their own small rooms. Small cellular spaces that can be enlarged or added if necessary are another perspective on habitation. Villa Skata by Heikki and Mirja Castrén is a good example of a whole gradually created in this way.

Structure in the Leading Role

In some villas structure or structural details are the leading idea behind the design. The plywood walls and steel supports of Mikko Pulkkinen's cabin (1967) are a bold experiment in the severe climatic conditions of the Finnish archipelago. At the time he designed the cottage, Pulkkinen was still an architecture student, and his early interest in the possibilities of expressing building structures continued in his later works. His design for the Turku Arts Academy (1993–97), situated in old machine workshop halls, combines structural clarity and graceful elegance.

Erkki Kairamo, Hanikka House, Espoo, 1970

Alvar Aalto in turn combined technology and artistic expression in the brick collage of the courtyard of his Muuratsalo Experimental House, while the steel frame of Pirkko and Arvi Ilonen's cottage represents the interest of the 1960s in experimenting with and developing quickly assembled structural solutions using manufactured parts.

At the core of Erkki Kairamo's buildings is a dynamic and poetic expression of structure, or, as architect Kirmo Mikkola called it, a lyrical and expressive constructivism, variations of which can be seen throughout his entire career, from the Hanikka houses built at the beginning of the 1970s to his last design, Villa Aulikki (1986–94, 1995–2003). Industrial projects were an important part of Kairamo's work, and his use of a highly rationalist framework, to which he added components in order to create poetry, is manifest even in his residential projects, such as the single-family houses at Hanikka near Helsinki. Kairamo's designs start with a distinct and simple leading idea and combine pure form and structural lyricism. In his works, dynamic lines dictate the possibilities of architecture and generate forms. Film also had a great influence on Kairamo, which is expressed in the importance of rhythm in his houses.

The simple wooden frame of Juha Kaakko, Ilkka Laine, Kimmo Liimatainen, and Jari Tirkkonen's Weekend Atelier at Puolarmaari is left exposed on the interior. The plastic sheeting covering the ceiling and walls of the studio is like a membrane around the building. This feature as well as the joints that are fastened with tape are representative of the architects' experimental approach to structural solutions.

A Place Amidst Nature

The Finnish landscape is characterized by small features. Tall peaks and broad vistas are lacking, while the mixture of small lakes and forests gives the landscape its typical continuity. The forest has always been an important source of livelihood for the Finns, from hunting and slash-and-burn-clearing to the processing of wood. The forest is respected and has a special place in the Finnish mental landscape, literature, and art. This relationship with the woods is marked by dependence and identification—the forest is a symbol of individuality and freedom. Even today it offers a place for silence and solitude. The outdoors in general are still an important part of spending leisure time in Finland. The varying rhythm of the woods and nature and their complex forms are the background of the Finns' conception of space. The landscape is seen between the trunks of trees, and continuity and indefinability are reflected in its expansiveness. The forest is an essential part of the lacustrine landscape, while the horizon opening up at the seashore offers a more open and freer view.

The seasons are an integral part of Finnish nature and its experience. For most of the year, the deciduous trees have no leaves and the dark greenery of conifers predominates. The abundant light of summer alternates with the sometimes severe darkness of winter. The horizontality and clarity of the northern light illuminate the landscape and its buildings in a different manner than the bright sunshine of the south. Dusk is long and soft. In the summer, the sun gradually sinks beneath the horizon—that is the right moment to sit quietly on the jetty of your summer cottage.

The summer villa has an obviously close relationship with nature. Most summer houses are situated in the untouched natural landscape apart from other development and preferably from each other as well. The only exceptions among the examples in this book are the cabins in the Kiljava vacation area by Kaj Englund and Pirkko and Arvi Ilonen.

Summer houses are often situated to capture views and to make the most of the warm, sunny days. On the other hand, the capricious weather of the short Finnish summer also leads to the desire to shut nature out of the building and to take shelter from wind, rain, and storms. Enclosed courtyards or the siting of buildings to shield against the wind are an excellent solution. At Villa Oivala, the Muuratsalo Experimental House, and Villa Sara the courtyards provide the first warm spaces in early summer and are the last places to capture the autumn sun. They offer residents the comforts of being inside while enjoying the fresh air and sunshine of the outdoors. As the designs of the houses on Lingonsö Island and Villa Skata show, a separate group of small buildings can also shield against the winds and open up toward the sun.

In the summer cottages the walls are the only boundary between nature and the interior. With its glass wall that can be opened, Kristian Gullichsen's Holiday Home (1996) appears to breathe, opening and closing. Being inside the house is like being outside, just as on Villa Oivala's semi-open terrace. In Kaija and Heikki Siren's sea pavilion only a thin membrane of glass separates those inside from the surrounding landscape. In their chapel for the Otaniemi campus (1953–57), the architects brought the landscape into the interior as the glass wall of the altar opens to a forest view. Kaija and Heikki Siren's works of the 1950s and 1960s capture the essential, relying on a distinct and solid use of structure and materials. Brick and wood appear repeatedly in many projects, and there is an unforced dialogue between the landscape and the buildings. Broad views give room for thought, and delimited exterior spaces create a sense of security. The controlled clarity of form in their works is reminiscent of classicism.

Views of the surroundings from the interior of houses may open up as broad panoramas or as selected views. Architects can thus frame the landscape in a deliberate way. Villa Silla, the Muuratsalo Experimental House, and Pallasmaa's Summer Cabin are impressive examples of how the landscape can become an integral part of the interior. Pallasmaa treats the landscape as a meditative element; in his philosophical discussions of the nature of architecture, he often refers to the importance of touch, perception, and remembering.

The works of Reima and Raili Pietilä are strongly original, drawing their inspiration from nature and the landscape in general as well the site of specific buildings. Their houses take root in their locations and seem to grow from them; they are attached to the specific rhythm of the place and its materials or colors. They have a life of their own, as it were. The Dipoli Student Union Building (1961–66) at the Helsinki University of Technology dynamically grows out of its site. Large boulders form the base of the building, tying it to the surrounding grounds. Though made of concrete, the wall surfaces mimic the scale and texture of logs or wood boards, giving the building its unique rhythm. The two saunas (1985) in Tenhola show a similar connection to place.

Kaija and Heikki Siren, Otaniemi Chapel, Espoo, 1953–57

Reima and Raili Pietilä, Dipoli Student Union Building, Espoo, 1961–66

Kristian Gullichsen, La Petite Maison, Grasse, France, 1972

J. S. Sirén, Finnish Parliament House, Helsinki, 1924–31

Bertel Saarnio and Juha Leiviskä, Kouvola Town Hall, Kouvola, 1968

Pekka Pitkänen, Chapel of the Holy Cross, Turku, 1965–67

Kristian Gullichsen combines elements of the site with general themes of architectural expression. He explicitly recycles various sources, with a focus on an architectural language of form compiled from modernism and the European architectural heritage. His buildings are contextual and ambiguous, containing messages in the guise of form. In his large public buildings cultural themes and references usually predominate, while his smaller and personal projects underscore the significance of place. The archetype of vernacular building is the shelter, the place that defines the boundaries of interior and exterior, relying on materials and colors from the nearby surroundings. The holiday residence Gullichsen designed for his mother in France, called La Petite Maison (1972), sits almost unnoticed as part of the terraces of an olive grove. The operable louvers allow the mood and character of the building to change, while the use of stone as a building material expresses locality.

Timelessness and Permanence

Some architects closely follow the spirit of the times and the various architectural trends of the international field, while the works of others have a sense of timelessness. The latter group often attempts to pass on the message of permanence through the specific nature of their designs.

J. S. Sirén's career spanned from the late 1910s to the 1950s. This long period saw a variety of architectural styles, but regardless of the decade, Sirén's works convey permanence, focusing on the clarity of classicism and careful finishes. The architect's main work is the monumental Parliament House in Helsinki (1924–31), a national symbol that expresses dignity and stability. Sirén's residential and office buildings also show a convincing dignity in both form and appearance. The same spirit prevails even in more everyday settings and buildings, with their carefully considered series of spaces and subtle symmetry. In the Blue House (1938–39) Sirén repeated the plan of the impressive spatial series of rooms in the Finnish Parliament House on a more homely scale.

Postwar architecture in Finland responded to the diversifying needs of society, while establishing a dialogue between landscape and space, and the unforced use of materials. Bertel Saarnio's works range from the 1940s to the 1960s. They express a subtle sense of scale, conveying an atmosphere of everyday dignity. His architecture is effortless and unassuming in character, and the same characteristics visible in his summer villa can be observed in the Kouvola Town Hall he designed with Juha Leiviskä (1968).

A unique subtleness and careful balance of spaces and details are typical of the works of Pekka Pitkänen. The architectural character of his Villa Sara (1994) is reminiscent of Pitkänen's design for the Chapel of the Holy Cross in Turku (1965–67). A sensitive unity results from interwoven spaces and views, which are complemented by the details.

Interpretations of Modern Perspectives

In Finland the prominent waves of twentieth-century architecture are crystallized in the functionalism of the 1930s, the modernism of the 1960s, and the pluralism of the 1990s. The perspectives entailed in these styles speak of enthusiasm, of the striving to create contrasts and order or to break down accustomed models.

Erkki Huttunen's works of the 1930s and 1940s have dynamic and vivid exteriors representing the optimistic vitality of the new architecture. In his industrial and commercial buildings the use of concrete permitted horizontal strip windows, bold protruding details, and impressive silos. But alongside these strong forms, Huttunen's designs, particularly their interiors and details, also express warmth and a sensitive touch. While the exterior is often monumental, a rich nuanced feel dominates on the inside. The main part of Huttunen's work is comprised of industrial and commercial buildings designed for the SOK Cooperative. Just as his Villa Huttunen, they convey energy and spatial continuity. This is also evident in

Erkki Huttunen, Sokos Commercial Building, Helsinki, 1938–52

Aarno Ruusuvuori, Weilin & Göös Printing Company, Espoo, 1964–66

Juha Jääskeläinen, Juha Kaakko, Petri Rouhiainen, Matti Sanaksenaho, and Jari Tirkkonen, Finnish Pavilion, Seville World Exposition, Seville, Spain, 1992

the lobby of the Hotel Vaakuna, forming part of the Sokos Commercial Building in central Helsinki.

Aarno Ruusuvuori defined order as the key to beauty. Characteristics of his architecture are clarity and extreme precision in forms, space, and details. Concrete predominates in his main works of the 1960s. His buildings appear ascetic and define distinct logical boundaries. The severity of his designs is softened by the use of contrasting colors and textures. Ruusuvuori's Weilin & Göös Printing Company in Espoo near Helsinki (1964–1966) is an impressive industrial building defined by its structural solution and expression. Now converted into a museum, this building dominates its setting in a monumental and unadorned manner.

In the early 1990s, the young generation of Finnish architects sought and expressed a new kind of abstraction in their works. They reduced buildings to forms and solids—to objects, in a sense—and effaced details illustrating scale or size. There was a tendency to condense the character of the building to volume, pure space, and simplified materials. The Finnish Pavilion at the 1992 Seville World Exposition by the office Monark: Juha Jääskeläinen, Juha Kaakko, Petri Rouhiainen, Matti Sanaksenaho, and Jari Tirkkonen, which is contemporary with Kaakko, Laine, Liimatainen, and Tirkkonen's Weekend Atelier, was an attempt to break down the form of a traditional building and to seek its abstract expression, with a focus on simplified structure and materials.

Finnish summer houses today continue the tradition of living amidst nature. Contemporary cottages often have the same conveniences as full-time city residences, and instead of small cabins larger houses are built. The time a family stays at their summer residence might be shorter than in the past, but many cottages are now also used during the winter months. Being able to live by a lake or by the sea and to walk in the forest is still an essential part of the Finnish lifestyle.

---

1 Pekka Korvenmaa, "Lars Sonck's life," in *Lars Sonck 1870–1956 Arkkitehti, Architect*, exhibition catalogue (Helsinki: Suomen rakennustaiteen museo, 1981), 15.
2 Bertel Saarnio, written on a drawing of his summer residence, 1955.

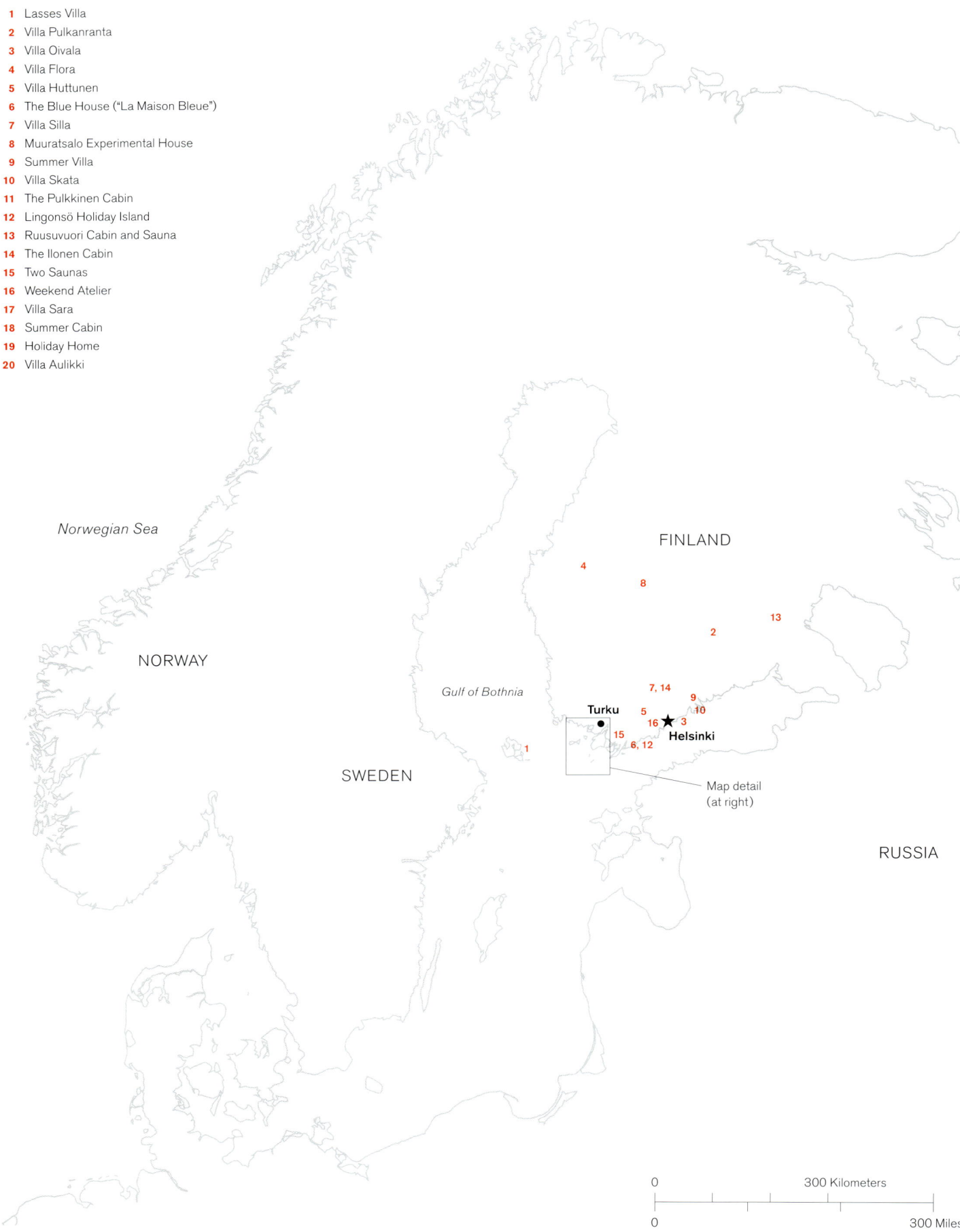

1 Lasses Villa
2 Villa Pulkanranta
3 Villa Oivala
4 Villa Flora
5 Villa Huttunen
6 The Blue House ("La Maison Bleue")
7 Villa Silla
8 Muuratsalo Experimental House
9 Summer Villa
10 Villa Skata
11 The Pulkkinen Cabin
12 Lingonsö Holiday Island
13 Ruusuvuori Cabin and Sauna
14 The Ilonen Cabin
15 Two Saunas
16 Weekend Atelier
17 Villa Sara
18 Summer Cabin
19 Holiday Home
20 Villa Aulikki

Lasses Villa

Finström, 1895
Lars Sonck

Lars Sonck was one of the most influential architects in Finland at the end of the nineteenth and beginning of the twentieth century. His generation made the new international architecture of the time an integral part of the Finnish culture and environment. Artistic expression in both arts and architecture indeed contributed significantly to the development of a Finnish national identity. It should be kept in mind, however, that these international trends, in particular art nouveau and Jugendstil, merged with themes that derived from the Finnish building tradition.

Early in his career, in 1894, Sonck won the competition for the St. Michael's Church in Turku and received the commission to carry out his winning proposal. This success enabled him, that very same year, to acquire a site and build his own summer villa in his home district of Finström on the Åland Isles. Around that time Sonck had intended to participate in a study trip to Karelia, a remote area in eastern Finland, together with his architect friends Yrjö Blomstedt and Victor Sucksdorff. This kind of trip was popular during the last decades of the nineteenth century among both artists and architects, who sought a "pure" form of Finnish culture in genuine and unadulterated landscapes, buildings, and folklore. The church project prevented Sonck from taking part in the trip, but he became well acquainted with its results, which became an important source of inspiration for the design of Lasses Villa. Other important influences were the rich forms and detailing of Swiss and Norwegian wood architecture.

Sonck's father had been the vicar in the Finström parish, and having spent part of his childhood there, the architect was familiar with the landscape. He bought a site on the western edge of a narrow bay dominated by an impressive and steep rock face and placed the building at the very edge of the precipice. Its dramatic location undoubtedly reflected the influence of his friends' experiences in Karelia, where houses were often situated by rivers or lakes and, with their impressive appearance and handsome gables, stand out in the landscape. On the forest side of the villa a rising slope demarcated a more sheltered yard area.

The character of Lasses Villa, especially its decoratively carved details, is a reflection of motifs derived from the traditional Karelian farmhouse. The gable facade, constructed of round logs, is accentuated by a balcony. From a veranda impressive views open out toward the bay. Originally, two porches framed each end of the villa, their round bulls-eye openings emphasizing the plasticity of the building. Together with the dark round logs, natural stone forms an essential part of the design and is used for both the foundation plinth and in the walls demarcating the perimeter of the yard. The long overhanging roof eaves, the ornamental ends of the cross-jointed logs, and the carved fretwork around the window frames add an exotic flavor to the building.

RIGHT
Site plan

OPPOSITE
The courtyard facade is reminiscent of a traditional Karelian farmhouse.

TOP
Lasses Villa seen from the other side of the bay, 1900

BOTTOM
Sonck on the balcony of his villa in 1905

Sonck altered and extended the villa several times over the course of his life. A fire in the building in 1951 brought about more substantial changes. In its earliest form, the facades facing the sea and the forest dominated the house. The lower kitchen wing extension enlarged the building in the direction of the slope on the rear side. In addition, a guest cabin and firewood shed were later built at the edge of the front yard. The yard itself is demarcated by a fence made of natural stone and logs. In the shelter of the forest high up on the slope, Sonck built a *ritsalen* (drawing salon), a small studio where he could sit and draw or generally work.

Sonck also designed other cottages and houses for himself, but Lasses Villa remained his most important point of reference: it was, after all, part of his home district. The architect worked on the villa intensively and shifted his office activities there during the summer. The house was always open for friends, and with his good humor and hospitality Sonck created a warm atmosphere for his guests. The importance of the building to him is best summed up in his own words: "There is only one thing that I do not regret as an architect, and that is my villa."

RIGHT
First-floor plan

BOTTOM
Lasses Villa and its dramatic setting

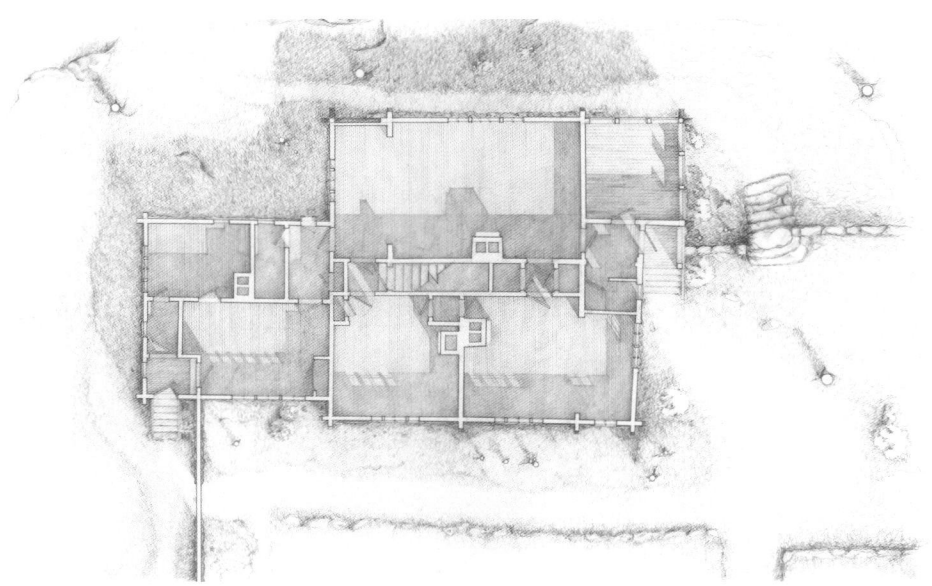

BELOW
The house seems to grow out of the steep cliffs.

OPPOSITE, TOP
Southwest facade

OPPOSITE, BOTTOM
Southwest facade

BELOW
Living room. The alcove at the end of the room was originally a porch.

OPPOSITE
Living room

Villa Pulkanranta

Mäntyharju, 1900–1901
Eliel Saarinen

Eliel Saarinen designed Villa Pulkanranta for his parents, Juho and Selma Saarinen, as a summer residence in Mäntyharju, in south Finland. Saarinen's mother was originally from this area, which is characterized by its many lakes and ridges. Another important factor in the selection of the location was the proximity of the railway, which made traveling to and from the summer home easy.

At the time the villa was being designed Saarinen was very busy. The Finnish Pavilion for the 1900 Paris World Expo was an important project for the architectural office of Herman Gesellius, Armas Lindgren, and Eliel Saarinen, and Saarinen was in Paris from the beginning of 1900 to supervise its construction. Their office also had several other extensive commissions, and Saarinen's parents were forced to wait for the final drawings for their villa. While the house was still under construction, Saarinen's mother described it in a letter to Saarinen's brother Hannes as follows: "The building looks peculiar, it is too early to say that it is beautiful, but it is unusual. I do not think that many will like it."[1]

The exterior of the villa is impressive with its log construction, painted with traditional red ochre paint, and its steep pitched roof. An open porch on the gable side faces the lake, which lies at the end of a gentle slope. On the other side of the house the landscape opens out toward fields. The immediate surroundings took on a more gardenlike form during the 1920s and 1930s, when the trees planted earlier were grown, and flowerbeds flourished. The heart of the villa is a tall living room with a pitched ceiling, an interpretation of the traditional Finnish farmhouse *tupa* (an all-purpose living space), as indicated by the unpainted log surfaces, the traditional farmhouse stove, and a bench along the wall. The other rooms of the house are located on two floors behind this open space.

Saarinen brought together both national and international features in the design of Pulkanranta. The materials and colors, such as the red-painted log walls, are reminiscent of traditional Finnish farmhouses. International elements are manifest in the small windowpanes, influenced by the English arts and crafts movement, and the Egyptian-style doorframes. The upper part of the gables is clad with shingles, suggestive of the American shingle style, although shingles were also a part of the Finnish building heritage: from the Middle Ages until the eighteenth century thick shingles were used as a roofing material for churches.

The Saarinen family would travel to Pulkanranta in the middle of May and return to the city after harvest in the middle of September. Summer life flowed easily: the piano was played and coffee was taken on the porch, but there was also a garden to tend and some farm work to do. Eliel Saarinen and his family moved to the United States in 1923 but returned each summer to Finland. During these trips Saarinen visited the villa every now and then, the last time in 1946, a few years before his death. He immortalized the view of the lake from the villa in a drawing for the country's first bank notes after Finland gained independence.

OPPOSITE
The villa seen from the lake

1 Letter to Hannes Saarinen, June 22, 1901. In *J. Kirjeitä Inkerinmaalta, Pietarista ja Suomesta* [Letters from Ingria, St. Petersburg, and Finland], ed. Pentti Voipio (Helsinki: Juho Saarisen sukutoimikunta, 1996), 42.

TOP
The villa in the summer of 1914

BOTTOM, LEFT
Painting of Villa Pulkanranta by Einar Saarinen, 1902

BOTTOM, RIGHT
Plans

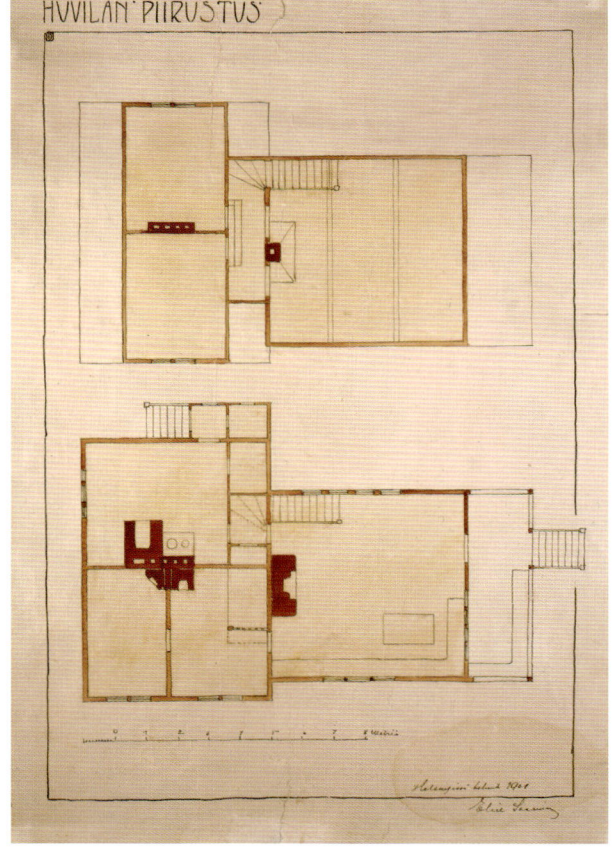

TOP
Drinking coffee in the living room, 1903. From left to right: Selma and Juho Saarinen, Einar, Siviä, Alma, and Siiri Saarinen.

BOTTOM, LEFT
Sections

BOTTOM, RIGHT
Facade drawings

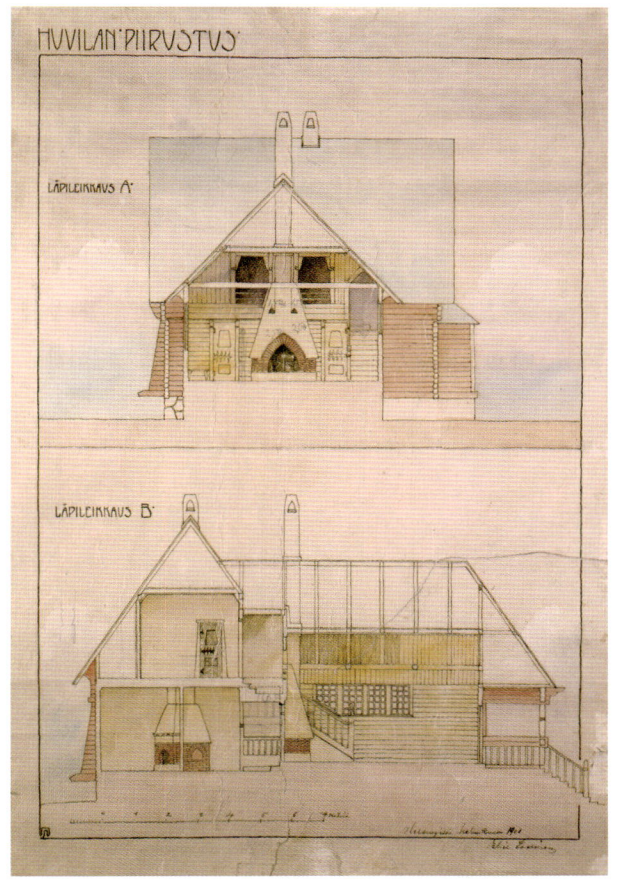

BELOW
The volume of the villa is divided into two parts with steep, pitched roofs.

OPPOSITE
Pulkanranta in the lush greenery of Mäntyharju

RIGHT
Drawings on the living room wall

BOTTOM
The sofa and chairs on the right were designed by Armas Lindgren.

OPPOSITE
The open porch faces the lake.

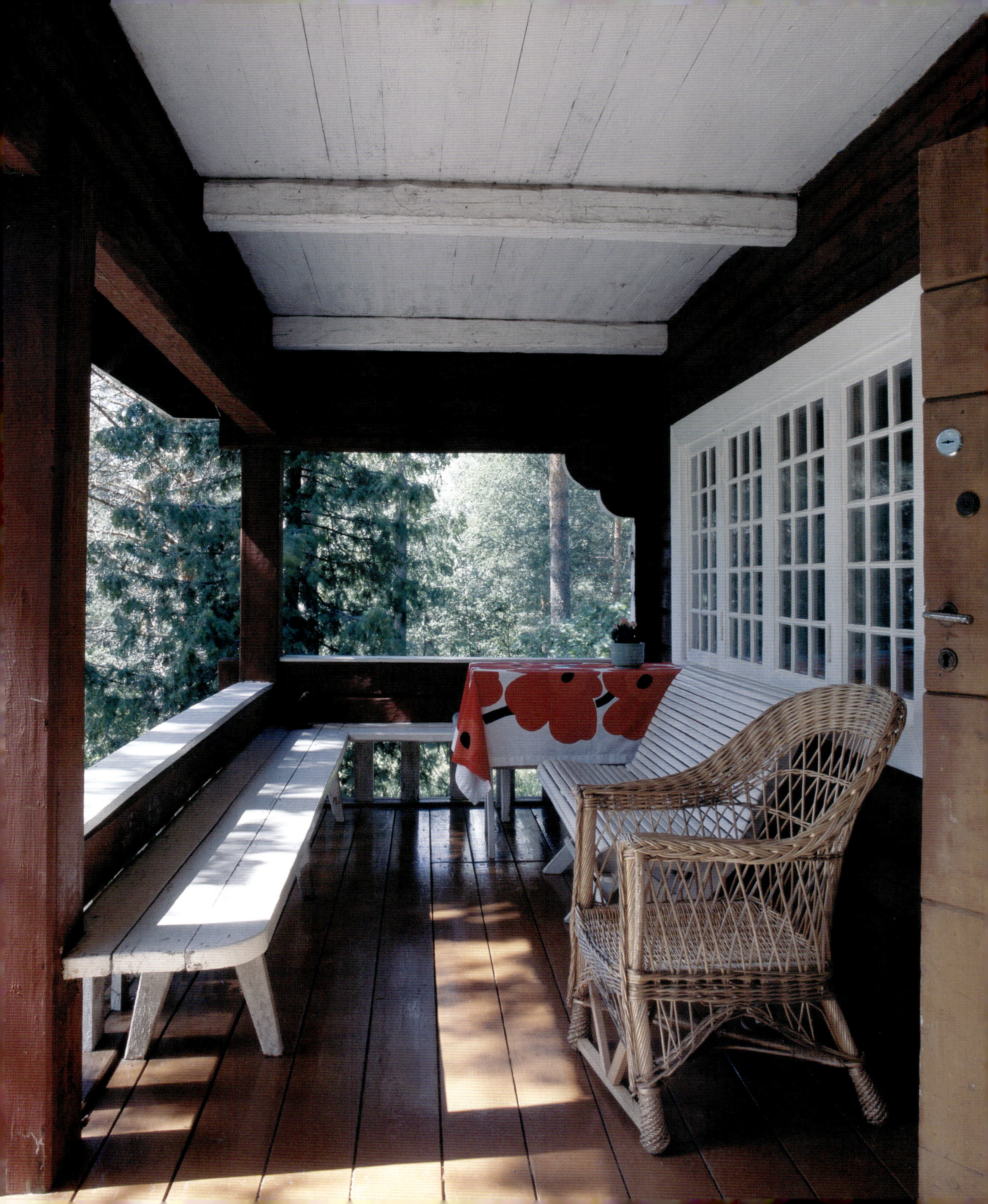

The *tupa* living room with a large fireplace forms the center of the villa. The stairs lead to the upper bedroom level.

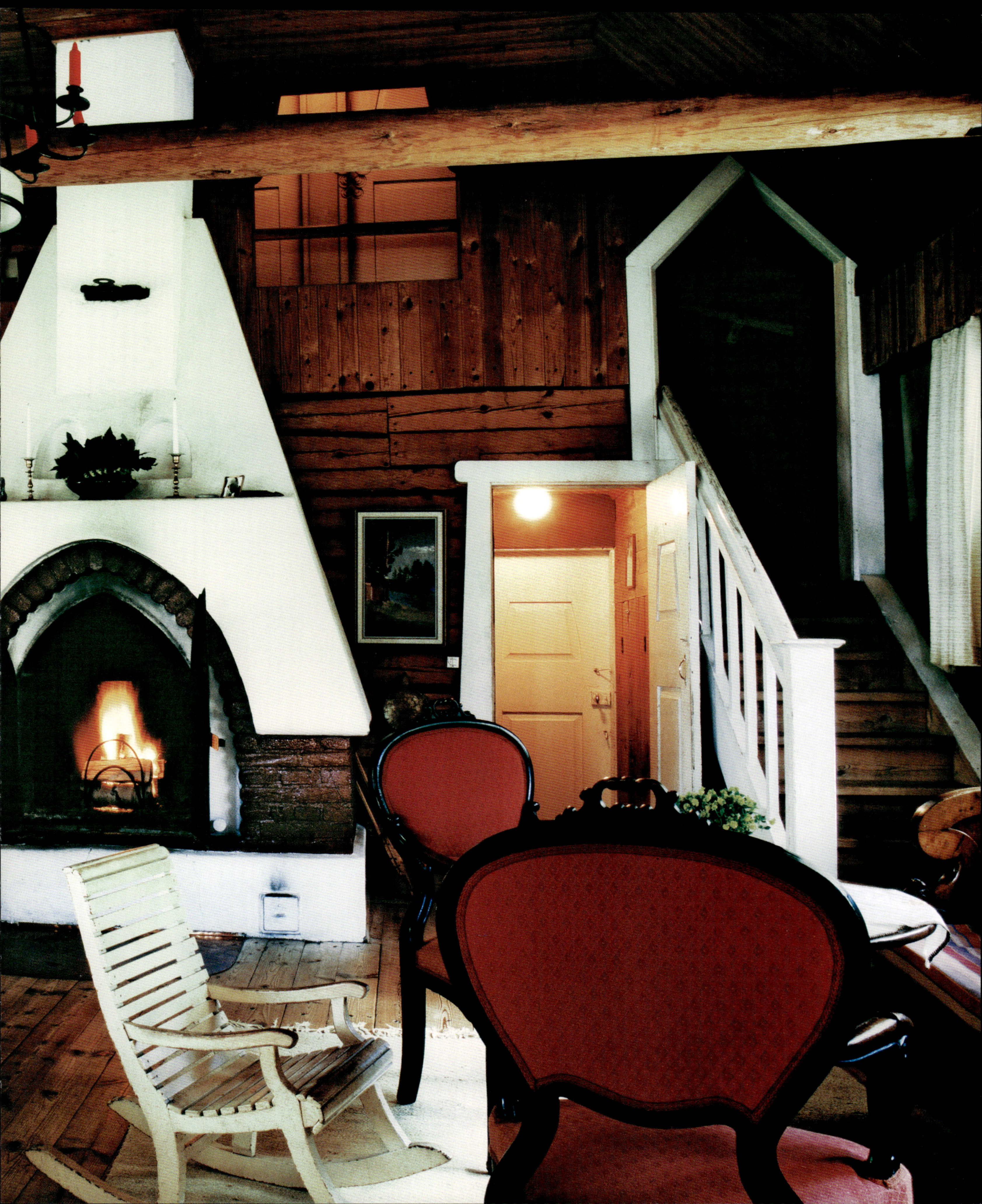

Villa Oivala

Villinge, 1924
Oiva Kallio

The island of Villinge near Helsinki has two faces: the surf-breaking rocks on the southern shoreline overlook the open sea, while a small forest along the sheltered cove offers calmer surroundings for Oiva Kallio's summer cottage. At first sight Villa Oivala appears to be almost completely closed off. Symmetry governs the facade on the seaward side, further emphasized by a colonnade and wide stairs. The facade facing the forest is marked by small windows and a solid gate, from which a path leads through tall grass to the overgrown garden. However, both openness and enclosure coexist in the house.

The heart of Villa Oivala is a sheltered atrium yard around which all the rooms are gathered, yet on which they turn their back. Both the small living room and the workroom are oriented toward the bay and the evening sun, while the sleeping alcoves face southwest and the kitchen is sited to receive the morning sun on the forest side to the east. The varied orientation of rooms is indeed an important part of the atmosphere in a Finnish summer house. People spend different times of the day in different rooms, enjoying the change of light.

In his villa Kallio interpreted the classical atrium motif in a way that was typical for the 1920s: asymmetry and symmetry, and the festive and the everyday come together here. On the narrow, sheltered terrace on the eastern side of the yard, a simple bench awaits a sitter to bask in the afternoon sun. The courtyard and veranda are simultaneously sheltered and open, offering a unique setting to enjoy the Finnish summer. The sun shines into the courtyard from early morning on, yet the veranda also offers shade and a cool place on a hot summer's day. The last rays of the evening sun setting beyond the bay also hit the veranda, and closing its glass doors, one becomes sheltered within it against the cool night air.

With its thin timber plank walls, the villa is structurally experimental in its minimalism. This economical solution also sped up the construction. The external wall consists of two one-inch-thick vertical planks nailed to each other, resulting in a total wall thickness of just two inches. The pillars only support the roof overhangs. Originally, the house had a shingle roof, which was later replaced by asbestos cement sheets. The interior includes numerous custom-designed pieces of furniture and details. The workroom, where Kallio built furniture for the villa and the sauna, takes up a significant part of the ground floor.

RIGHT
Site plan

OPPOSITE
The villa from the forest side

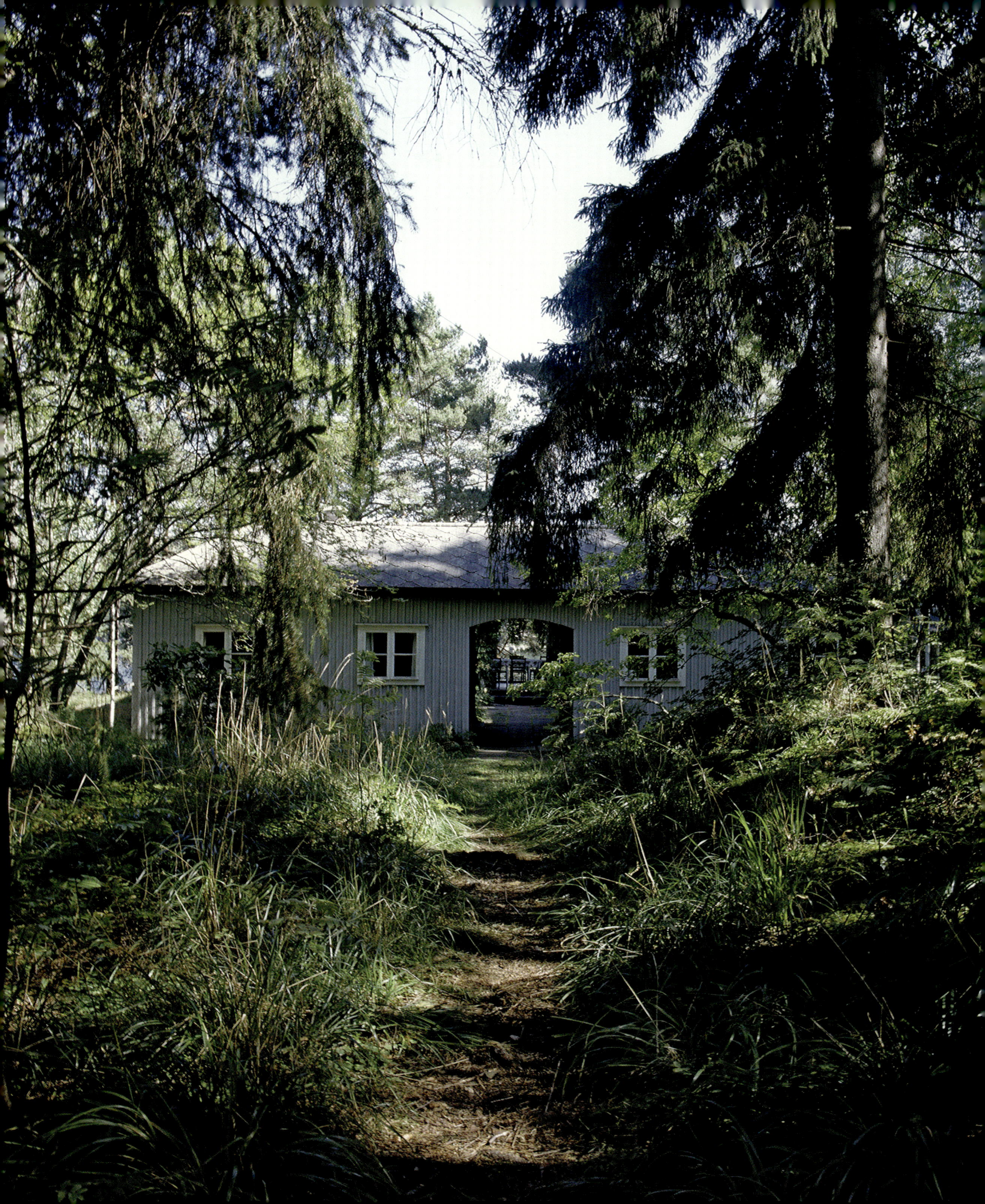

TOP
Plan

BOTTOM
Villa Oivala in the landscape

OPPOSITE, TOP LEFT
The veranda opens to the atrium courtyard.

OPPOSITE, TOP RIGHT
The house invites the visitor to step in.

OPPOSITE, BOTTOM
The narrow terrace creates an asymmetrical accent to the atrium courtyard.

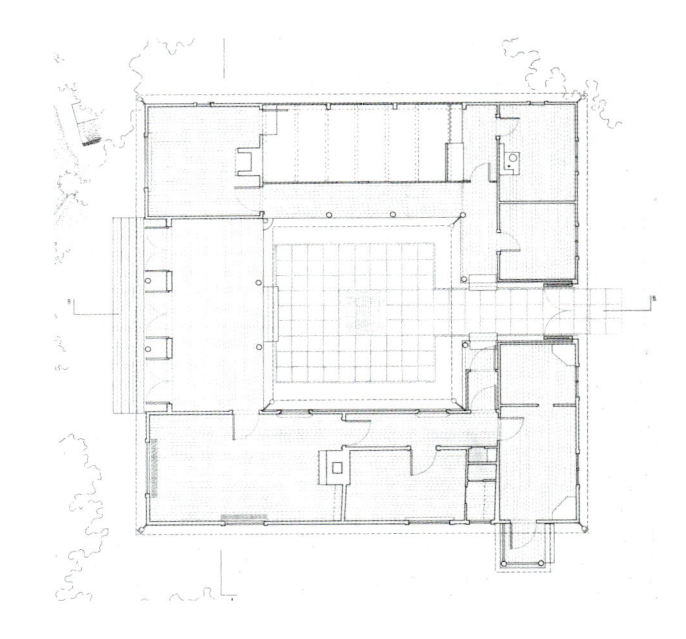

Kallio was very interested in the Finnish sauna culture and built a separate log sauna nearby a few years later. In addition to the sauna bath itself, the building contains a small room, where one can sit and relax after taking a sauna or where guests could sleep over. The open fireplace, the grandfather-clock motif of the cupboard, the roof purlin, and the bed in the guest room bring to mind the *tupa* of a farmhouse in Ostrobothnia, where Kallio grew up. Fronting the sauna is a small veranda that faces the evening sun and is protected by long overhanging gable eaves. Apart from the round logs, there are also details, such as the decorative woodcarvings along the eaves, that refer to the Karelian building tradition.

The sauna is a good example of the prototypical Finnish log sauna, a model that is still popular in modern-day summer villas. Kallio used the sauna during the wintertime as a small weekend cabin, but in his last years he lived there during the summer months as well, leaving the summer house for the use of the younger generation.

An important joint hobby of Kallio and his wife was to tend the garden and forest around their summer cottage. They made a clearing in the copse behind the house and planted flowers. In general, the outdoors was an important part of life at the villa, including daily morning swims in the sea and trips with Kallio's motorboat. Villa Oivala can be seen as a self-portrait of the architect: calm and reflective, but at the same time enterprising and productive.

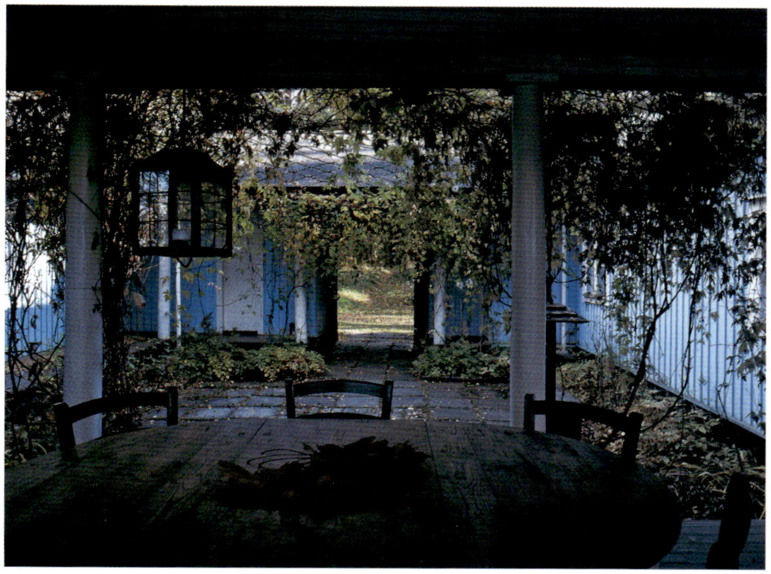
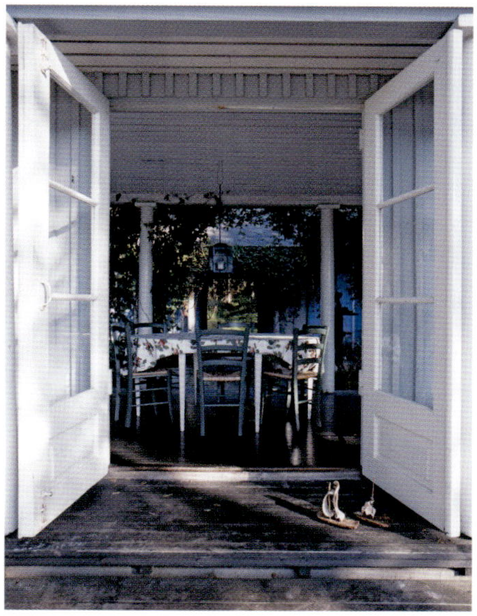
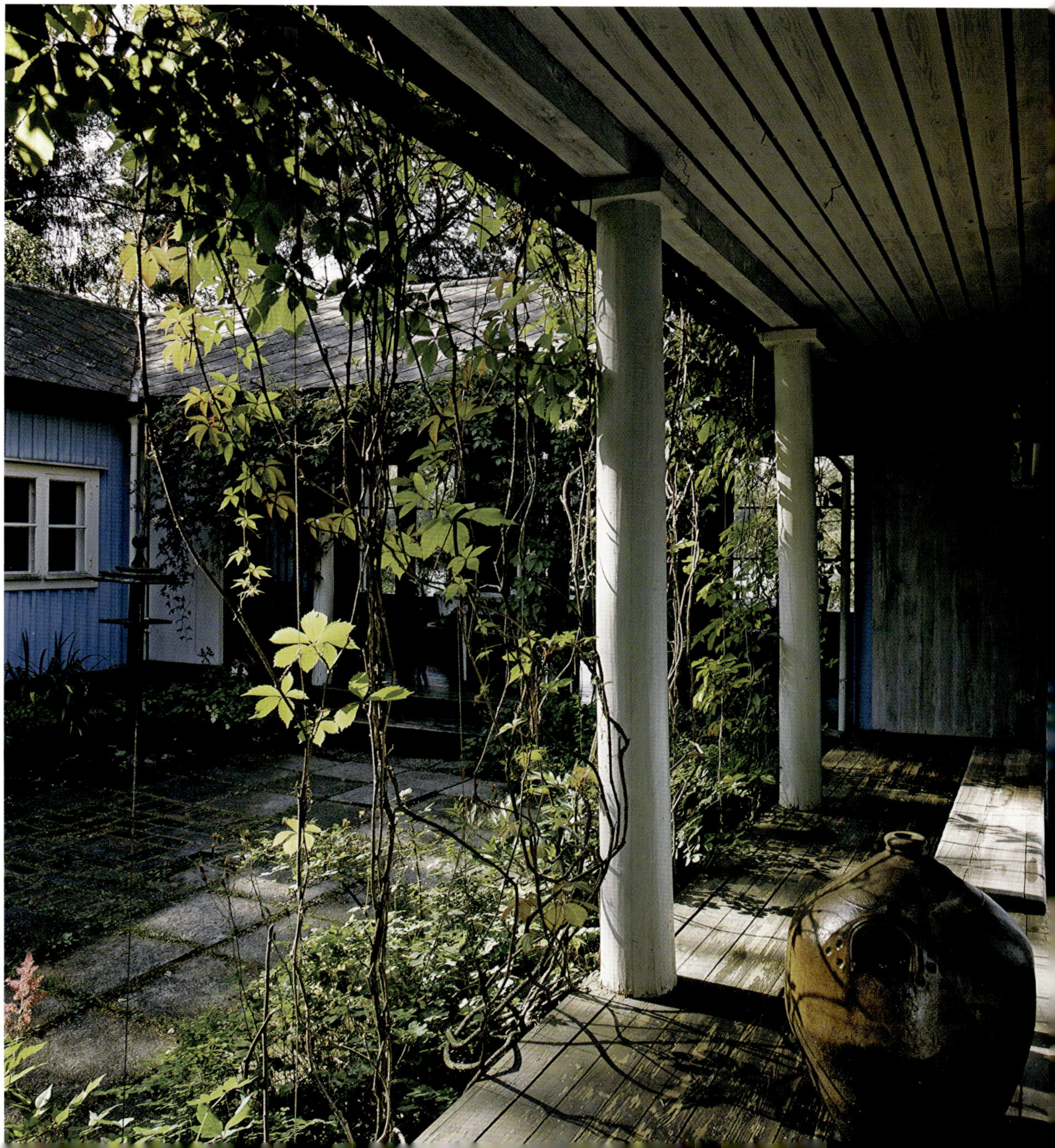

Evening light enters
the space.

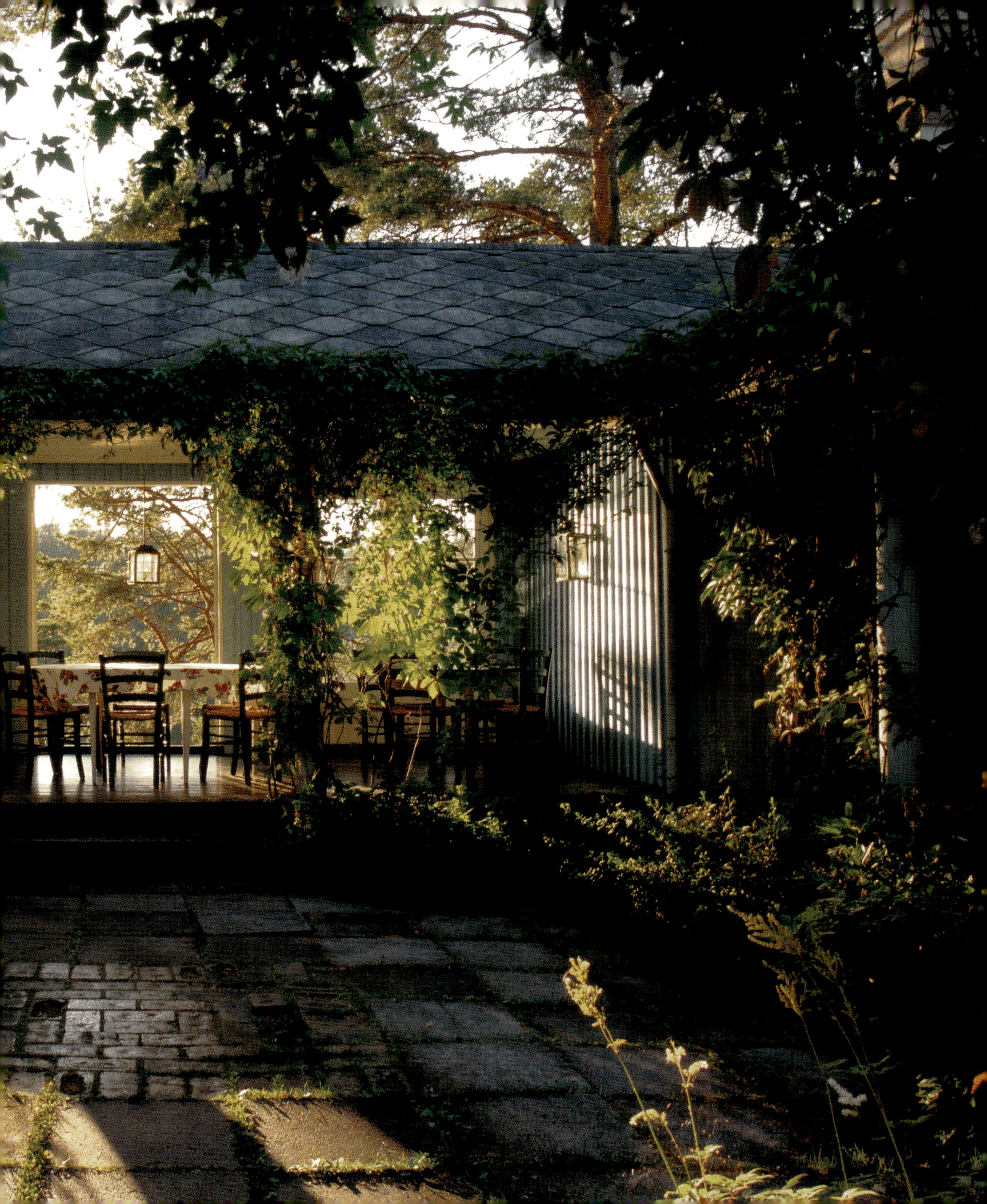

The living room opens to the atrium through the veranda.

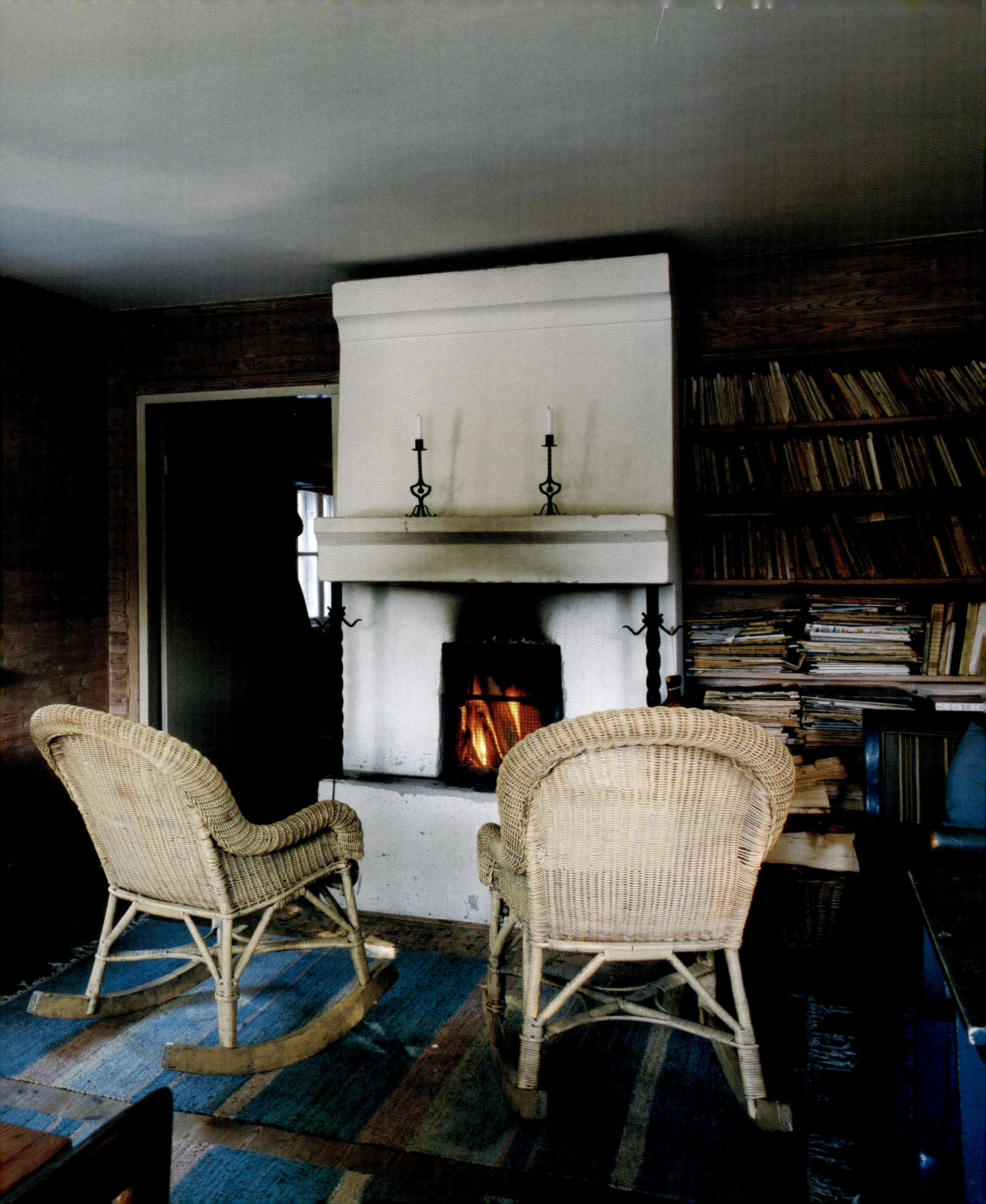

RIGHT
Section of the sauna room showing the custom-made bench

BOTTOM, LEFT
The sauna is located on the slope of a mossy cliff.

BOTTOM, RIGHT
Interior of the sauna room

OPPOSITE
Kallio designed and made most of the furniture for the small changing room in the sauna himself.

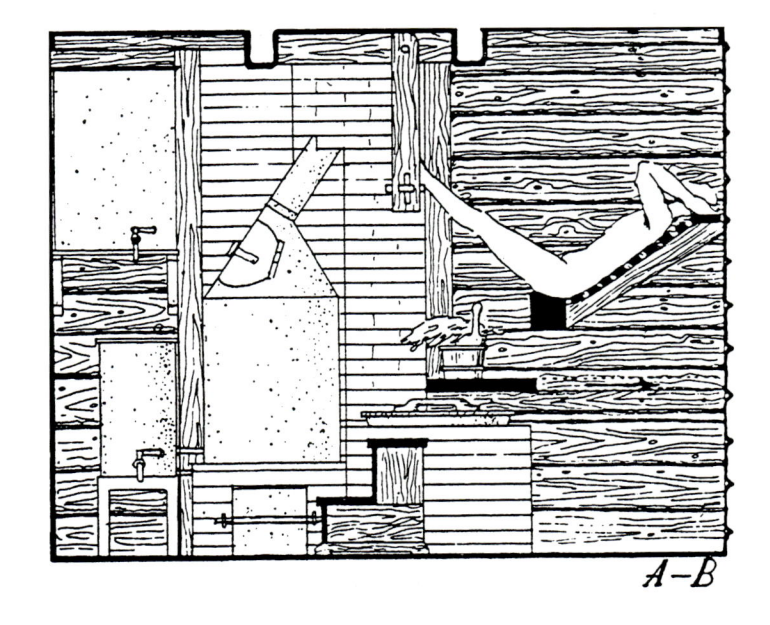

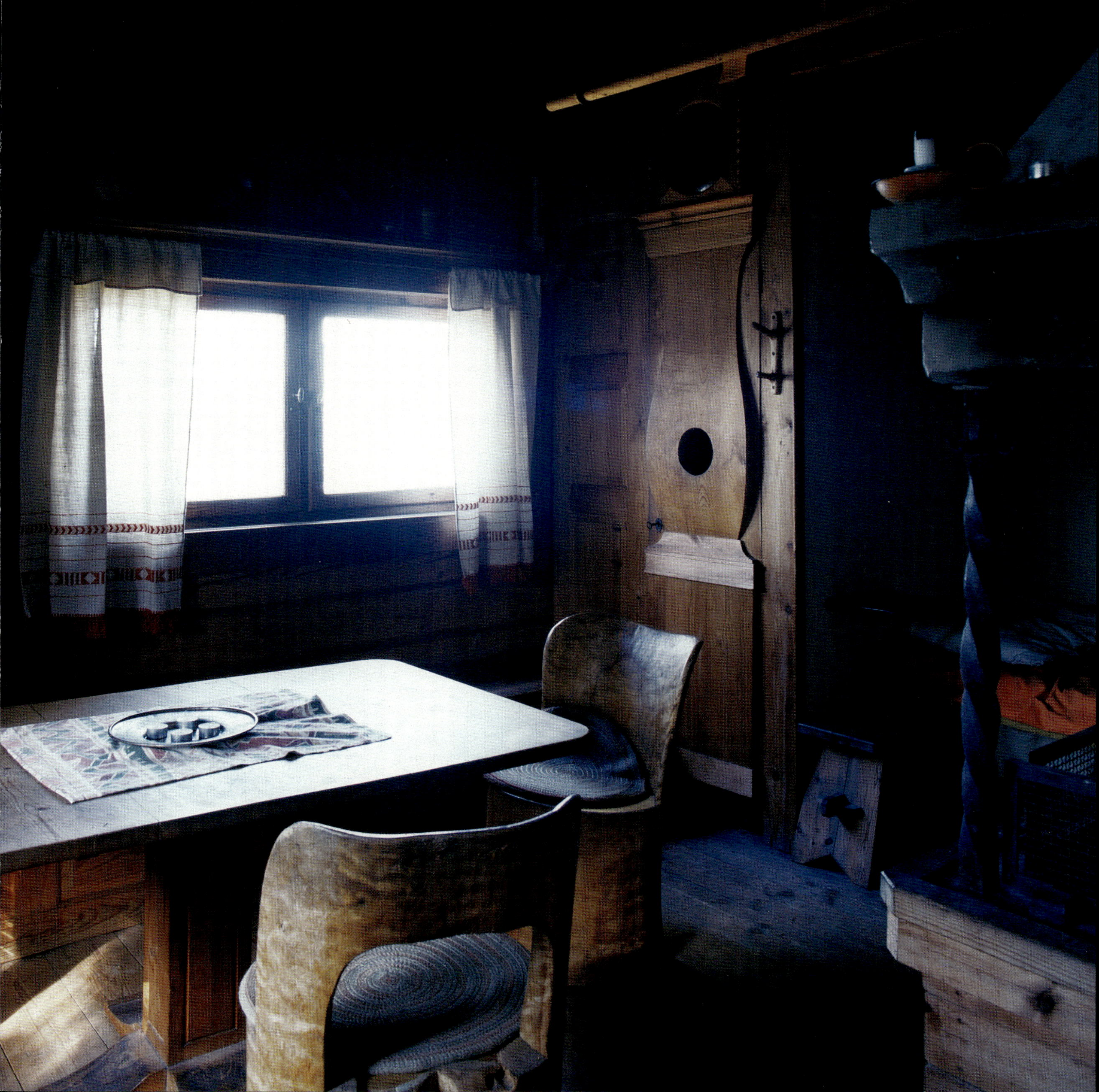

Villa Flora

Alajärvi, 1926, alterations 1938
Aino Aalto

Aino Aalto has been described as a quiet, even shy, person, yet nevertheless someone who possessed great determination and strength. She was a steady rock next to the extrovert and bohemian Alvar Aalto. The works that she and Alvar Aalto created in their joint office form an inseparable whole. Aino's role was to be a key partner beside Alvar as he rose to world fame. She mostly focused on the design of interiors and furniture, but also acted as the artistic director of Artek, founded in 1935, and in the 1940s as its managing director.

Villa Flora was, according to Aino Aalto's own description, "a holiday cabin for the hottest time of the summer."[1] The house is situated in the heart of the countryside, on an embankment at the edge of a lake and with a landscape of flat fields to its rear. The villa resembles a robust farmhouse, with its light-rendered external walls, mullioned windows, and wooden shutters. Originally, a turf roof enhanced the overall impression. On the lakeside an arcade of wooden columns runs the whole length of the facade. Its wooden barrel vault brings a delicate classical flavor to the otherwise simple exterior. The architecture expresses the simplicity of rural houses, in particular the rural architecture of Denmark, which was admired in Scandinavian design during the 1920s.

When it was first built, Villa Flora contained a living room, bedroom, and a small kitchen, but Aino added additional bedrooms at the end of the 1930s. The ceilings and walls are covered with untreated wooden panels. Classical elements in the interior include the temple pediment patterns in the internal doors and the classical relief pattern of the original fireplace. Although the house is located close to the lake, only one window, the one in the living room, faces the water. The building and the surrounding nature live naturally side by side. It is the villa's simplicity that allows us to relate to it: in the daytime it offers cool shade, while in the evening a homey light glows from its windows.

The location of the house and its name closely tie it to the Aalto family. Aino Marsio and Alvar Aalto married in 1924 and lived in Jyväskylä in central Finland during the time Villa Flora was under construction. They chose Alajärvi as the location for their summer residence because Alvar's father and family had lived there since 1918; Alvar had also built his first works in this municipality. Flora was an important person in Alvar's life; she was his mother's sister, and became his stepmother after the early death of his mother. Life at the summer residence was spent with the children and extended family. Aino also relaxed there by painting watercolors. After Aino's death in 1949 Villa Flora was mainly used by the Aaltos' children and their families.

OPPOSITE
View of Villa Flora from the lakeside

1 "Villa Flora," Aino Aalto, *Arkkitehti* 5 (1929): 74–75.

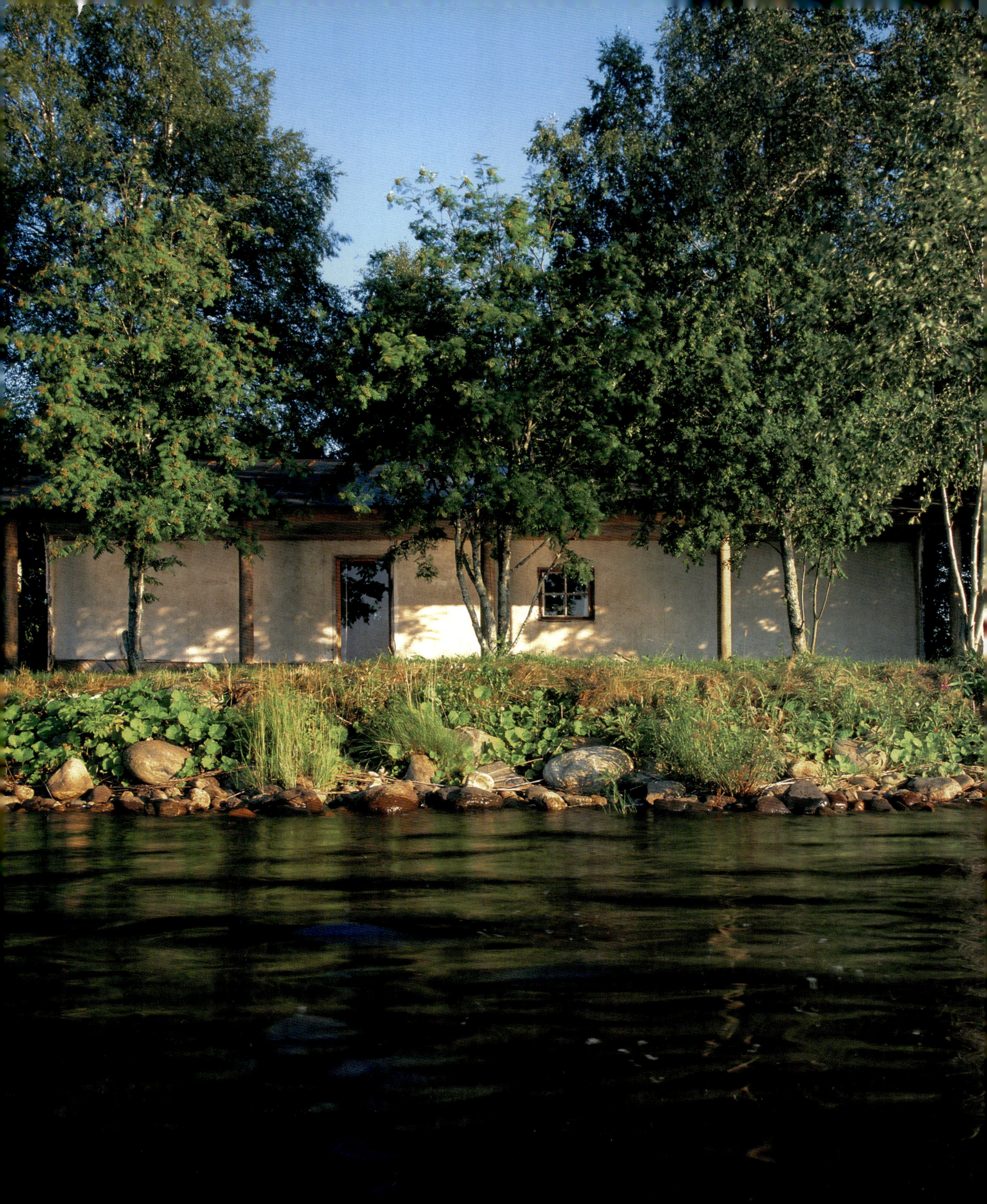

RIGHT

Alvar Aalto sitting by the fireplace on a rainy day. Sketch by Aino Aalto, 1944.

BOTTOM

Plan, section, and facade drawings

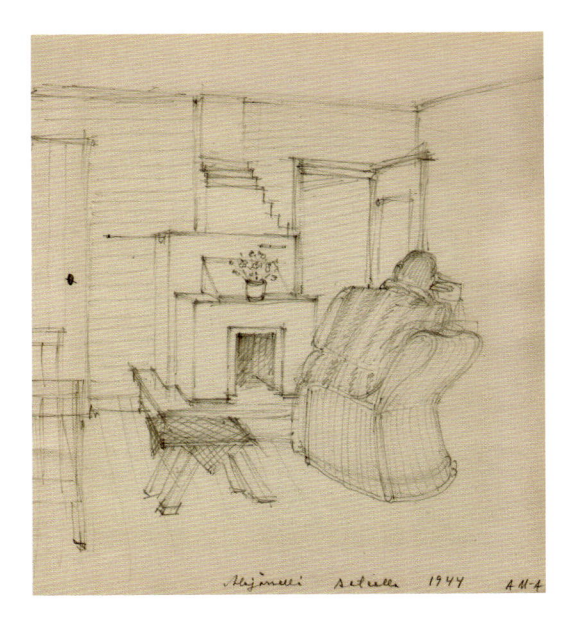

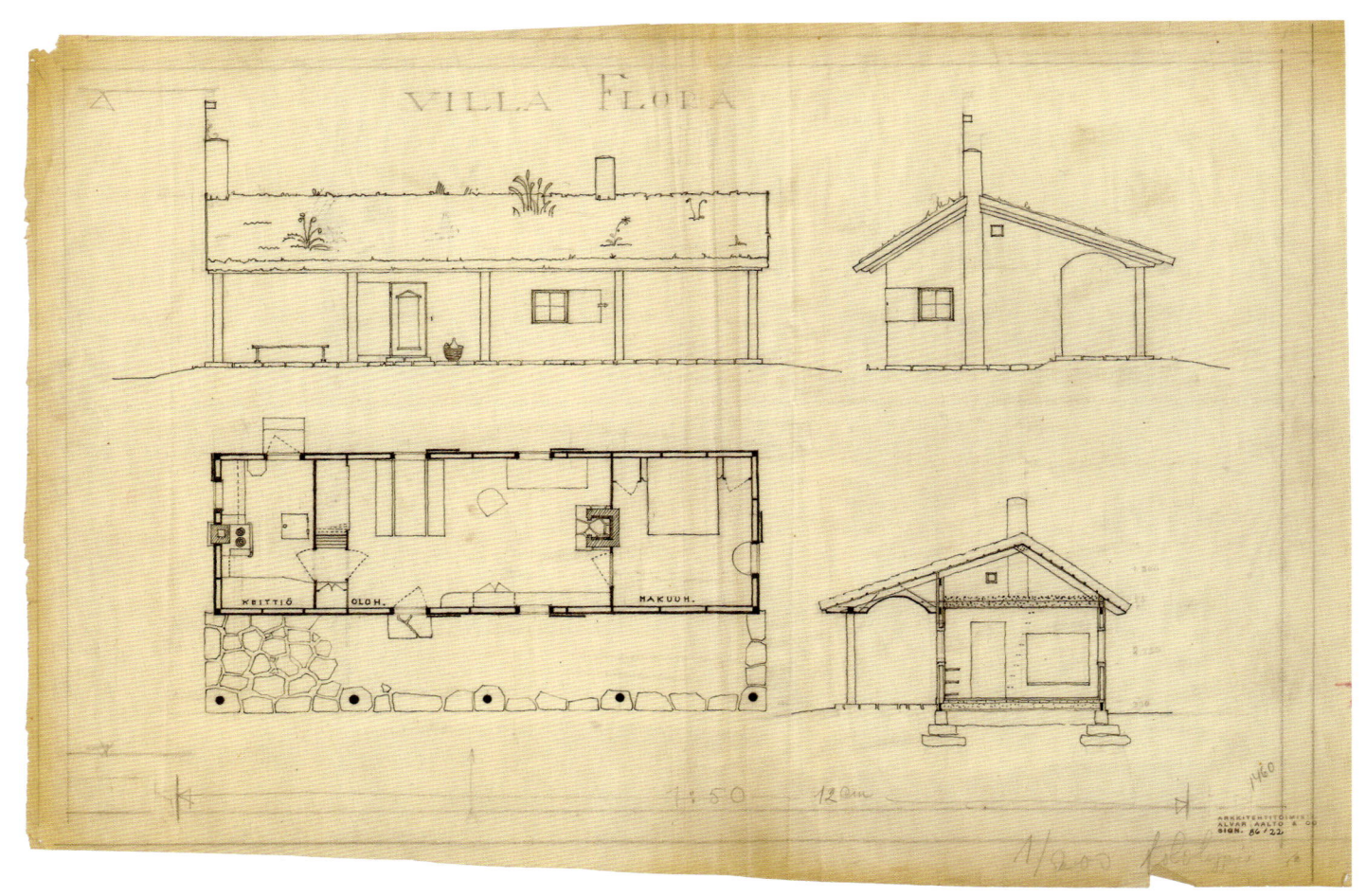

TOP
A summer day at Villa Flora, late 1920s or early 1930s

MIDDLE
Aino Aalto and her children in a hammock, late 1920s or early 1930s

BOTTOM
Alvar Aalto painting near the lake, 1940s

RIGHT
Living-room corner with the dining table. A photograph of Aunt Flora is visible on the back wall.

BOTTOM
The living room incorporates a dining area.

RIGHT
The furniture in the master bedroom was specially designed for Villa Flora.

BOTTOM
A 1938 extension added additional bedrooms for the children.

Villa Huttunen

Nuuksio, 1937–38
Erkki Huttunen

Erkki Huttunen's architectural career can be divided into three parts. He worked in the building department of the SOK Cooperative, where his main task was to design the cooperative's retail and industrial buildings, from the end of the 1920s until 1941. He was central in creating a uniform architectural appearance for the SOK buildings, which were dominated by white functionalism. In 1931 Huttunen founded his own private practice and specialized in the design of offices and commercial buildings. During the third part of his career, from 1943 to 1953, he was head of the Finnish National Board of Building.

Despite the administrative nature of a large part of his career and despite the practicality and rationality of his buildings, Huttunen is often described as an artistic type of architect. He sketched his buildings as if he was sculpting them. Art—drawing and painting—as well as singing were among his hobbies throughout his life.

Huttunen's summer house is located on a slope that descends steeply toward an elongated lake. The cubic shape of the building forms a strong contrast to the surrounding landscape. Partly raised on pillars, the house has light-colored walls and large windows, and is crowned by a roof terrace—it is a functionalist villa in its purest form. Huttunen himself emphasized the openness and refreshing quality of the building: "There is also the aspect of the quietness of rural life, which is said to be disturbed by Functionalism; yet it should be clear that what would fit there—and anywhere—better than anything is Functionalism, whose calm and smooth surfaces allow the shadows of trees and foliage to play freely, and whose open and natural appearance seems to have been especially created for nature."[1]

The most important space in the villa is the tall living room, which is dominated by a large corner window overlooking the lake. The interior spaces are seamlessly joined together, with the living room continuing into the dining area. This continuity in several directions creates a dynamic atmosphere and emphasizes the importance of movement. The furniture, designed by Huttunen himself, forms an integral part of the interior, and the animal hides, such as that of a zebra, hanging on the walls add an exotic touch. The upstairs bedrooms are accessed from the living room via a straight flight of stairs and an internal balcony.

Huttunen once described the exterior balcony facing the lake as a place to "rid oneself of morning drowsiness and to down a cup of coffee in an early morning state of undress in the spirit of the sun, freshly risen from the lake."[2] The house had no modern comforts, not even a bathroom. The intention was for everyone to "run down the gravel and spruce-log-edged steps to the sauna for a wash—and a swim."[3] Such statements by Huttunen vividly describe the ideals of the outdoors and the idea of hardening oneself that prevailed during the 1930s.

OPPOSITE
Winter view of the villa

1 "Huvila Nouksin-Pitkäjärven rannalla" [Villa by Lake Pitkäjärvi], Erkki Huttunen, *Arkkitehti* 5 (1938): 77–78.
2 Ibid.
3 Ibid.

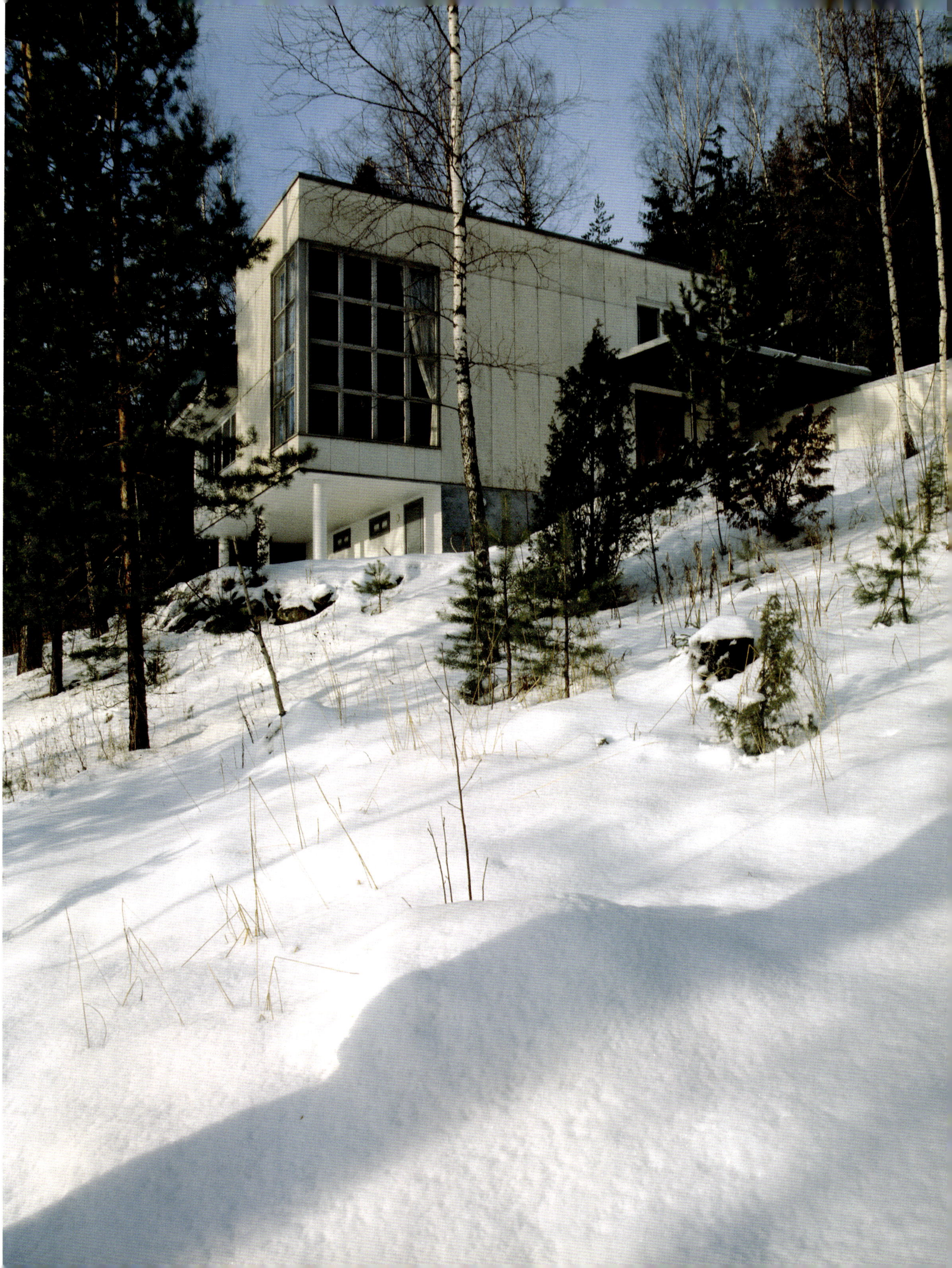

RIGHT
Perspective drawing by Huttunen

BOTTOM
Plans, sections, and facade drawings

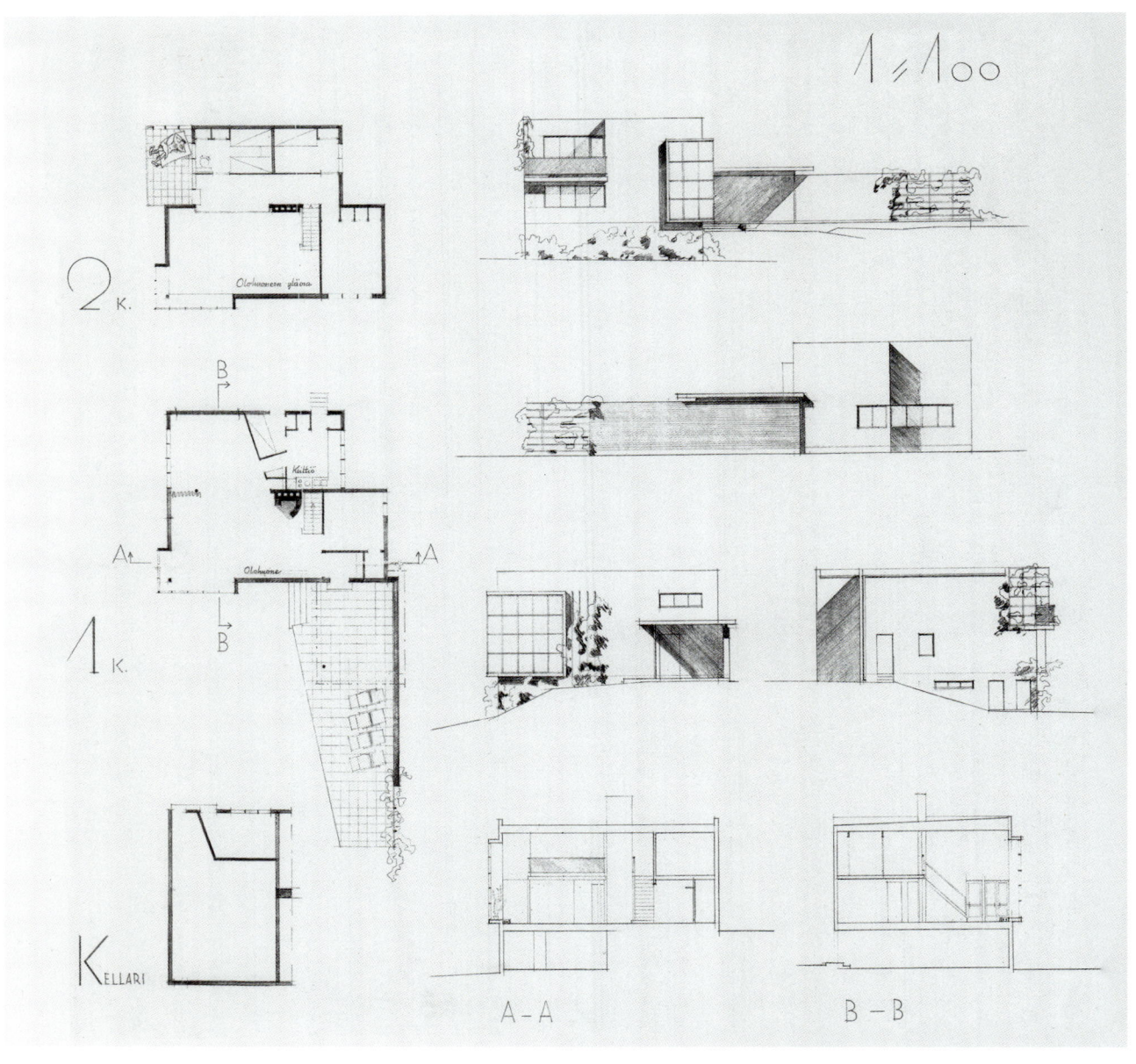

RIGHT
Erkki Huttunen and his son in the living room

BOTTOM
A photograph from the late 1930s shows the villa between birch trees.

BELOW
The animal skins bring warmth to the living room.

OPPOSITE
The staircase leads to the second-floor bedrooms.

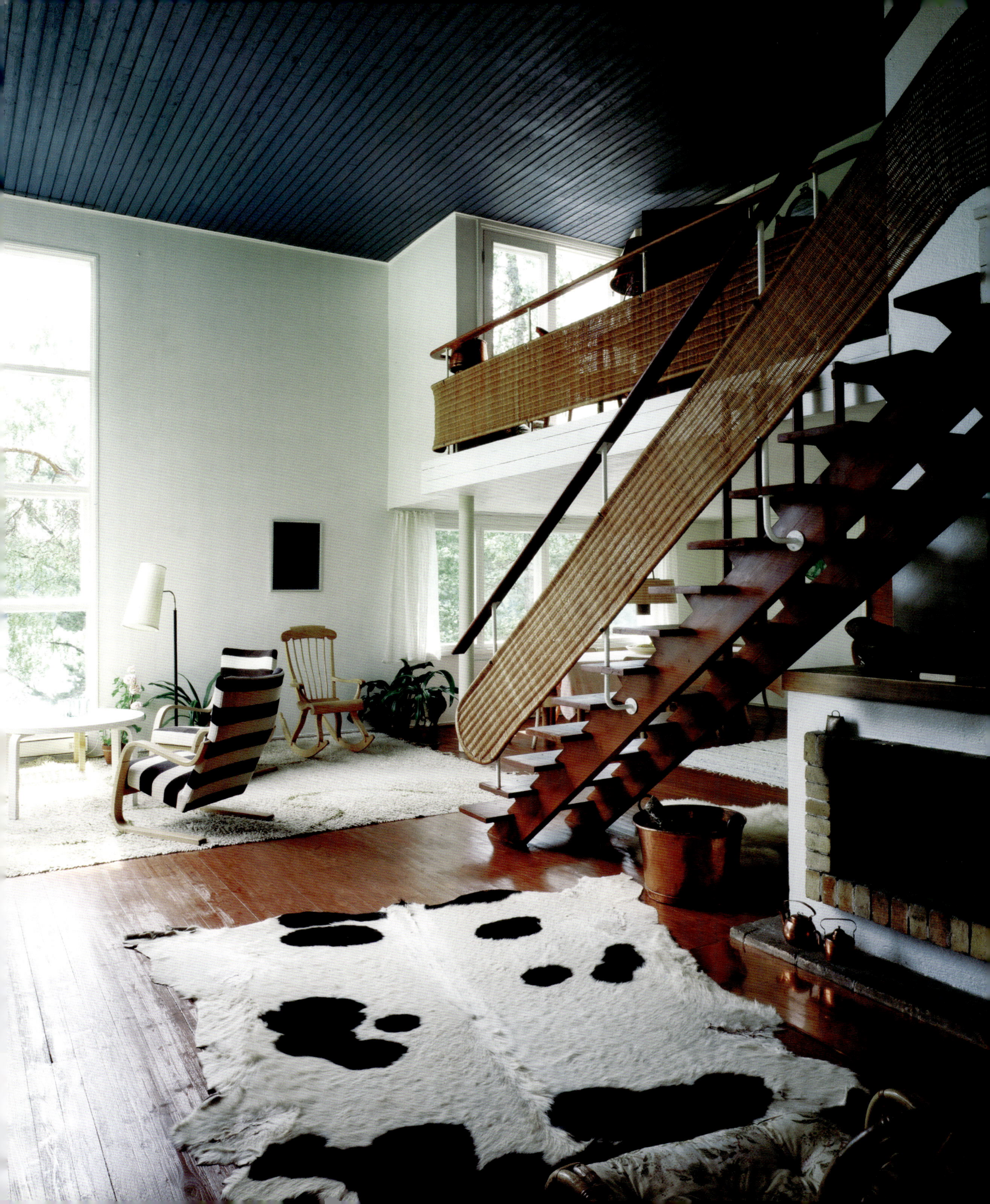

BELOW
Dining space with furniture designed by Huttunen

OPPOSITE, TOP
Watercolor still life by Huttunen

OPPOSITE, BOTTOM
First-floor bedroom

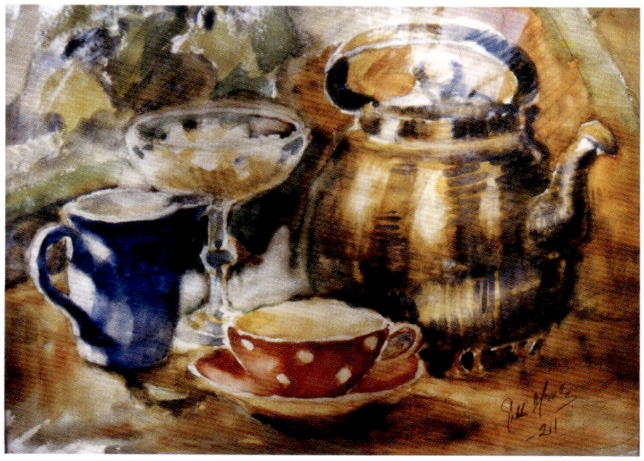

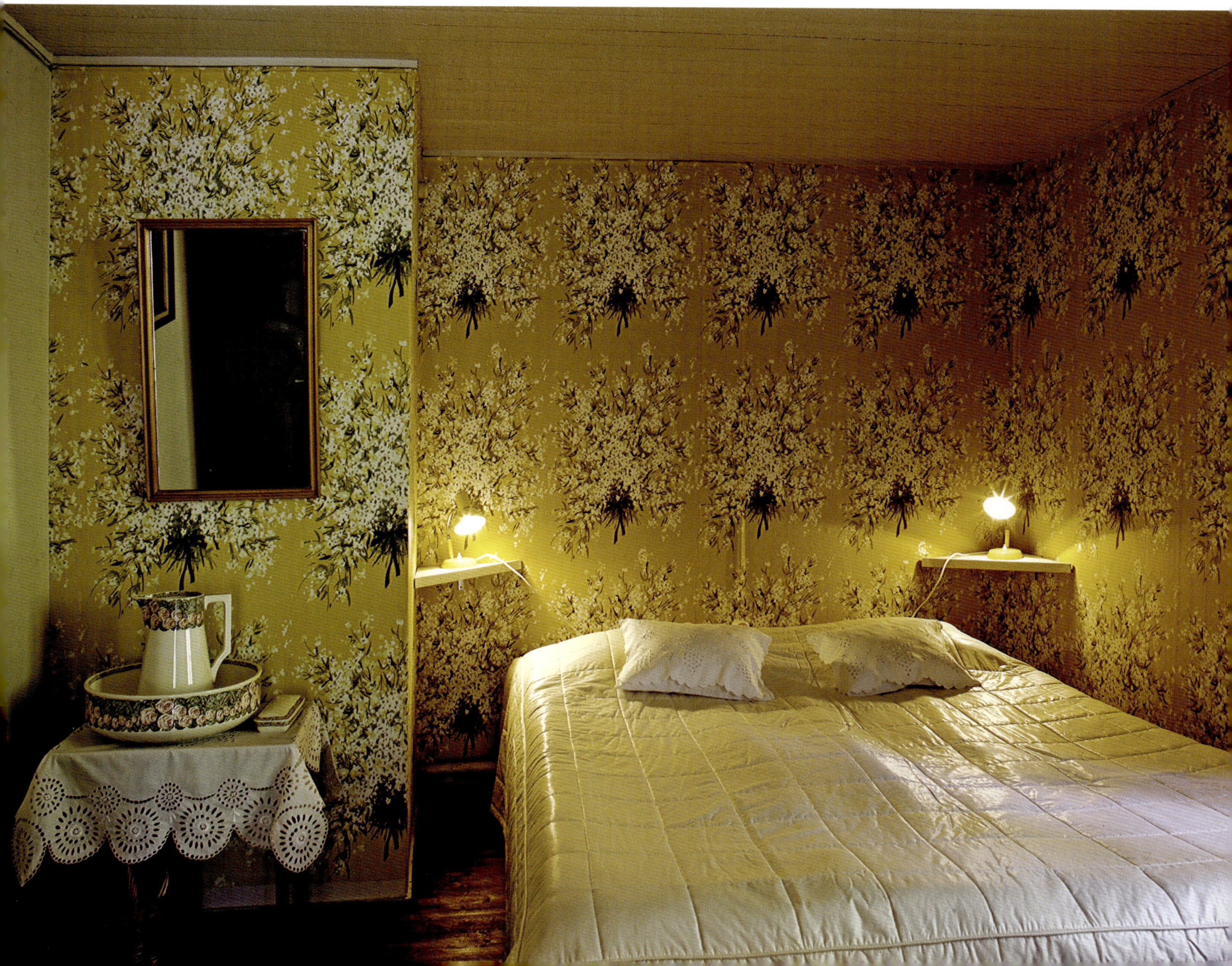

View from the dining space
to the living room

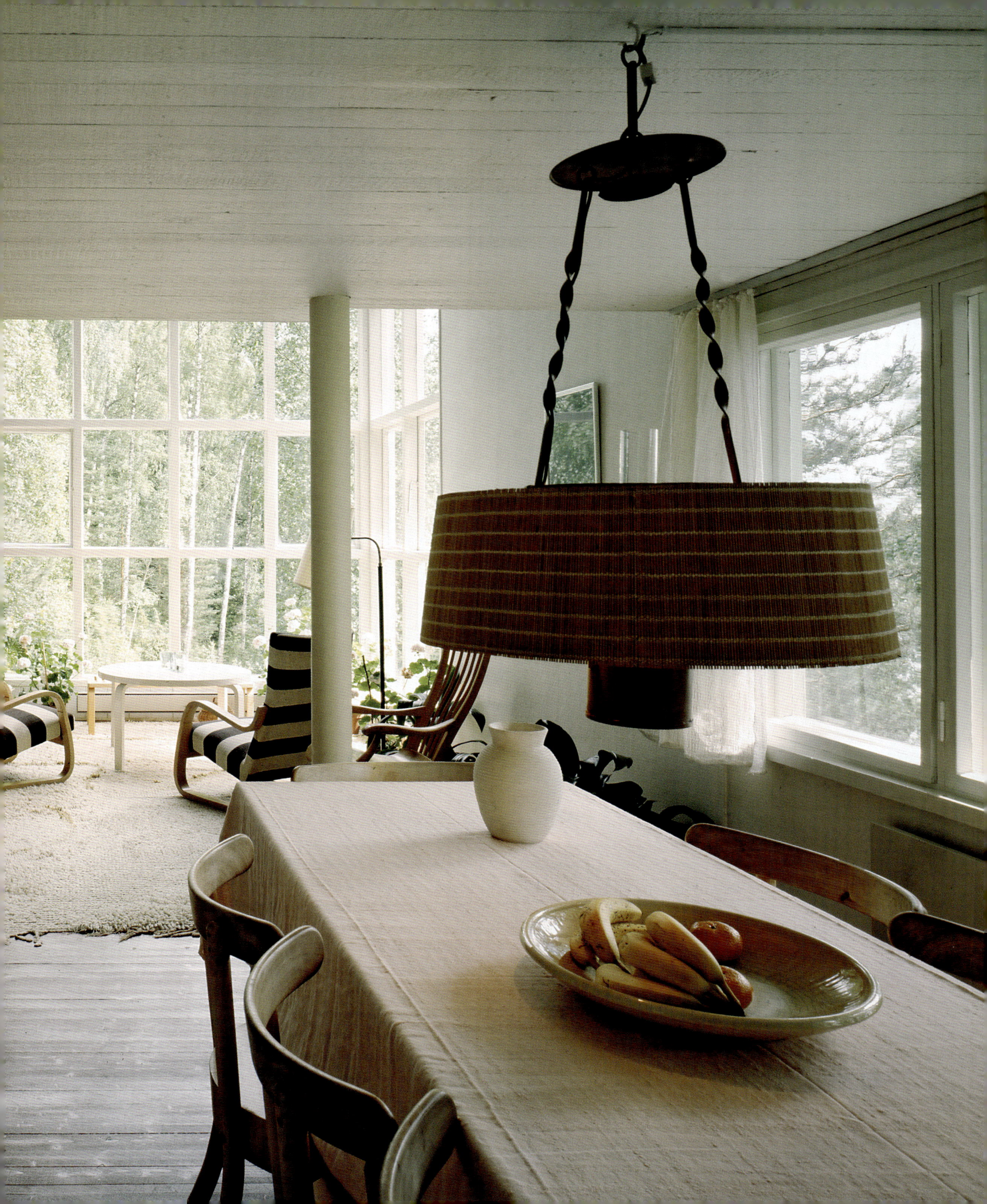

The Blue House (La Maison Bleue)

Borgholm, 1938–39
J. S. Sirén

J. S. Sirén's most well-known design is the Finnish Parliament Building in Helsinki: it was completed in 1931, at a time when modernism had already taken hold in Finland in the works of the younger generation of architects, such as Alvar Aalto and Erik Bryggman. In contrast, Sirén's entire architectural œuvre exhibited academic classicism, and both in his buildings and in his teaching as a professor at the Helsinki University of Technology for almost thirty years (1931–57) he emphasized timeless, basic elements such as functionality and usability as well as the correspondence between the spatial solution and the appearance of a building. Sirén's roots were in Ostrobothnia in western Finland, where vernacular stability and reliability were valued characteristics. Many impressive two-story farmhouses dot the countryside, and Vaasa, Sirén's hometown, was the wealthy regional center of seafaring and trade. The heritage of this area was an important influence on the architect.

Sirén built the Blue House on an island off the south coast of Finland at the end of the 1930s. Its overall appearance and detailing show virtually no features of the new modern architecture but rely heavily on classical themes. The villa consists of two separate wings, one containing the living spaces and bedrooms, the other the kitchen and sauna, set amidst shoreline birch trees. Between the two wings is an open space facing a garden, providing a place to sit and relax. The outdoor living spaces are thus protected against the winds blowing in from the sea.

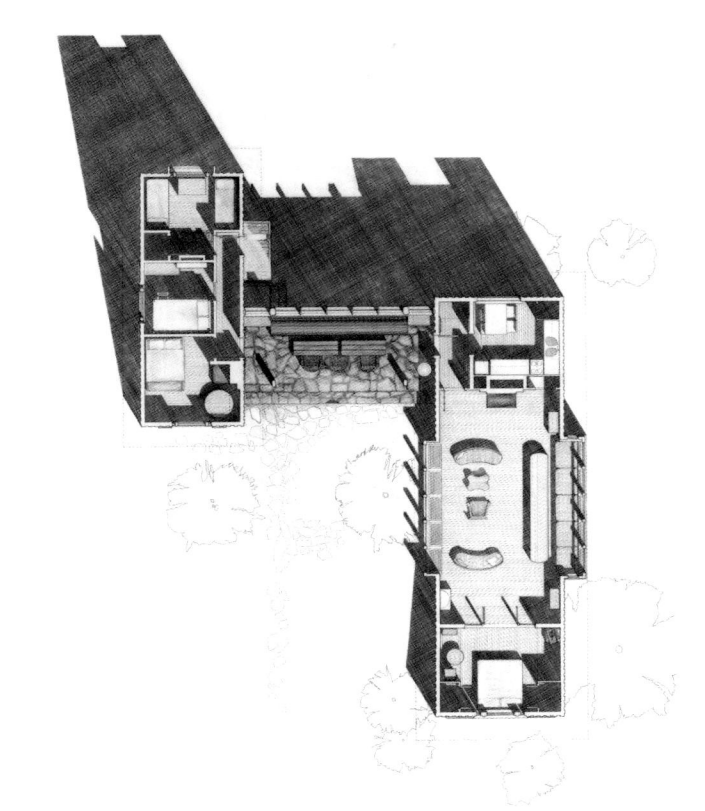

The main wing is dominated by a long living room with broad views in two directions. A large window on the sea-facing side, subdivided into even squares, looks out onto the jetty and visitors approaching by boat. Glass doors open toward the lush garden. The roof beams and the wooden surfaces create a solemn appearance, which is underscored by the use of neutral colors in the furnishings. In the bedrooms at the end of the house horizontal windows provide views of the sea and the horizon.

The architecture of the Blue House is calm, refined, and timeless. Sirén offset symmetry in a delicate way, both in the overall appearance of the building and in the main rooms of the house. The interior and exterior spaces are linked together in a balanced sequence, and the harmony of the design is evident even in the smallest details. Furniture forms an important part of the spirit of the house. Sirén designed the furnishings together with interior designer Arttu Brummer, with whom he also collaborated on other projects, including the furniture for the Finnish Parliament House.

Sirén used to spend long periods of time at the Blue House during summers, where he would stroll around in a white summer costume with a walking stick when he was not busy working on lectures or other projects.

ABOVE
Plan

OPPOSITE
The Blue House is situated near the seashore.

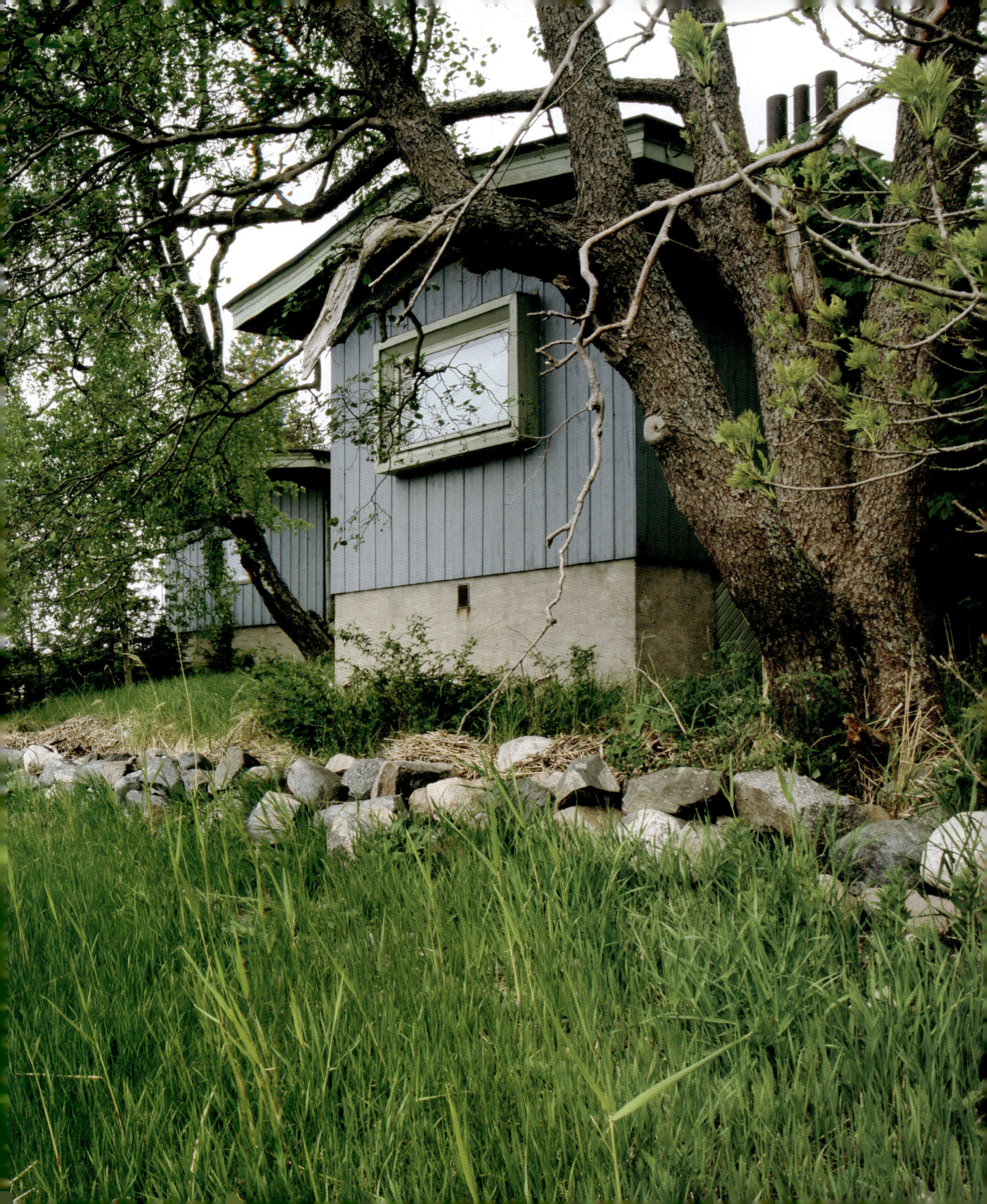

RIGHT
Facade drawing and sections

BOTTOM, LEFT
J. S. Sirén on a warm summer day by the shore

BOTTOM, RIGHT
J. S. Sirén in the living room

RIGHT
View of the Blue House from the sea

BOTTOM
View of the living-room wing

RIGHT
A broad horizontal window provides a panoramic view of the seashore.

BOTTOM
The terrace between the two wings

OPPOSITE, TOP LEFT
French doors in the living room open to the garden.

OPPOSITE, TOP RIGHT
A chair designed for the Blue House

OPPOSITE, BOTTOM
The custom-made chairs and sofas are light and comfortable.

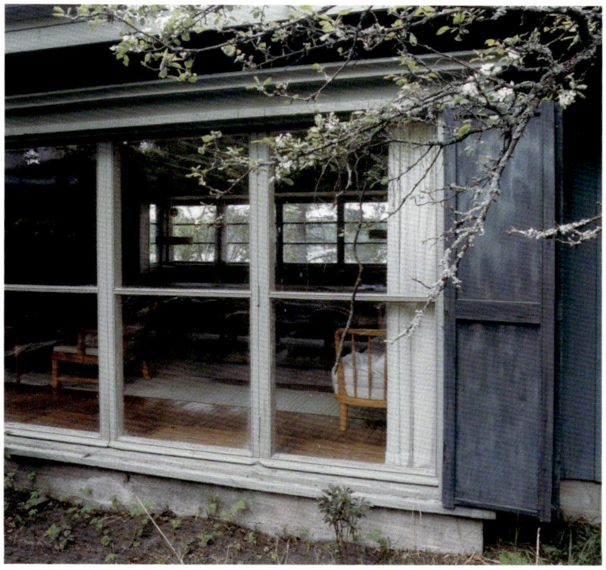

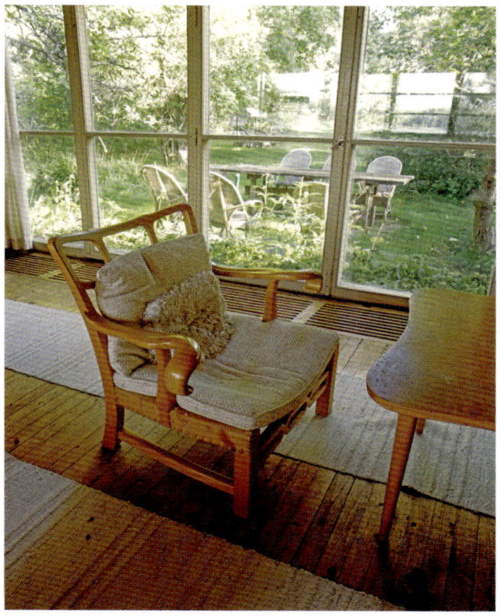

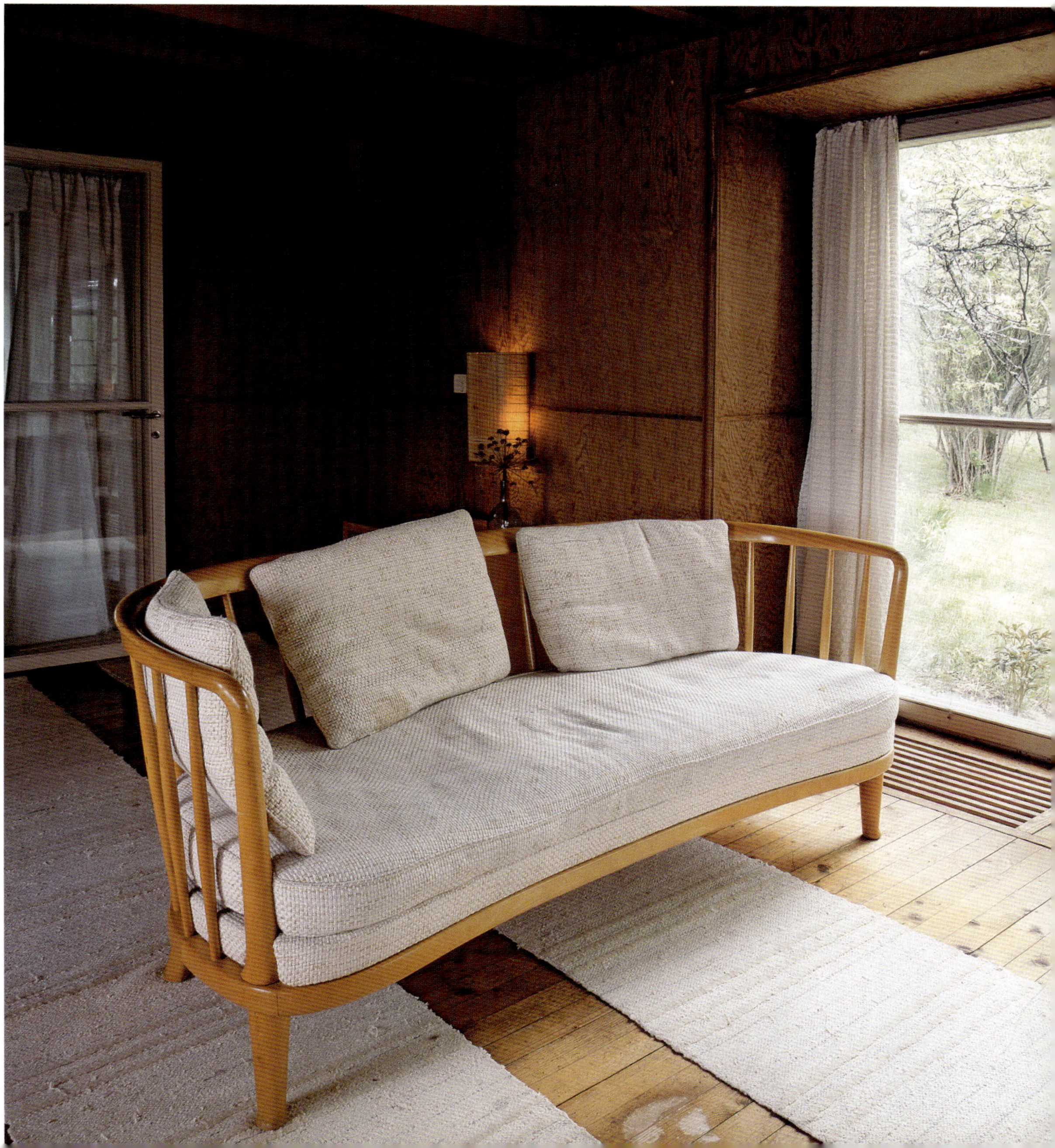

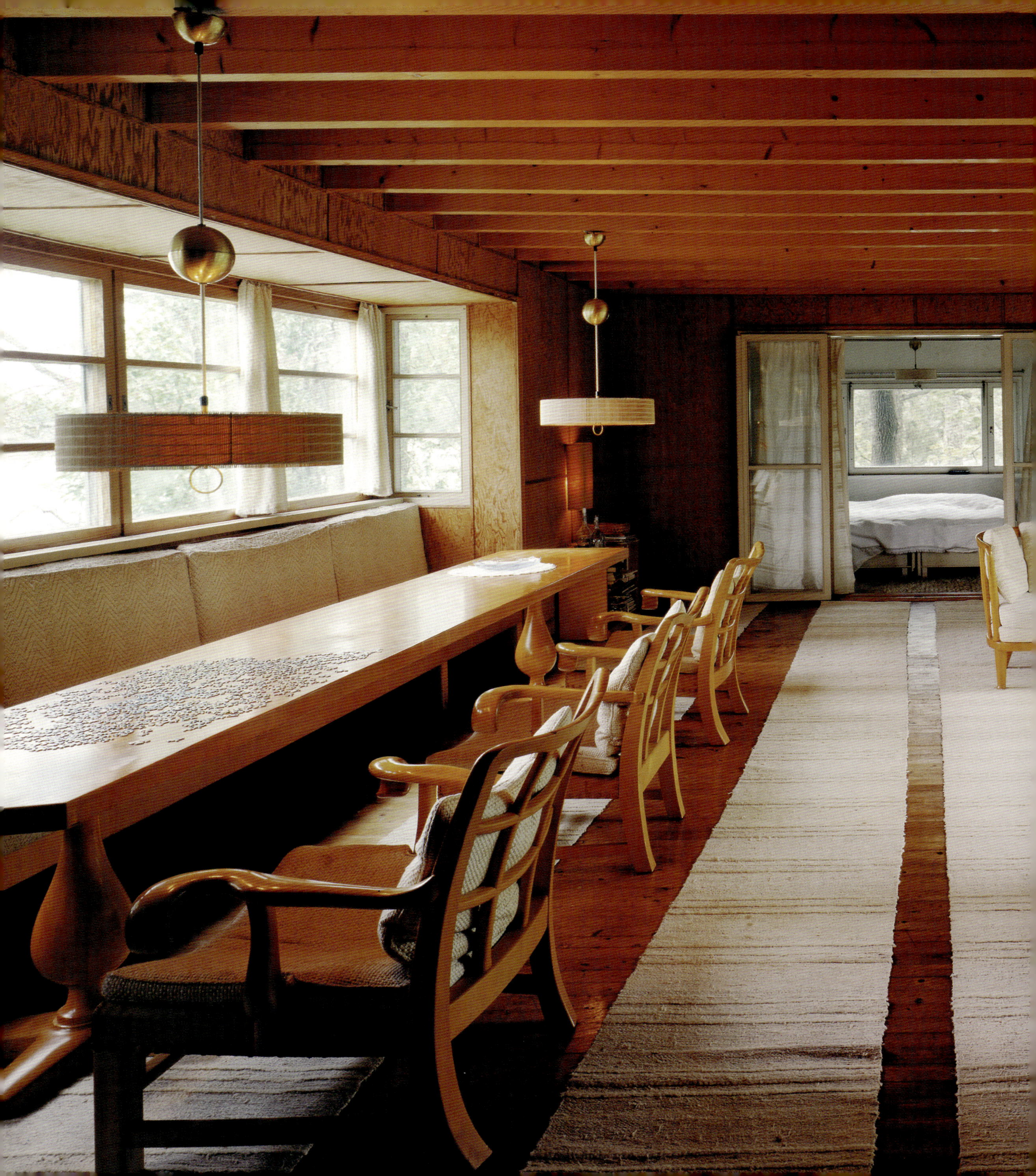

The living room offers views in two directions.

Villa Silla

Kiljava, 1947
Kaj Englund

In the 1930s architect Väinö Vähäkallio donated a seventy-four-acre piece of land in south Finland to the Association of Finnish Architects (SAFA). Named Vähä-Kiljava after its donor, the area is located on the shore of a lake renowned for its clear water. It was intended to serve as a place where SAFA members could relax and spend their leisure time. At the end of the 1930s a two-story main building, called the casino, was constructed as a common social space with small hostel-type bedrooms and a dining area. A separate one-story hostel building was erected at the same time. SAFA members were allowed to build their own summer cabins in other parts of Vähä-Kiljava.

The building of individual summer villas began in the 1940s. Most of these cottages were small in size and simply equipped because dining facilities in the casino and a sauna building on the shore brought the summer residents together. Villa Silla, designed by Kaj Englund, was one of the first of the summer houses to be built. Named after the Englunds' daughter, Silla, it was intended for summer and weekend use, and its design emphasized the theme of minimal living.

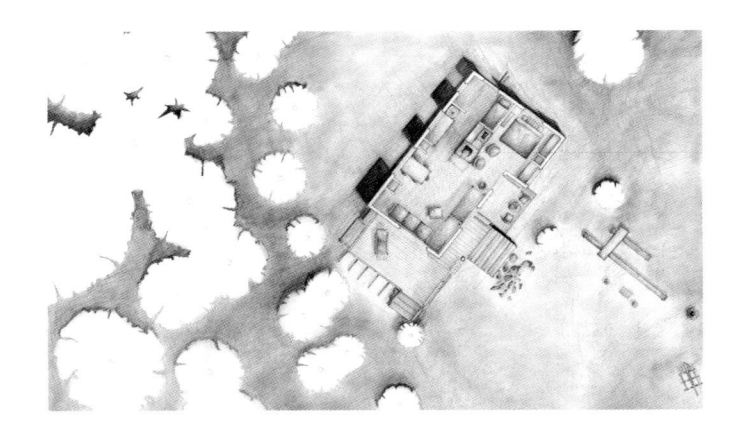

Situated on a gentle slope and surrounded by a natural sandy pine heath terrain, the villa's exterior appearance is modest. The timber boarding on the external facades is stained a dark pine tar, except for the back wall of the small veranda whose light color (originally light yellow) draws the visitor in. On one corner of the veranda a densely branched tree trunk supports the roof eaves, which Englund painted white on the underside in order to bring in as much natural light as possible during the fall and winter. The exoticness of the interior surprises the visitor. Bold black-and-white mural decorations designed by Kaj Englund's wife, artist Li Englund, dominate the continuous space, which is divided into kitchen, dining, living, and sleeping areas.

Windows opening out in four directions further increase the feeling of spaciousness, with daylight streaming in from the early morning until sunset. Positioned at the eye level of a seated person, they frame views that emphasize the close connection with the earth and trees of the forest. The blueberry and moss brushwood and the tree trunks are, as "living pictures," inseparable parts of the room.

Englund made his career as a residential architect, and one of his particular interests was the single-family house. Villa Silla crystallizes in a single space the study of the importance of place even in a small house. The modest exterior unfolds in the interior into a multilayered spatial experience.

ABOVE
Plan

OPPOSITE
The southeast facade in the morning sun

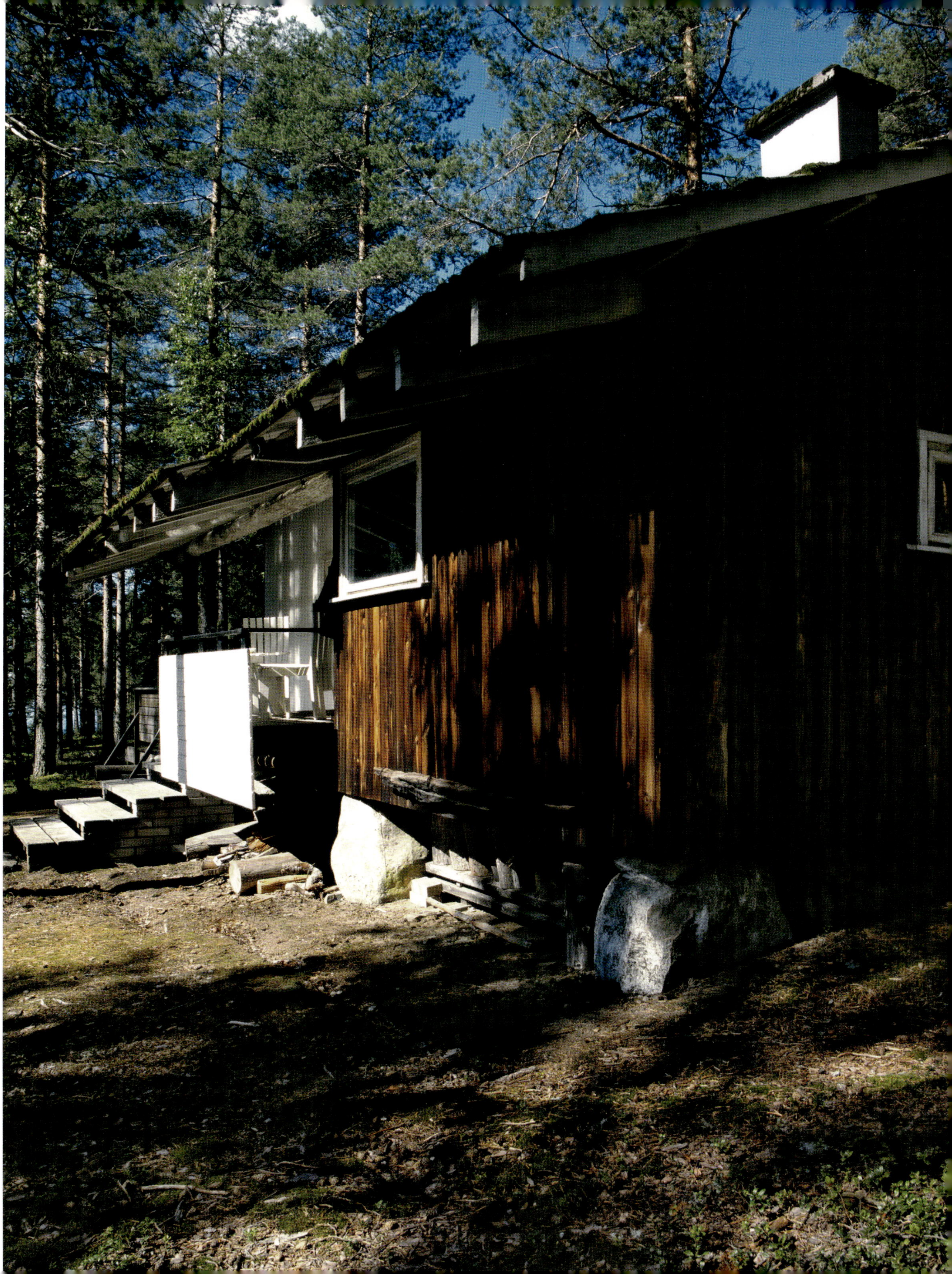

RIGHT
Cross-section and longitudinal section

MIDDLE, LEFT
Kaj and Li Englund at the dining table, 1948

MIDDLE, RIGHT
Interior of the villa, 1948

BOTTOM
Winter view of Villa Silla, 1948

RIGHT
View of the main facade

BOTTOM
Villa Silla is almost hidden between trees.

BELOW
Southwest facade

OPPOSITE
The small porch is painted white.

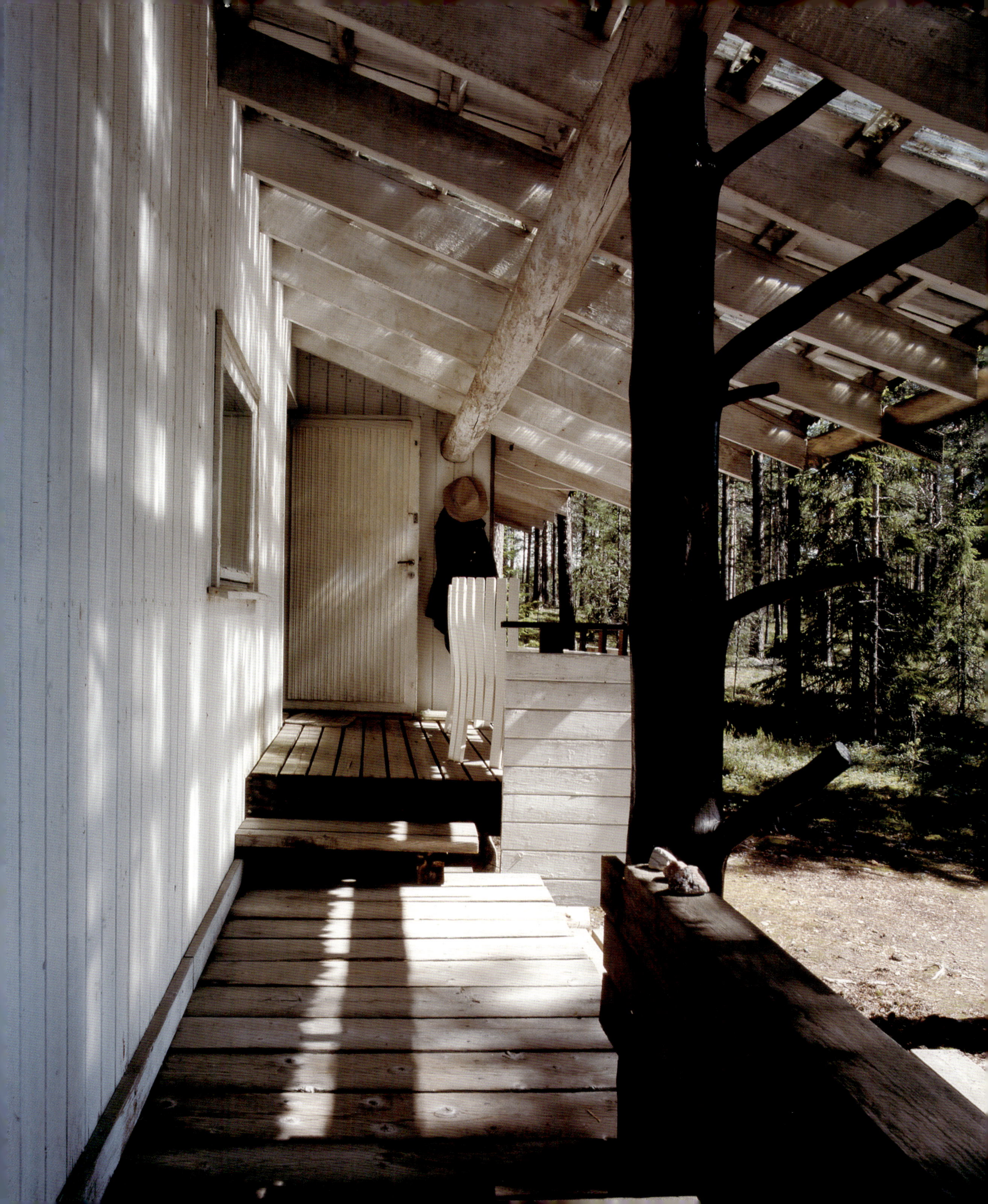

Li Englund's black-and-white murals enliven the interior.

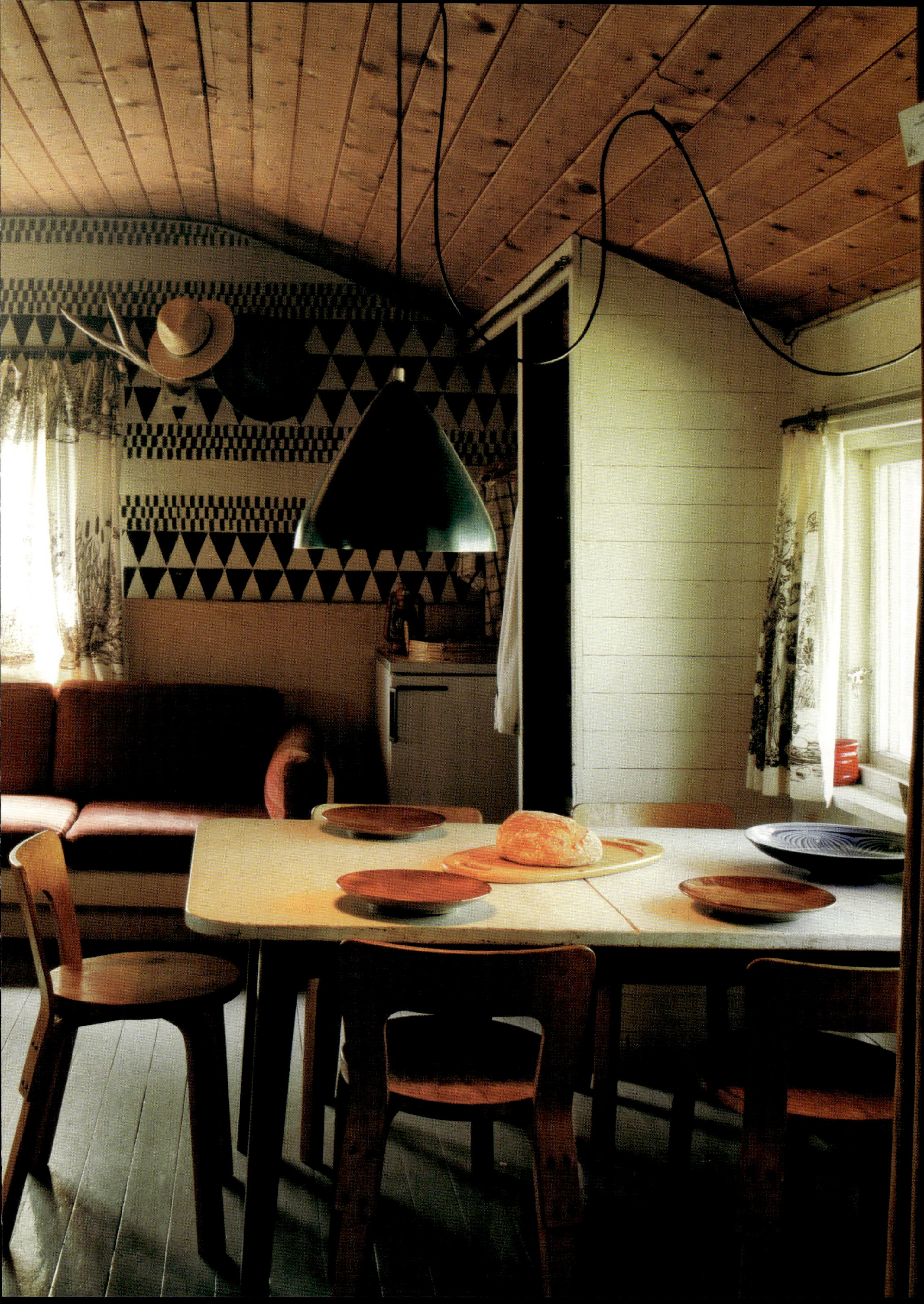

Muuratsalo Experimental House

Muuratsalo, 1952–54
Alvar Aalto

The Muuratsalo Experimental House is closely linked to an important stage in Alvar Aalto's life and œuvre. His Säynätsalo Town Hall was under construction at the end of the 1940s and beginning of the 1950s. One day, after visiting the building site, Aalto and a young architect who worked in his office, Elissa Mäkiniemi, later to become his second wife, came across a rocky outcrop on Muuratsalo Island while on a boating trip. They fell in love with the place and later purchased it as the site for their summer residence. Alvar and Elissa Aalto got married in 1954, and the Muuratsalo Experimental House became an important symbol for this new stage in Aalto's life.

Standing on bare rock adjacent to the lake in a steep, featured landscape typical of central Finland, the white-walled villa appears almost like a temple when approached from the lake, the original direction of arrival. On the forest side the house transforms into a small-scale building cluster. The third face of the villa, draped in red brick and colored tiles, turns inward toward a central courtyard.

The nearby lake and rolling landscape were important for Aalto in many ways, reminding him of both his childhood in Jyväskylä and the rolling Italian landscape that was so dear to him. Another link to his youth and Italy (where he spent his honeymoon with Aino Aalto) was the Muurame Church, one of the architect's early works from the 1920s, whose bell tower is visible on the other side of the lake.

The house is divided into two main wings, one containing the living room, the other bedrooms and a bathroom, with the kitchen at the intersection. The tall living room includes a dining area next to the fireplace, as well as a space for drawing tables and an elevated loft that Aalto used as an atelier, working on oil paintings in his free time. The exposed wooden roof beams and the loft structure contribute to the organization of the open space, demarcating the various areas. Aalto described the house as a combination of a tranquil architect's atelier and an experimentation center. It was both an important retreat in the heart of nature and a place where friends came together to relax and find peace. As Aalto once said: "Between swims I can work completely in peace."[1]

The courtyard and the open fireplace at its center form the focal point of the building. From here a view framed by the courtyard wall opens up toward the expanse of the lake. The evening sun enters the yard through the louvers on the west wall, warming the space. The open fireplace is reminiscent of the ancient custom of gathering around a campfire, while the surrounding walls create a feeling of safety.

The wall surfaces of the courtyard served as a testing ground for the durability of various ceramic materials and the æsthetic impressions of different surfaces. Aalto also experimented with several different structures for the walls and the roof of the building. The plan included tests for other free-form brick structures and solar heating, but they were never realized. The additions to the main volume were built of wood: a guest wing, whose basic structure consisted of logs set at an angle, and a woodshed. In the nearby smoke sauna, built about a year after the house, Aalto implemented a unique variation of the traditional log structure. The trapezoid-shaped building found its form from the rocks on the site. Aalto placed the logs of the walls so that their narrow and wide ends always faced the same direction, resulting in an automatically mono-pitched roof.

The brick courtyard of the main house is a good example of the multi-layered weave of possibilities in Aalto's works. Writing about the blend of experimentation and playfulness, Aalto described the Experimental House as "being made for the architect's own amusement and play. But it is also made for serious experiments, mainly for problems that the architect cannot resolve in ordinary building tasks."[2]

1 Göran Schildt, *Inhimillinen tekijä* [The Human Factor] (Helsinki: Otava, 1990), 261.
2 "Koetalo, Muuratsalo" [Experimental House, Muuratsalo], Alvar Aalto, *Arkkitehti* 9–10 (1953): 159.

OPPOSITE
The atrium courtyard is framed by high brick walls.

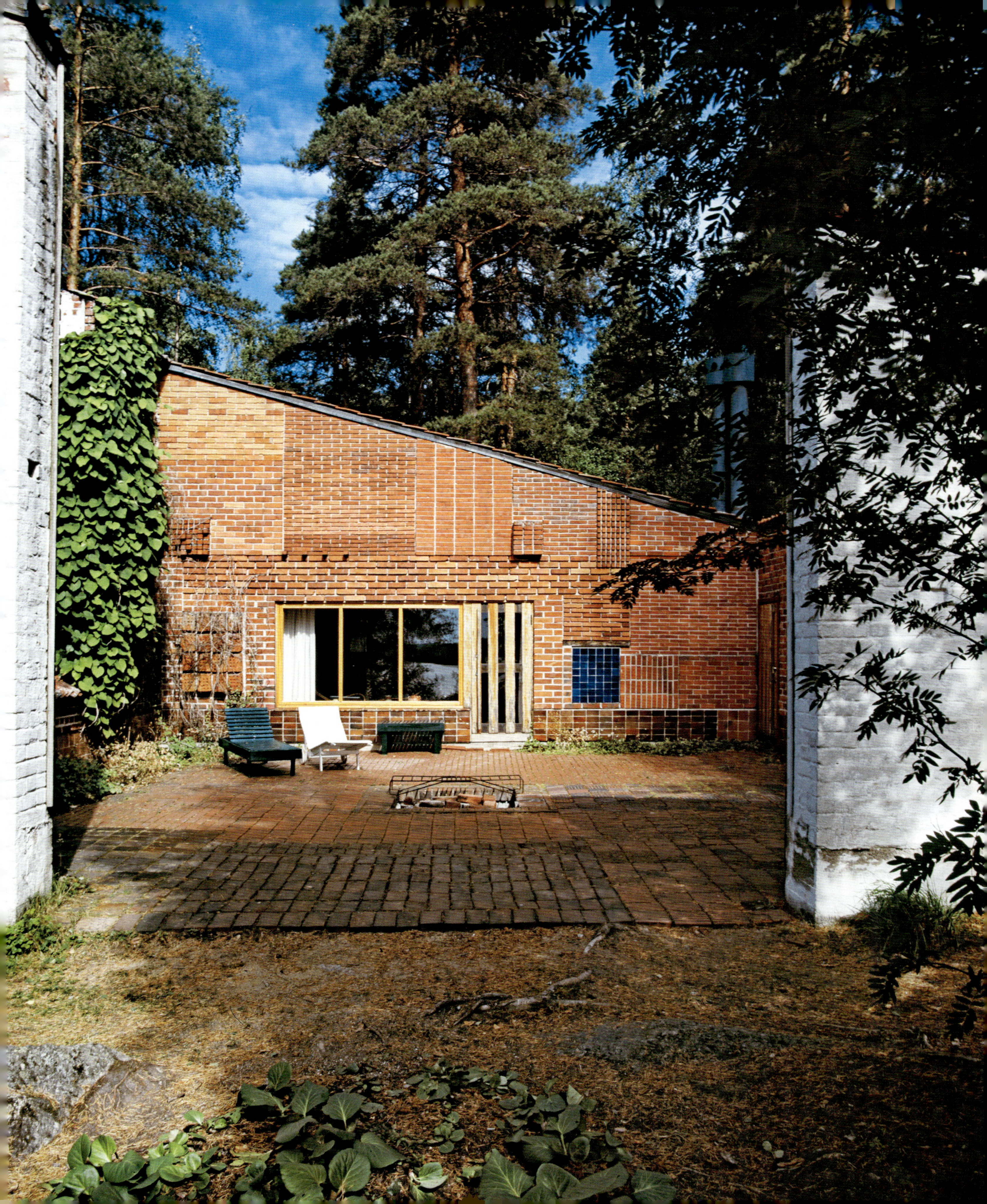

TOP
Perspective drawing by Aalto

MIDDLE
Sketch of site plan by Aalto

BOTTOM
Plan

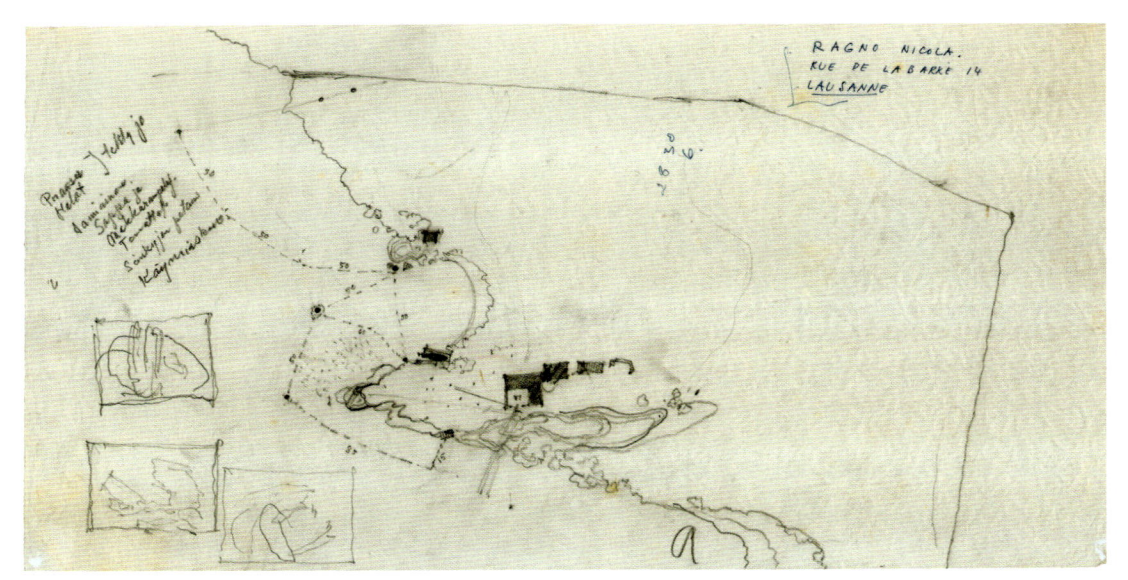

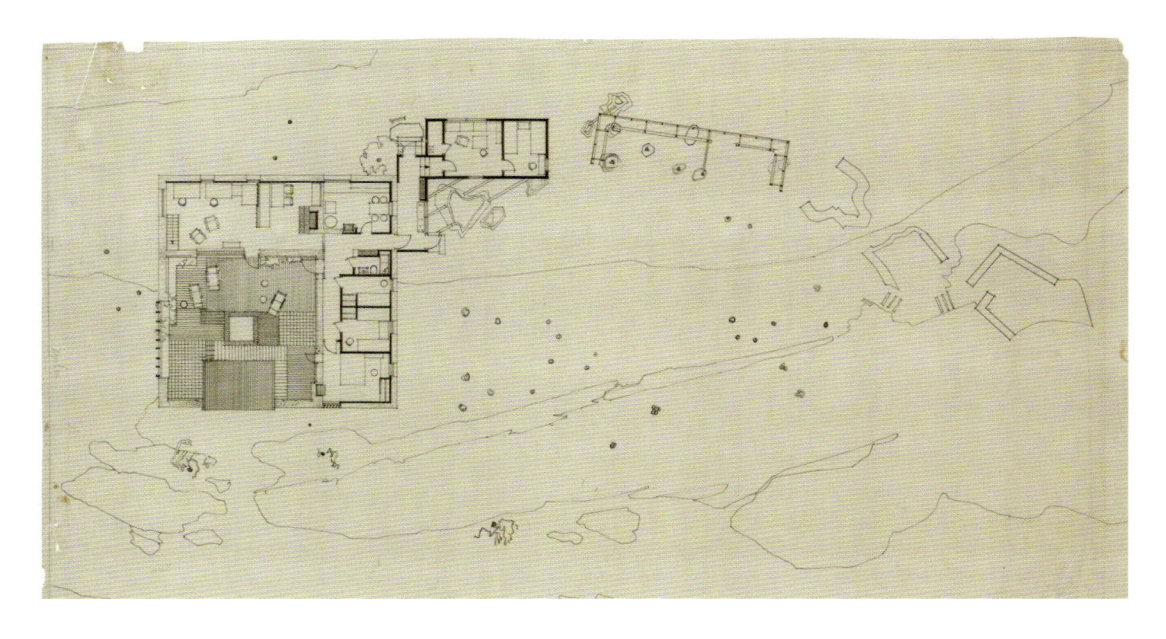

RIGHT
Göran Schildt (left), Alvar Aalto (right), Mona Schildt, Maire Gullichsen, and Maija Heikinheimo (back from left to right) in Aalto's boat *Nemo Propheta in Patria*, 1954

BOTTOM
Alvar and Elissa Aalto with guests in the courtyard. On the left are Alvar Aalto and Sigfried Giedion, on the right Carola Giedion and Elissa Aalto.

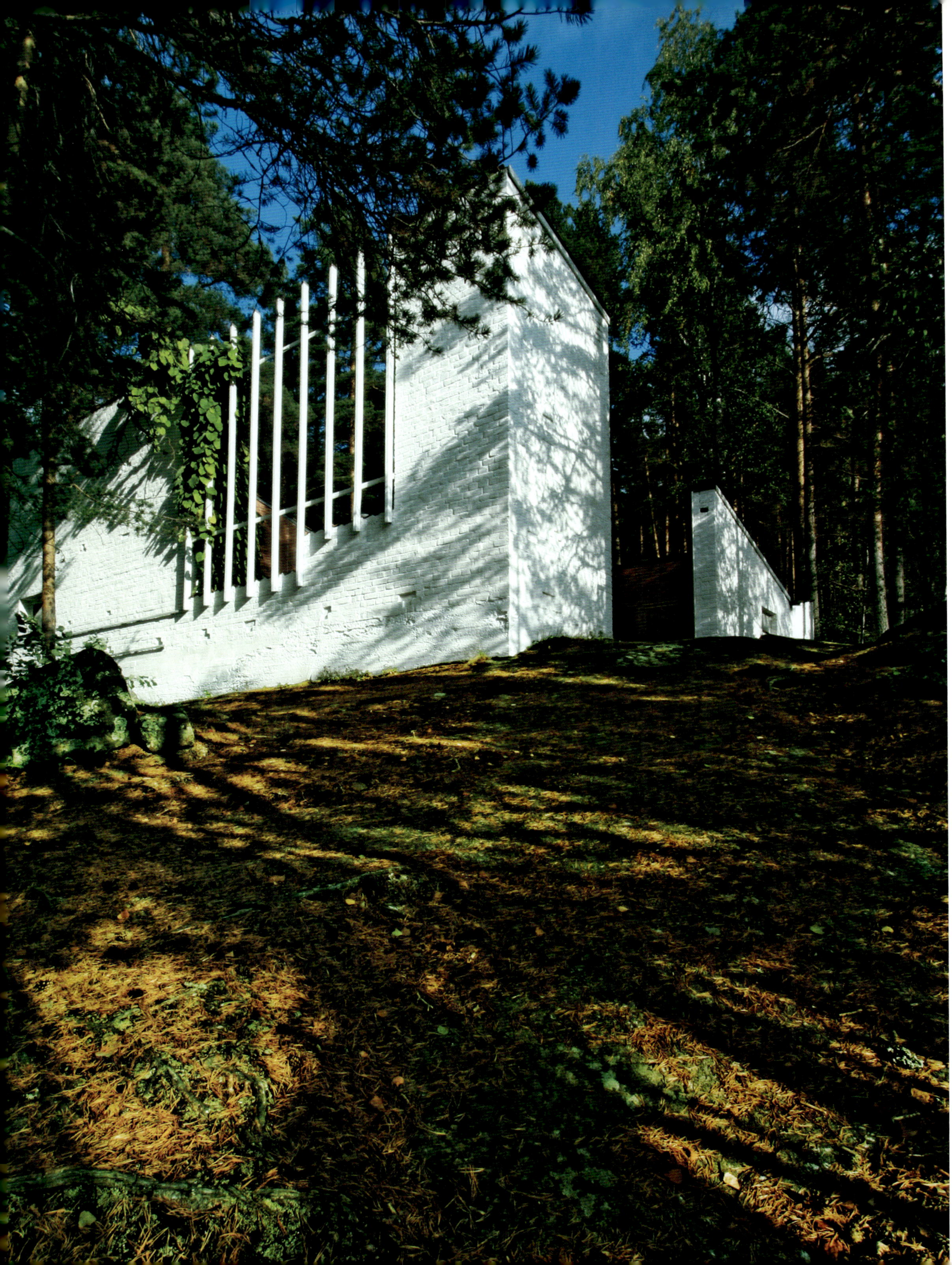

OPPOSITE
View of the house from the lakeside

RIGHT
Oil painting by Aalto

BOTTOM
Brickwork detail from the atrium courtyard

BELOW
Sequence of spaces from the living room through the atrium courtyard to the lake

OPPOSITE, TOP
Living room cabinet

OPPOSITE, BOTTOM
The living-room captures the evening sunlight.

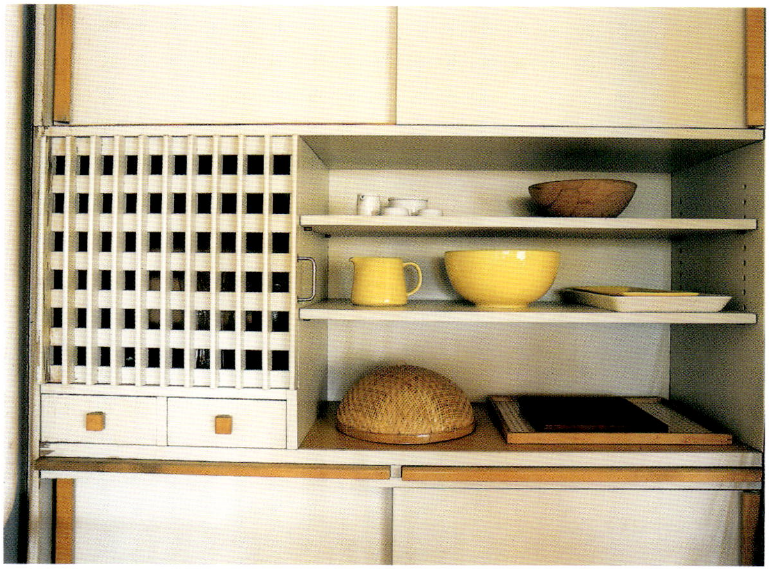

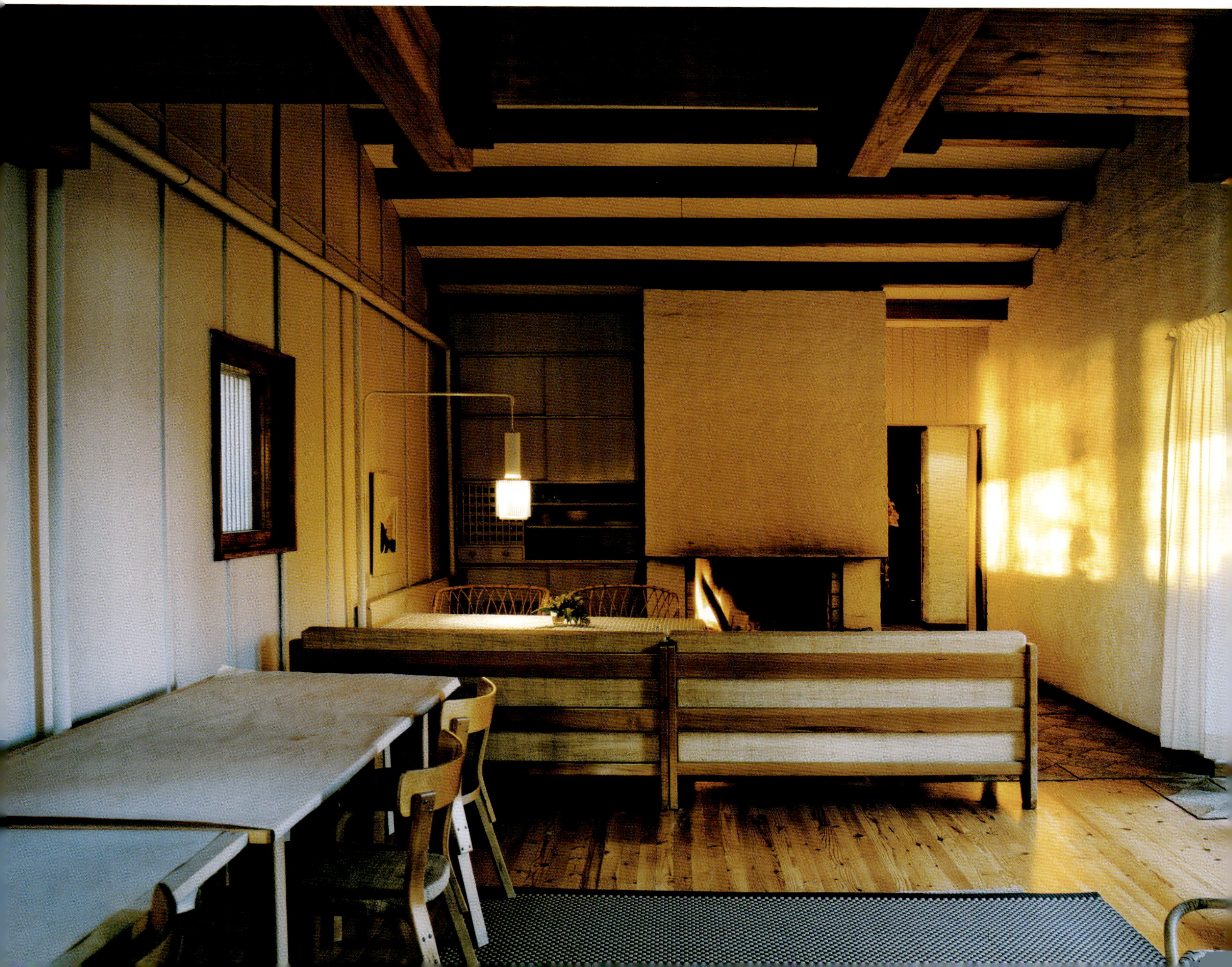

RIGHT
The fireplace in the living room

BOTTOM
Living room with loft

OPPOSITE
Window between the kitchen and back entrance room

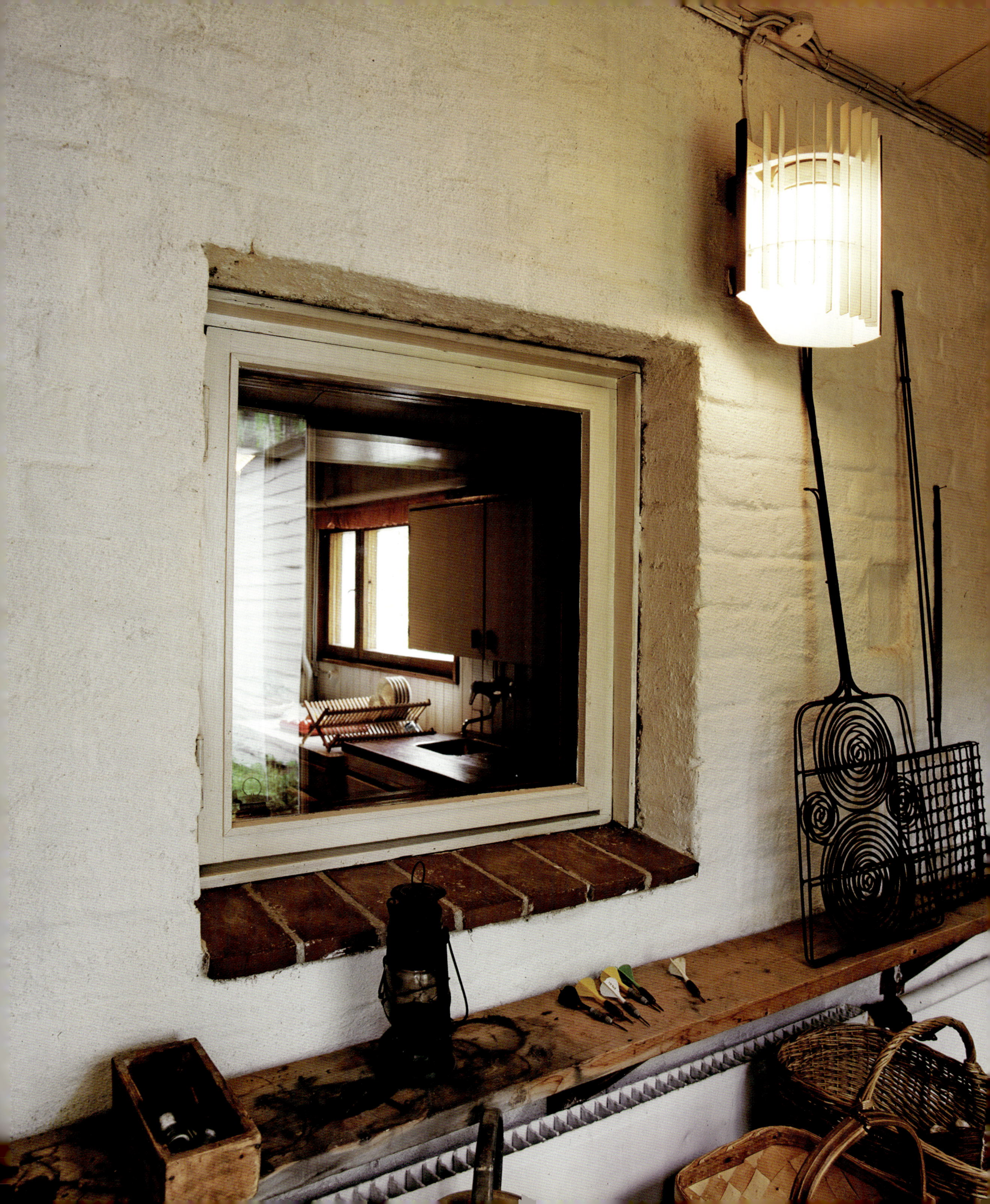

RIGHT
Smoke sauna interior

BOTTOM
Smoke sauna

OPPOSITE
View of the house from the forest side

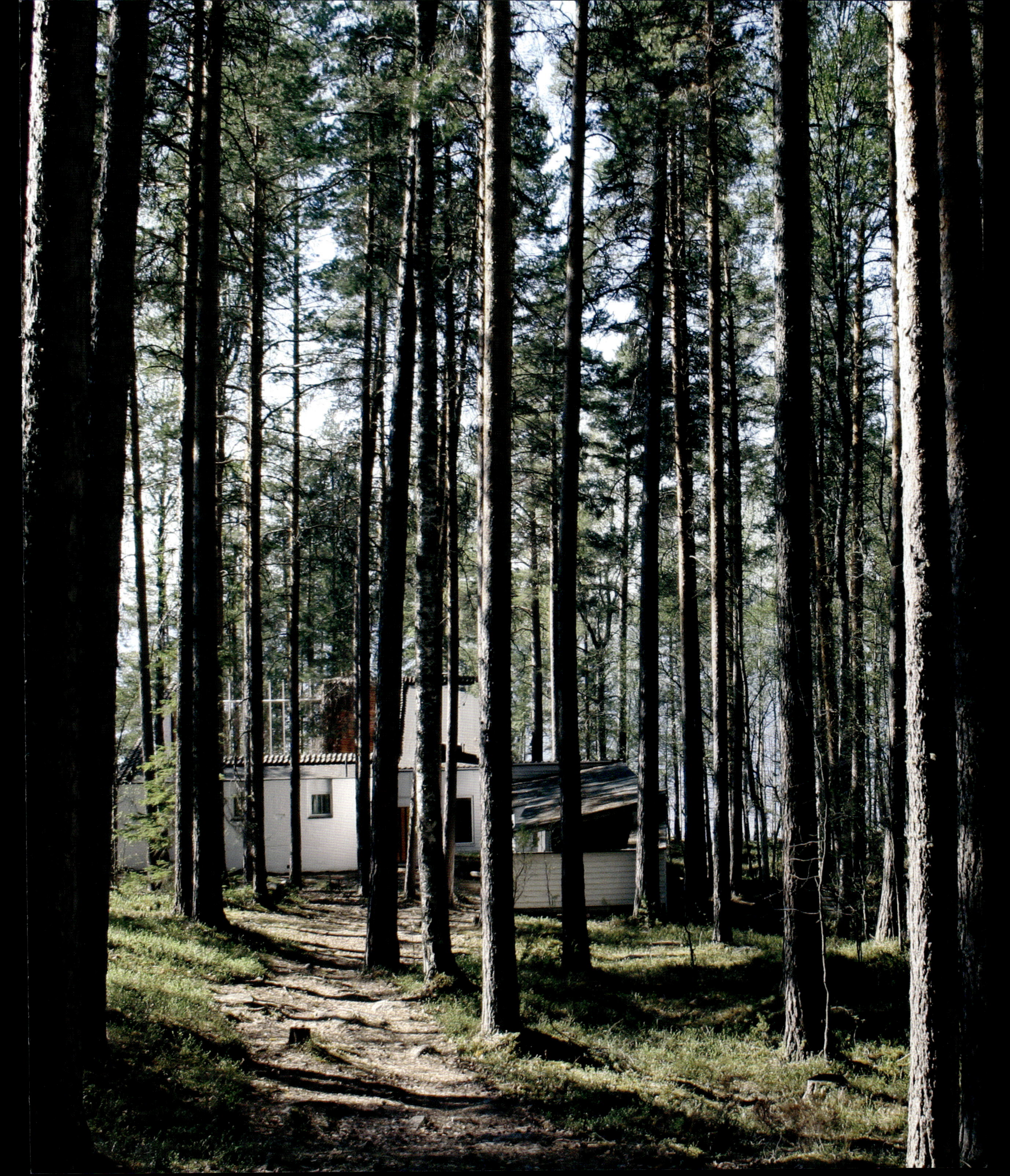

Summer Villa

Bökars, 1955
Bertel Saarnio

In his "dream house," as Bertel Saarnio described his summer villa, comfort and a homey atmosphere come together with elegant clarity. The two-story building is partly raised on pillars and sits in the shade of a small forest near a gentle sea bay. In front of the house is a low hillock, but the elevated living spaces provide an unhindered view of the sea. The raised building also preserves the natural shoreline with its numerous moss-covered boulders. The ground floor holds sauna facilities, which are bordered by two covered outdoor spaces: a terrace and a carport.

The upper floor has an open plan arrangement. Saarnio gave different functions their own zones through the placement of furniture. These furniture clusters, such as a table and chairs, a drawing table and bookshelves, a built-in sofa and a coffee table, are grouped around the brick wall of the fireplace and chimney, while the sleeping spaces are separated by cupboards and light partitions. Wooden pillars and beams also subdivide the space, which is otherwise dominated by unplaned wood surfaces. The exterior walls are clad with dark-painted boards, which are interrupted by large areas of glazing.

The glazed wall on the seaward side of the villa is the most open and accentuated of the facades. On the west side a window catches the evening sun, while an opening in the north facade near the stairs provides a view of the meadow behind the house.

The villa served as the summer home for Saarnio's six-person family but was also used on weekends during the spring and fall. Even though the house was meant as a place for relaxation, Saarnio also made provisions to work there. The plan includes space for a drawing table in the corner of the living room.

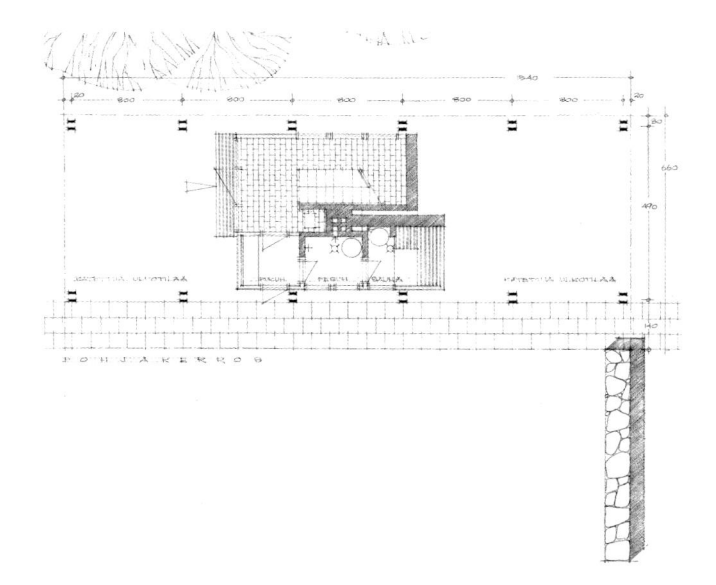

RIGHT
First-floor plan

OPPOSITE
View of the cabin from the seaside

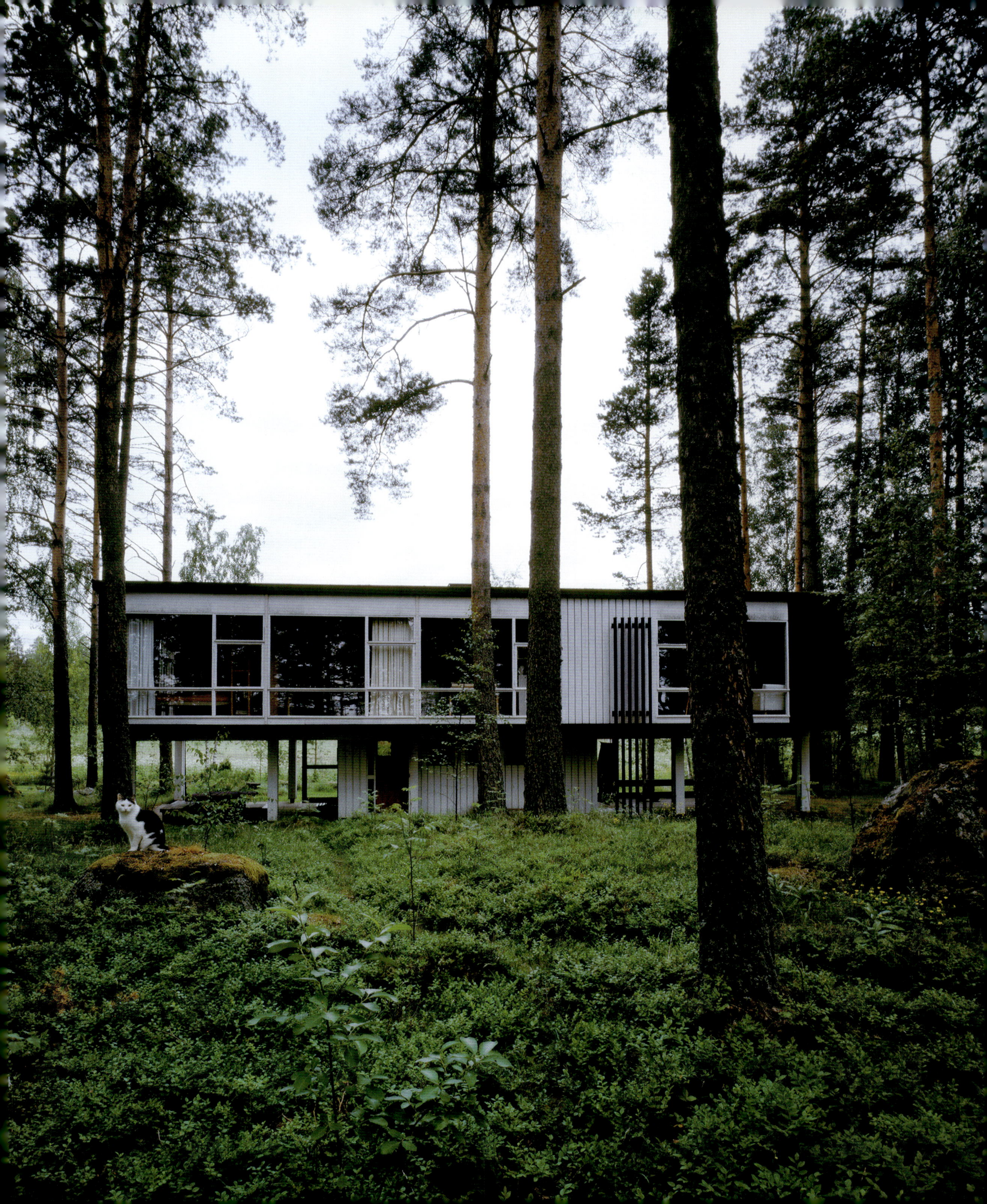

TOP
Second-floor plan

MIDDLE, LEFT
Bertel Saarnio with his children Ulla, Timo, Satu, and Meri, 1955. Before the construction of the cabin, the family used to camp on the site.

MIDDLE, RIGHT
Saarnio's employees, Juha Leiviskä and Pentti Helenius, visiting the cottage and playing cards with Saarnio's daughters, 1962

BOTTOM
On the construction site, 1950s

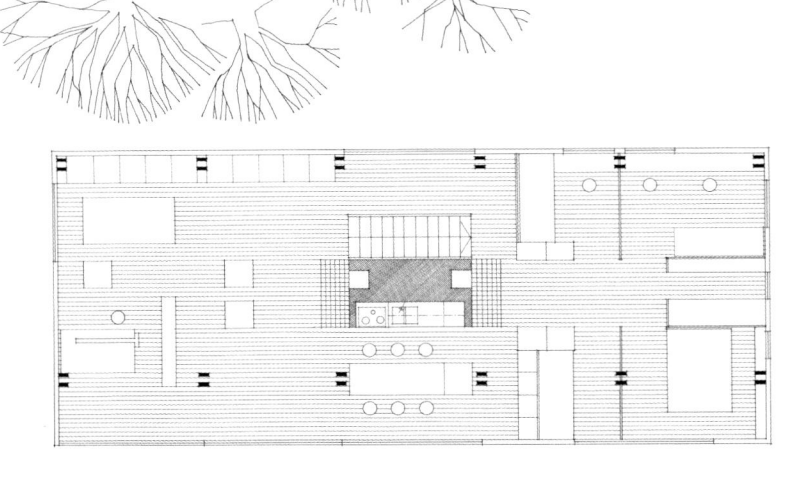

94

RIGHT
View of the entrance facade

BOTTOM
A view of the cabin in the early summer landscape

BELOW
View of the entrance

OPPOSITE
The terrace at the end of the building

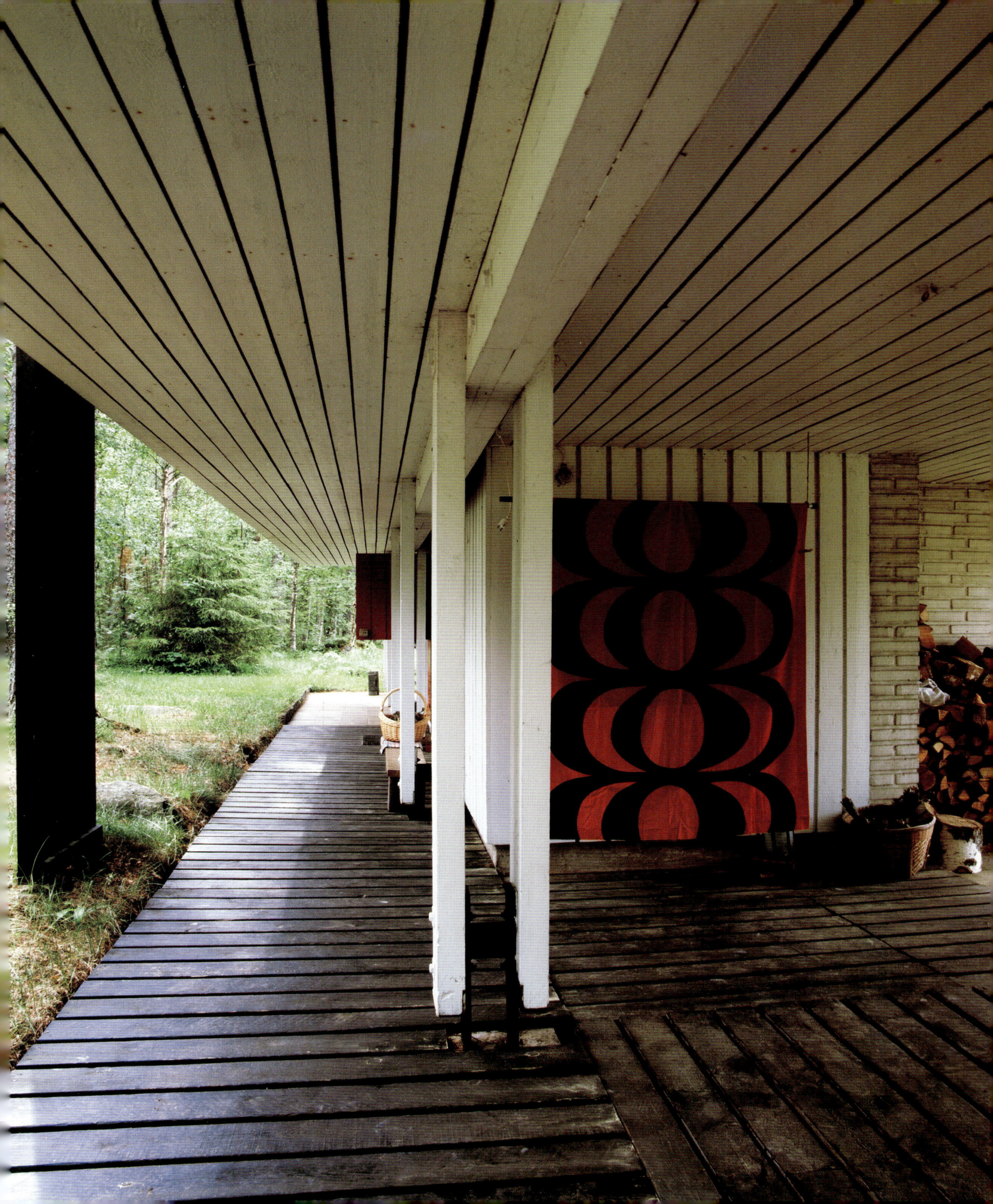

BELOW
Windows near the staircase look out onto the meadow landscape.

OPPOSITE
Dining area

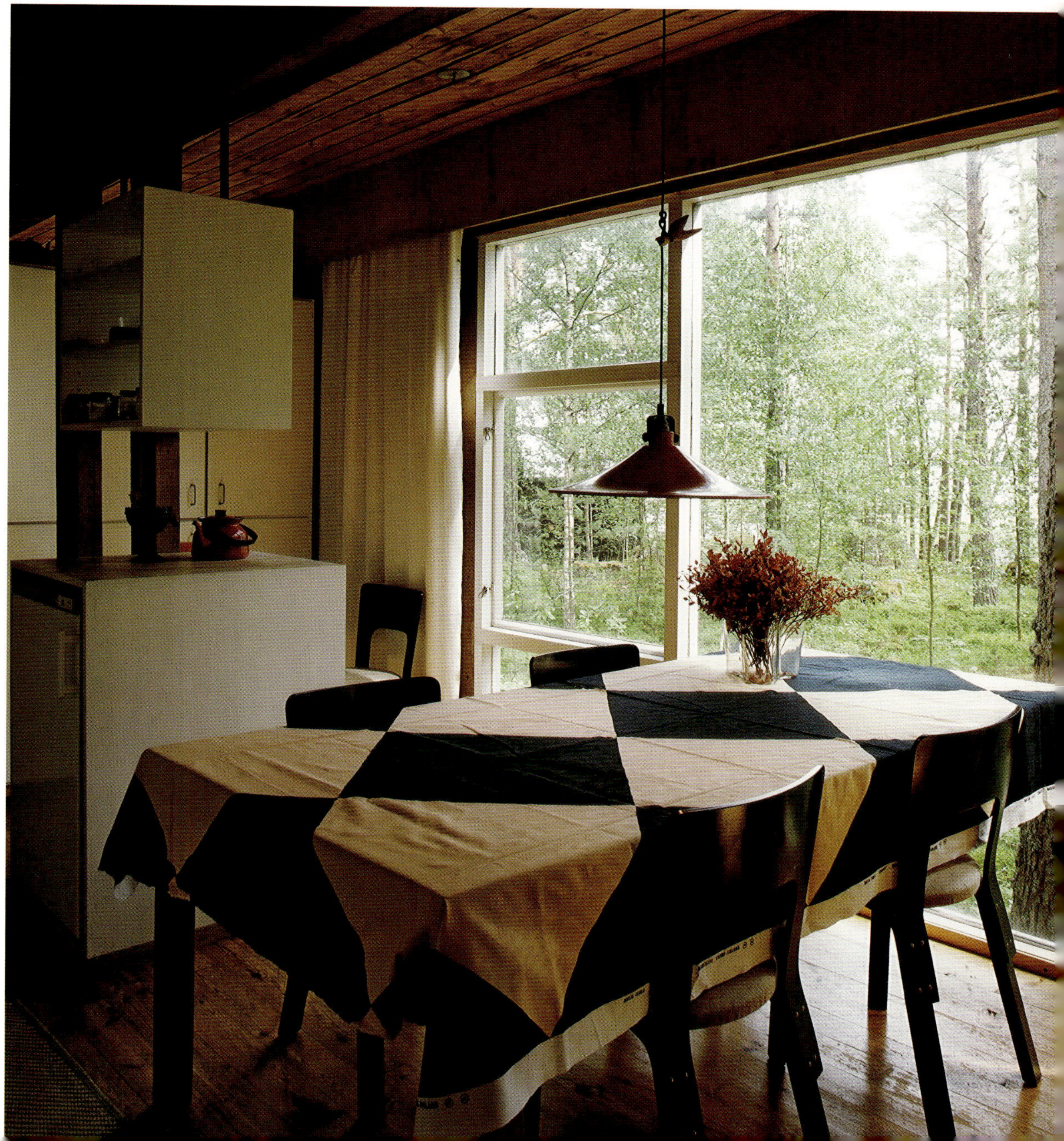

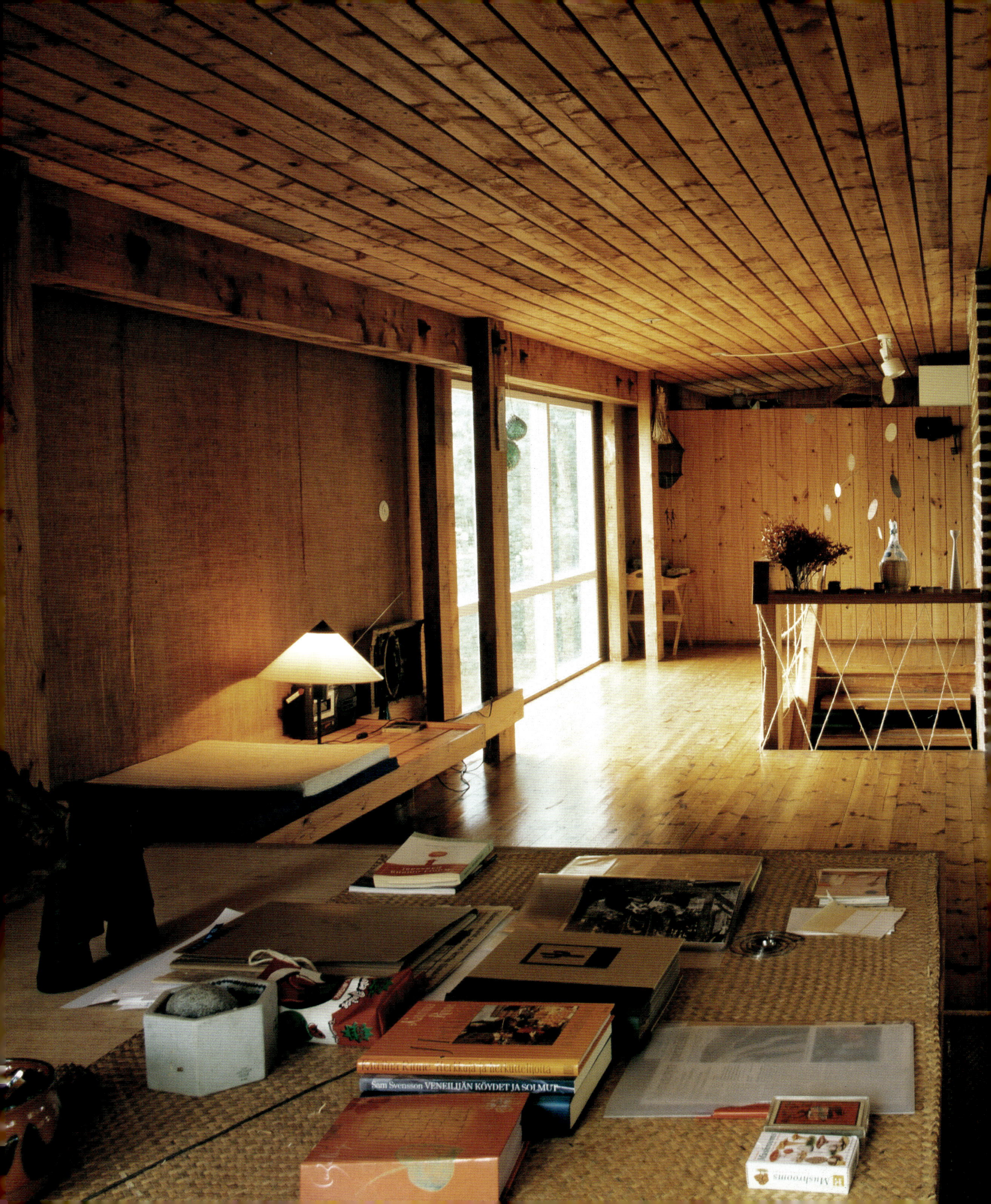
Sam Svensson VENEILIJÄN KÖYDET JA SOLMUT

The open space is divided only by a central fireplace.

Villa Skata

Löparö, 1953–55, 1962–67
Heikki and Mirja Castrén

The group of buildings that comprise Villa Skata developed over a period of time. Heikki and Mirja Castrén designed the first small log cabin of eighty-six square feet while they were still architecture students. Together with relatives they built the small structure themselves over the course of three years, felling trees, researching traditional log-jointing techniques, and fetching moss from a bog. Sitting on a beautiful cape with exposed, smooth rocks, somewhat sheltered from the wind by a small island in front of the cape, the cabin was often approached from the sea by boat. From the main landward side only a narrow footpath leads to the building.

For some years the couple and their growing family spent their summers in the small cabin—which provided space to sleep—while everyday chores, cooking, and eating initially took place outdoors, in a kitchen shelter. Gradually, the Castréns built a more spacious cottage, whose interior is dominated by a vertical log-frame construction, as well as a small sleeping cabin and storage facilities. The exterior spaces between the various buildings are as important as the cabins themselves. Through their careful placement, the architects created a yard space that is protected from the sea winds. The Castréns built a rhomboid-shaped sauna on a nearby small island facing the Villa Skata buildings. Situated in a rocky crevice, the small sauna merges into the landscape.

The cabins, which over the years have acquired a grey patina, are partly hidden among the shoreline trees, and their backs are guarded by a stepped rock face. The buildings express both a feeling of generosity and a natural settling into the landscape. Experimentation is manifest in the cabins in various ways: the first cottage is the cell of minimal living; in the second villa the structure plays the leading role; while a third and final building was constructed on the adjacent island. The family spent their summers together at Villa Skata, from where Heikki and Mirja Castrén would routinely boat to work in the center of Helsinki. The family occasionally visited the cottages during the winter, arriving over the frozen sea. In the early years they enjoyed living at the mercy of nature in simple camp-like conditions as a meaningful experience.

Heikki Castrén, a designer of large office buildings, brought out his more sensitive side in his summer residence. He once stated that he directed all of his romantic thoughts into this design. He constructed some of the later cabins himself, continuing the do-it-yourself tradition. It is possible to see his summer residence as a counterpart to the demands and scale of his commercial and office buildings, but an essential feature common to both is their clear structural principle.

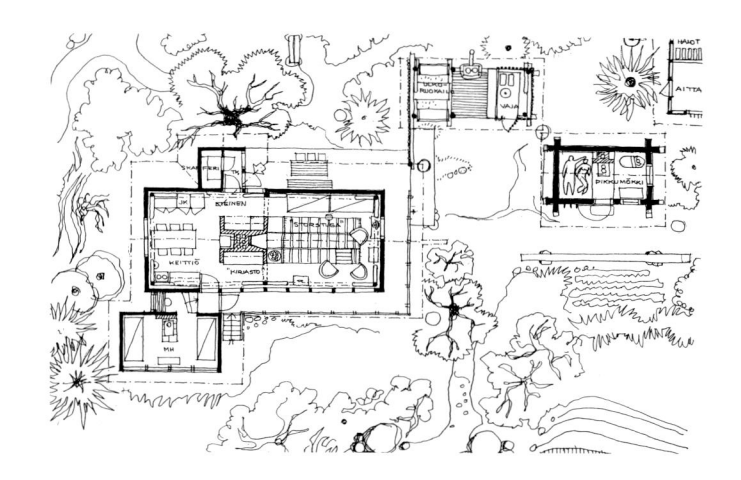

RIGHT
Site plan and plans of the cottages

OPPOSITE
The cottages are located at the edge of the forest.

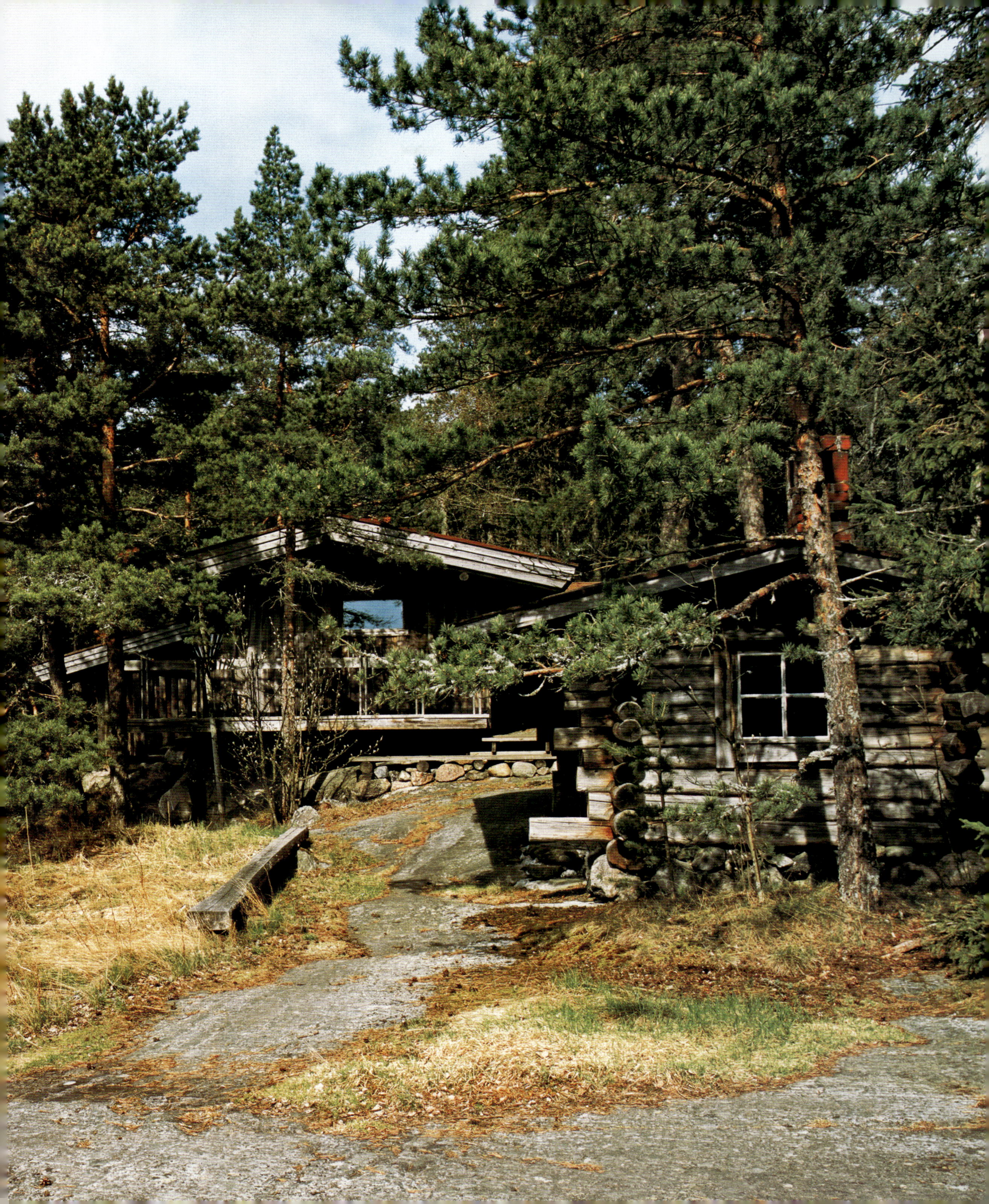

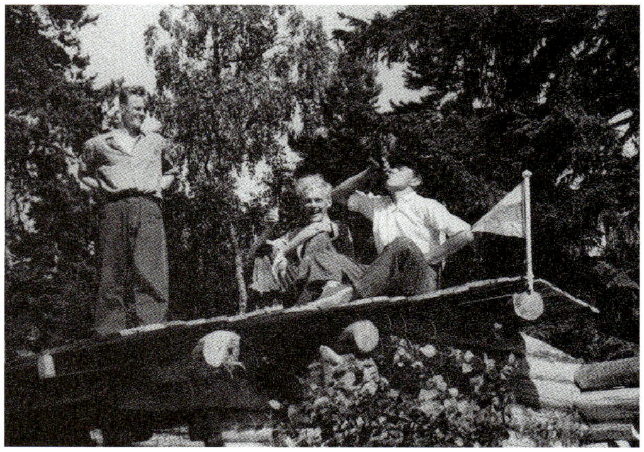

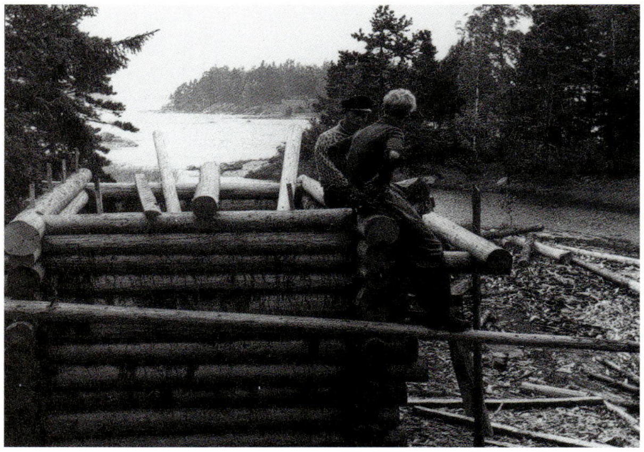

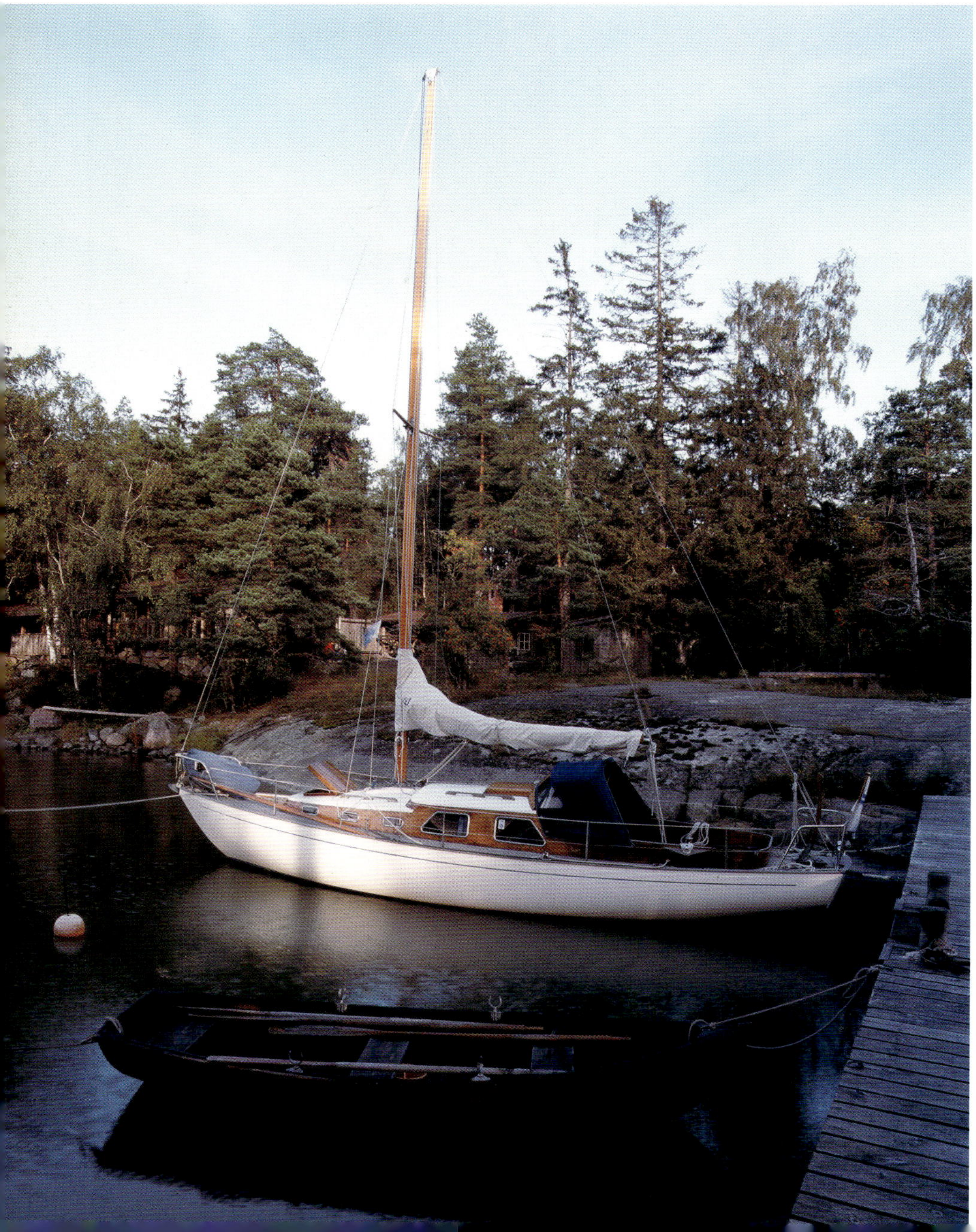

OPPOSITE, TOP LEFT
Celebrating the construction work (Heikki Castrén is in the middle)

OPPOSITE, TOP RIGHT
The cabin log frame is almost finished.

OPPOSITE, BOTTOM
Villa Skata's sheltered harbor

RIGHT
The sauna in the evening sun

BOTTOM
Seaside view of the buildings

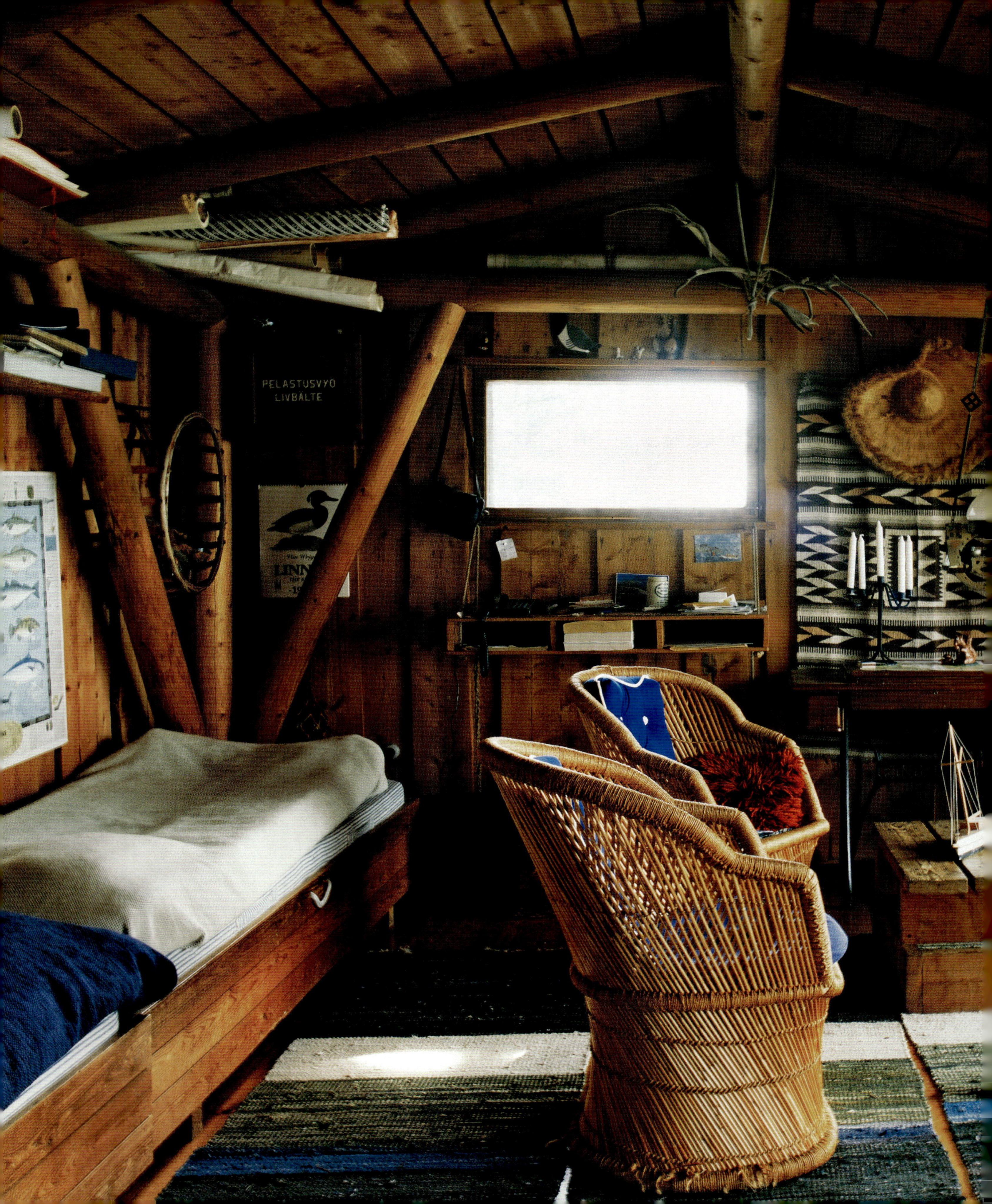
PELASTUSVYO
LIVBALTE

Interior of the villa

The Pulkkinen Cabin

Kustavi, 1967
Mikko Pulkkinen

With its steel structure and vibrant colors, the Pulkkinen Cabin stands in contrast to the surrounding landscape, yet, nestled in the rocky terrain among low pine trees, it also respects its surroundings. The cabin was built on a west-facing cape in the southwest Finnish archipelago. The windy conditions of the site determined the location of the building, which is protected from the southwest winds by undulating shoreline rocks.

The various parts of the cottage differ in their materials and structure, depending on the use and character of each area. Except for the terraces, which have a steel construction, Pulkkinen used wood for the main load-bearing structure. The canopy is supported by a triangular arrangement of thin steel rods and can be lowered down to form a window shutter during the winter. The plywood terrace roof is coated with plastic to withstand the harsh climatic conditions of the outer archipelago. From the outside, the cabin looks like a box with openings cut into the sides. Colored lines create a playful effect on its dark-stained plywood walls.

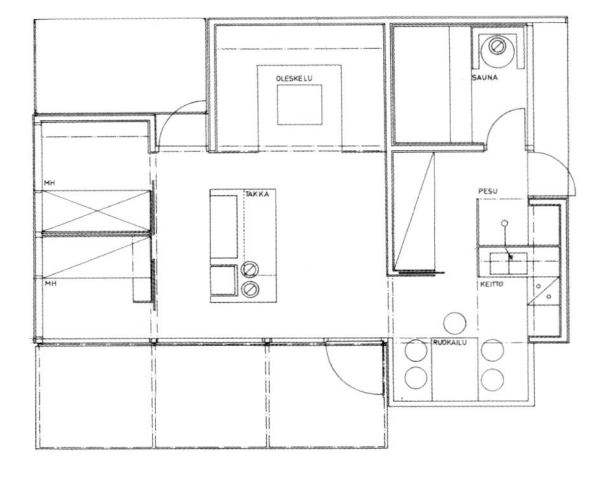

The main focus of the open plan interior is the fireplace in the living space, which directly links to a small kitchen and dining area. Furniture separates the sleeping spaces, forming individual small rooms. Multiple windows provide an unhindered view toward the sea from almost every point in the cabin. Pulkkinen carefully placed these openings at the height of the viewer. For instance, a broad vista of the horizon opens up from the dining table. Some of the interior walls are painted red, and the sunlight that enters through the skylight further emphasizes their warm atmosphere. Three small exterior terraces, each facing a different direction, extend the small cabin into the landscape: the sauna terrace is on the south side; the largest terrace—linked with the interior living spaces—faces west, capturing the evening sun; while the third terrace functions as an entrance on the landward side of the island.

The whole interior is only 592 square feet because the family spends as much time as possible outdoors. The Pulkkinens visit the cabin frequently. Even though the building has a light appearance, it can be used in the winter. During these times, activities such as skiing and ice-skating on the sea provide a different view of the archipelago landscape.

ABOVE
Plan

OPPOSITE
While contrasting with the landscape, the cabin shows respect for its surroundings through its siting.

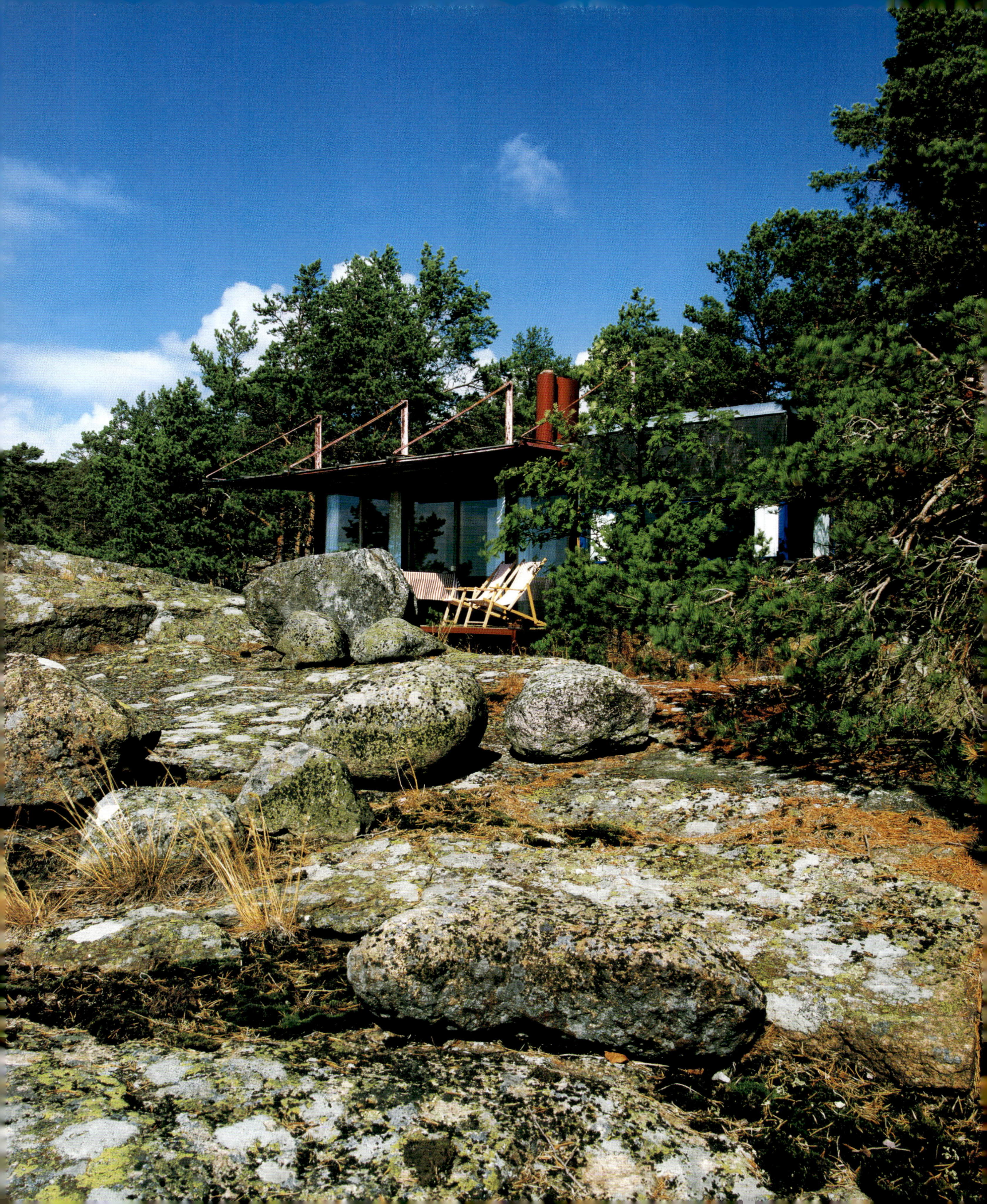

RIGHT
The Pulkkinen Summer Cabin is located on a small cape.

BOTTOM
The cabin under construction

RIGHT
Skylight in the living space

BOTTOM
Its steel structure and bright colors give the Pulkkinen summer cabin its unique character.

RIGHT
Kitchen corner

BOTTOM
View of the sea from the living room and terrace

OPPOSITE
View from the bedroom

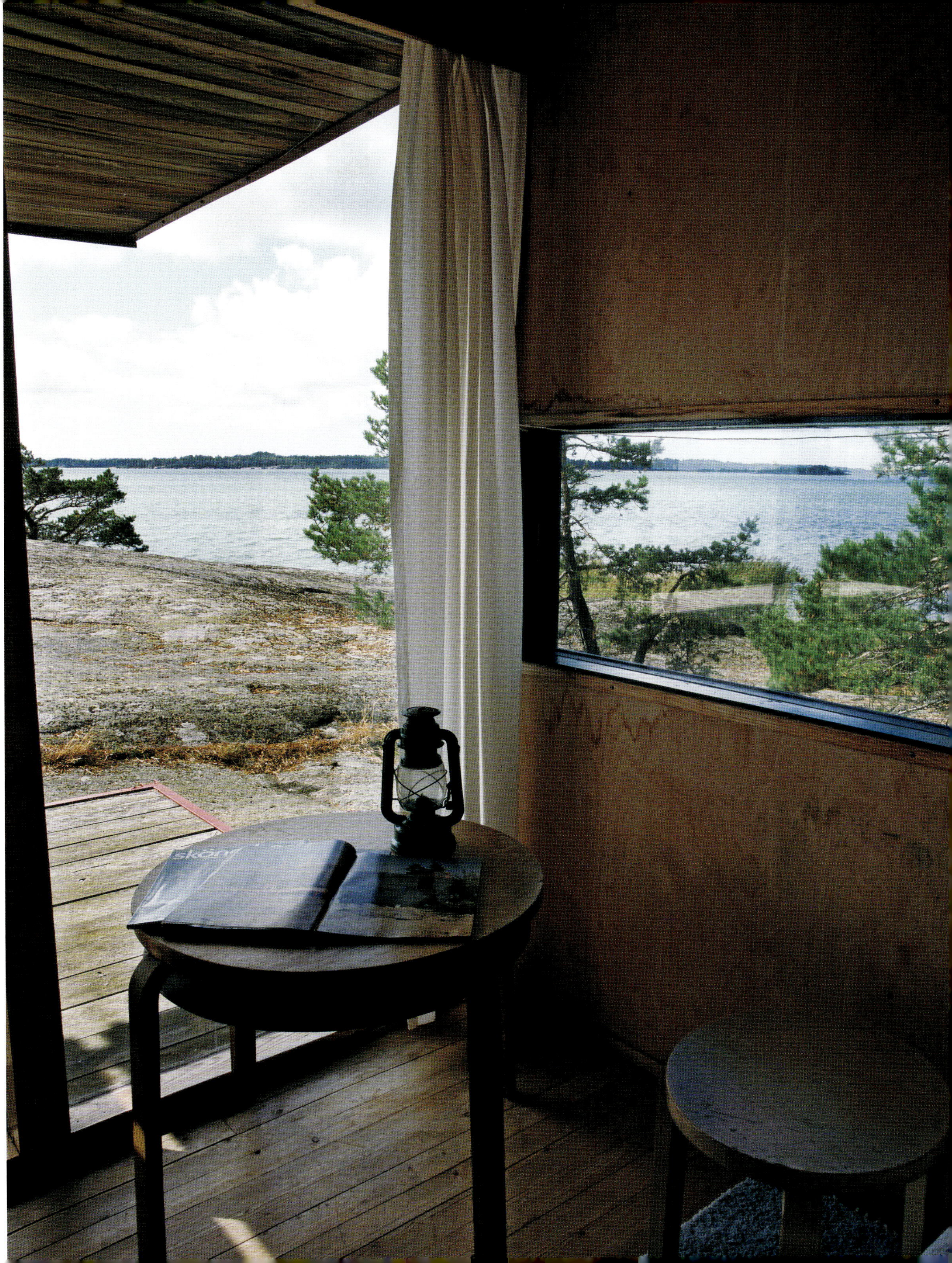

Living space

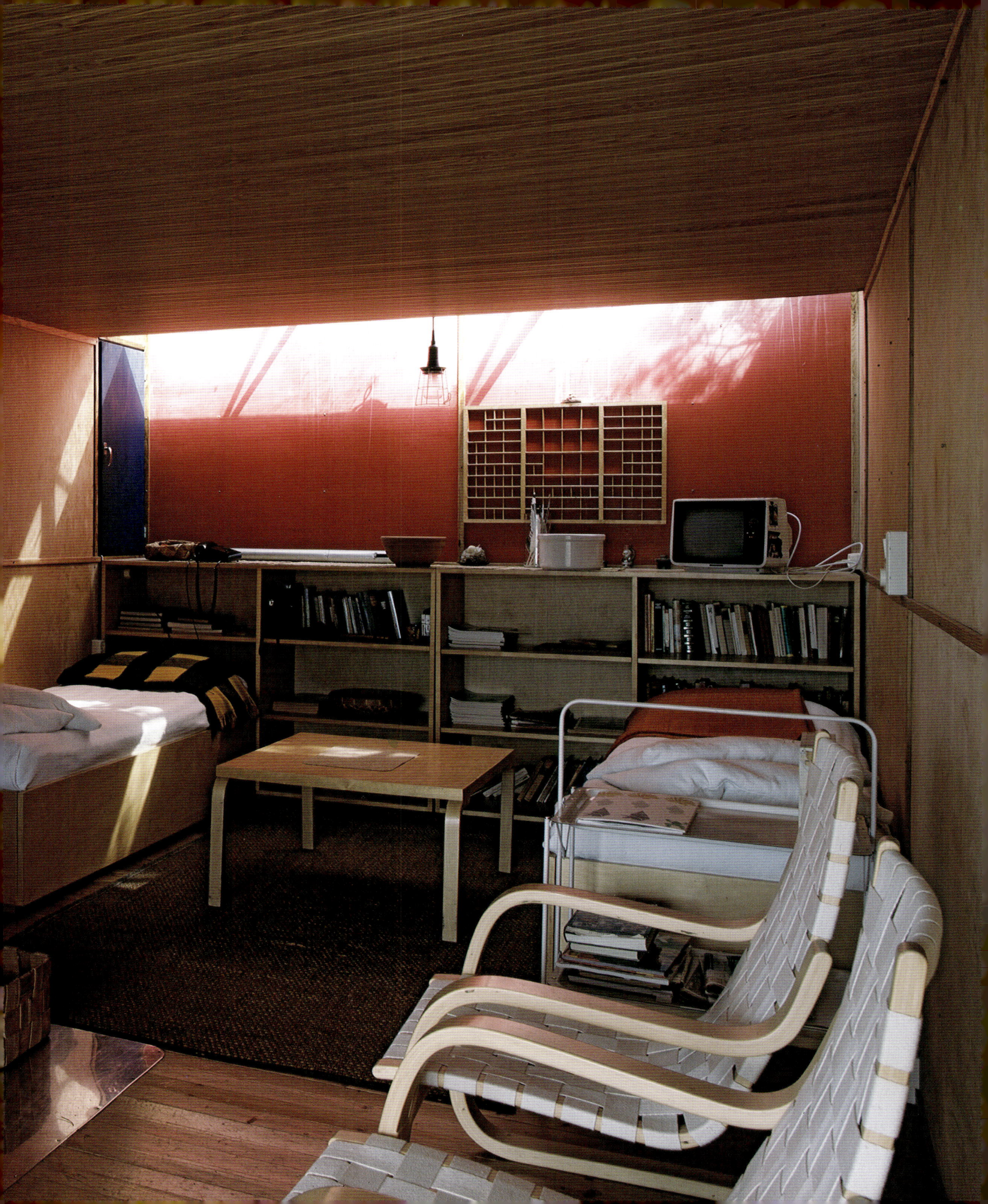

Lingonsö Holiday Island

Barösund, 1966–69
Kaija and Heikki Siren

Kaija and Heikki Siren belong to the generation of prominent postwar Finnish architects. In the 1950s and 1960s they were involved with the design of residential buildings in Tapiola Garden City and also worked on projects in Otaniemi, the University of Technology's student village. They built their summer residence on Lingonsö— a fishermen's island in the outer archipelago—in stages during the latter half of the 1960s. A wave breaker and boat mooring were the first necessities the Sirens constructed, as well as a sauna and adjoining room providing shelter for sleeping. There is a long tradition in rural Finland to build a sauna, which acts as a multipurpose space, before the main house. Along with these practical and sensible structures, the Sirens also immediately built a sea pavilion—the only one of their buildings facing the open sea. It was intended as a place for meditation and concentration, where they could experience the strong presence of nature. The pavilion, also called the chapel, is simultaneously ethereal and transparent—with its glass walls—and heavy and sturdy—with its round-log construction. The harsh climate and the small-scale monumentality of the rocks and the trees—typical for the outer archipelago—were an important inspiration for its robust structure.

On the opposite side of the island the main residential buildings form a village-like grouping; the sauna, the traditional *tupa* farmhouse-style kitchen, and the sleeping spaces each have their own separate log cabin. The kitchen building is adjacent to the sauna, which is situated at the edge of the shoreline rocks. Large windows in both cabins look out onto the sea and the setting sun. In front of them a narrow terrace marks the transition from the buildings to the rocks and provides a place for common activities and socializing. The sleeping cabins—which are more enclosed and private—are behind the kitchen and sauna buildings, grouped around a small yard. Terraces form a connection between the cottages, whose scale is typical for traditional archipelago buildings. In addition to acting as circulation links—and delicately connecting the cabins to the natural terrain and landscape—the terraces are important living spaces. The spot best sheltered from the winds is the central southwest-facing yard between the buildings. Wood is the dominant material of the interior, where the architects introduced variation through different ceiling designs.

The Lingonsö Holiday Island demonstrates how facilities for varied functions—leisure activities, daily chores, and retreat—can complement one another in a special way. The group of buildings by the jetty was created for an active vacation lifestyle and the completion of chores, while the sea pavilion offers a quiet place for meditation and rest. The pavilion is reached via a path that travels across the island. En route, one withdraws from everyday life and forgets mundane issues, gaining instead a peace with oneself, and an awareness of the colors of the surrounding landscape and the sounds of the birds. At the pavilion one encounters an ever-changing atmosphere, as determined by windy or calm weather, by rain or sun. The sun either shines as a strong glare or faintly through the clouds, or sets beneath the horizon.

OPPOSITE
In the sea pavilion only a thin glass wall separates the inside from the outside.

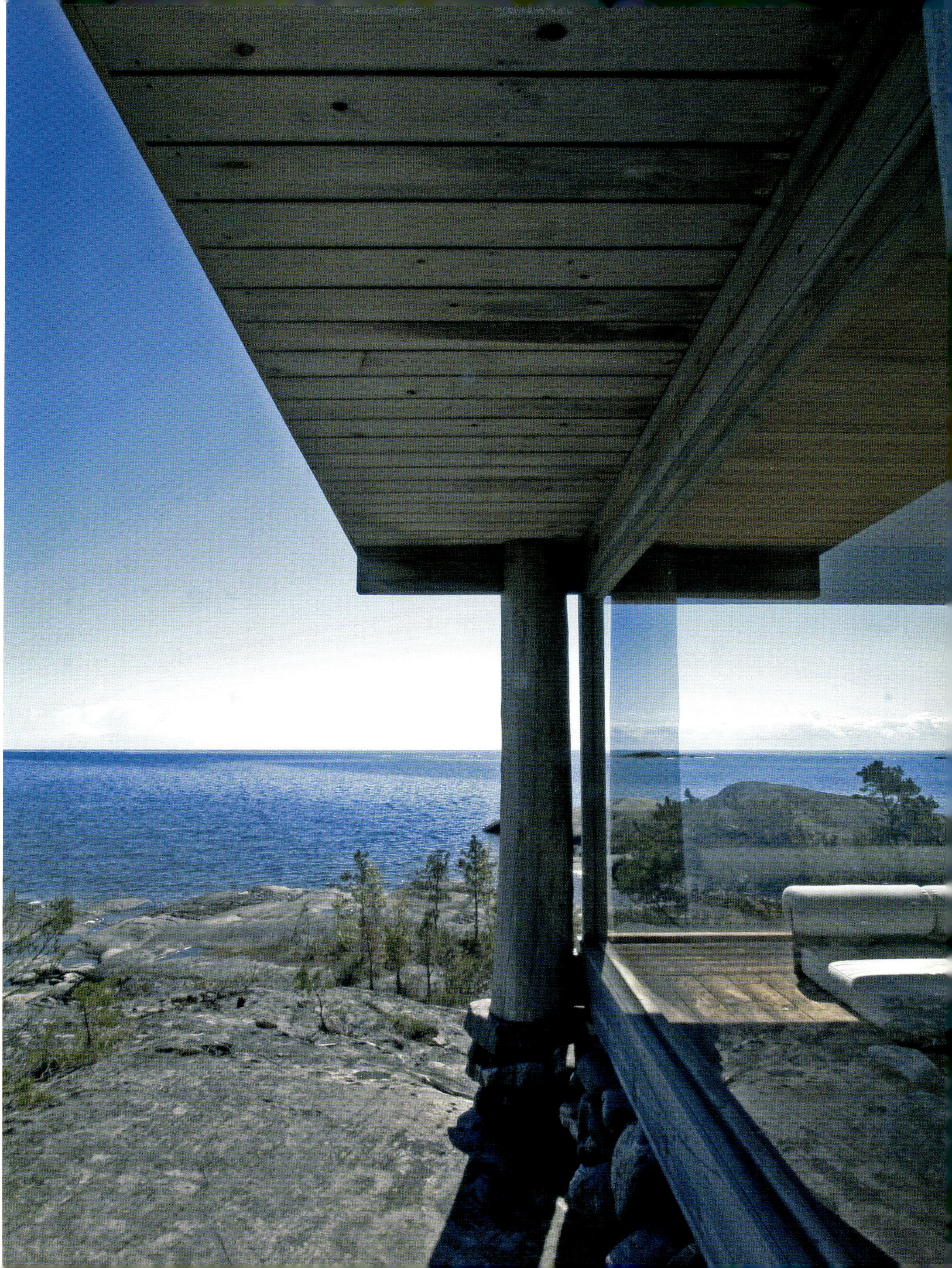

TOP
Plan

MIDDLE
The two seaside buildings have large windows that look out onto the shoreline.

BOTTOM, LEFT
Sunset moment at Lingonsö

BOTTOM, RIGHT
Drying racks for fishing nets by the shore

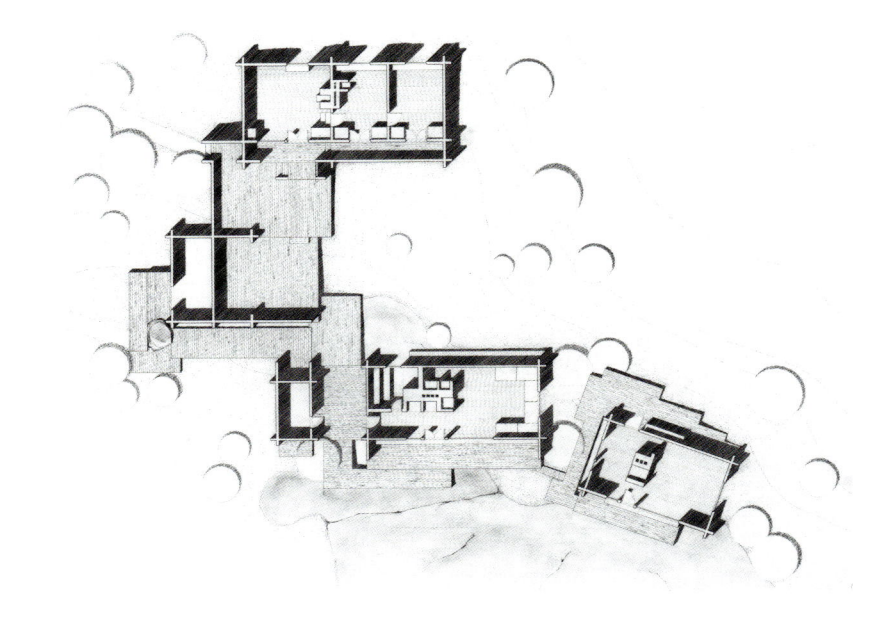

TOP
Northeast and northwest facades

BOTTOM
Seaside facades and terraces

BELOW
Terraces link the buildings together.

OPPOSITE
The sauna with a small bedroom was built first.

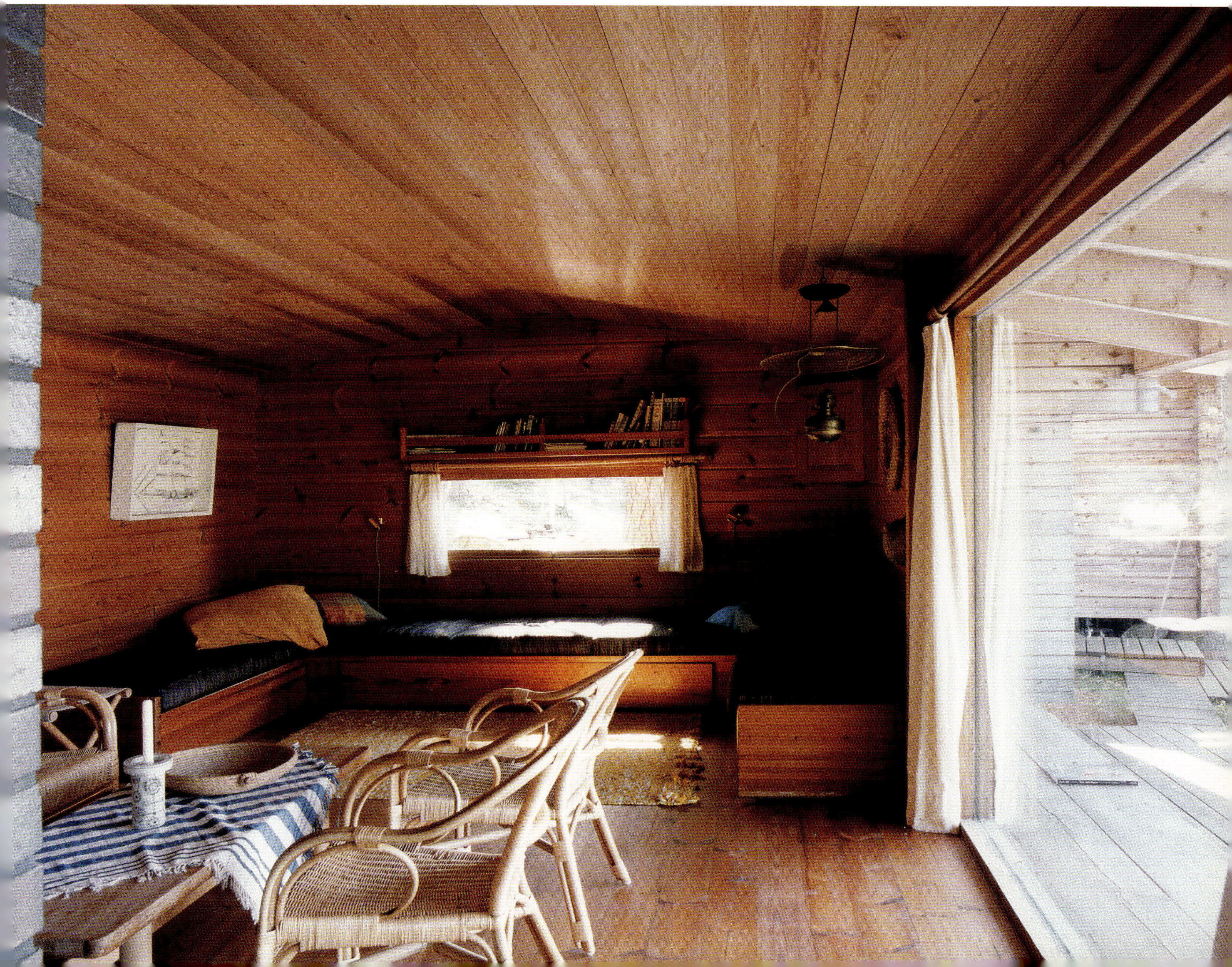

RIGHT
The simplicity of its details gives the pavilion a strong character.

BOTTOM
The sea pavilion, or chapel, stands on a cliff.

OPPOSITE
The open view to the sea is meditative.

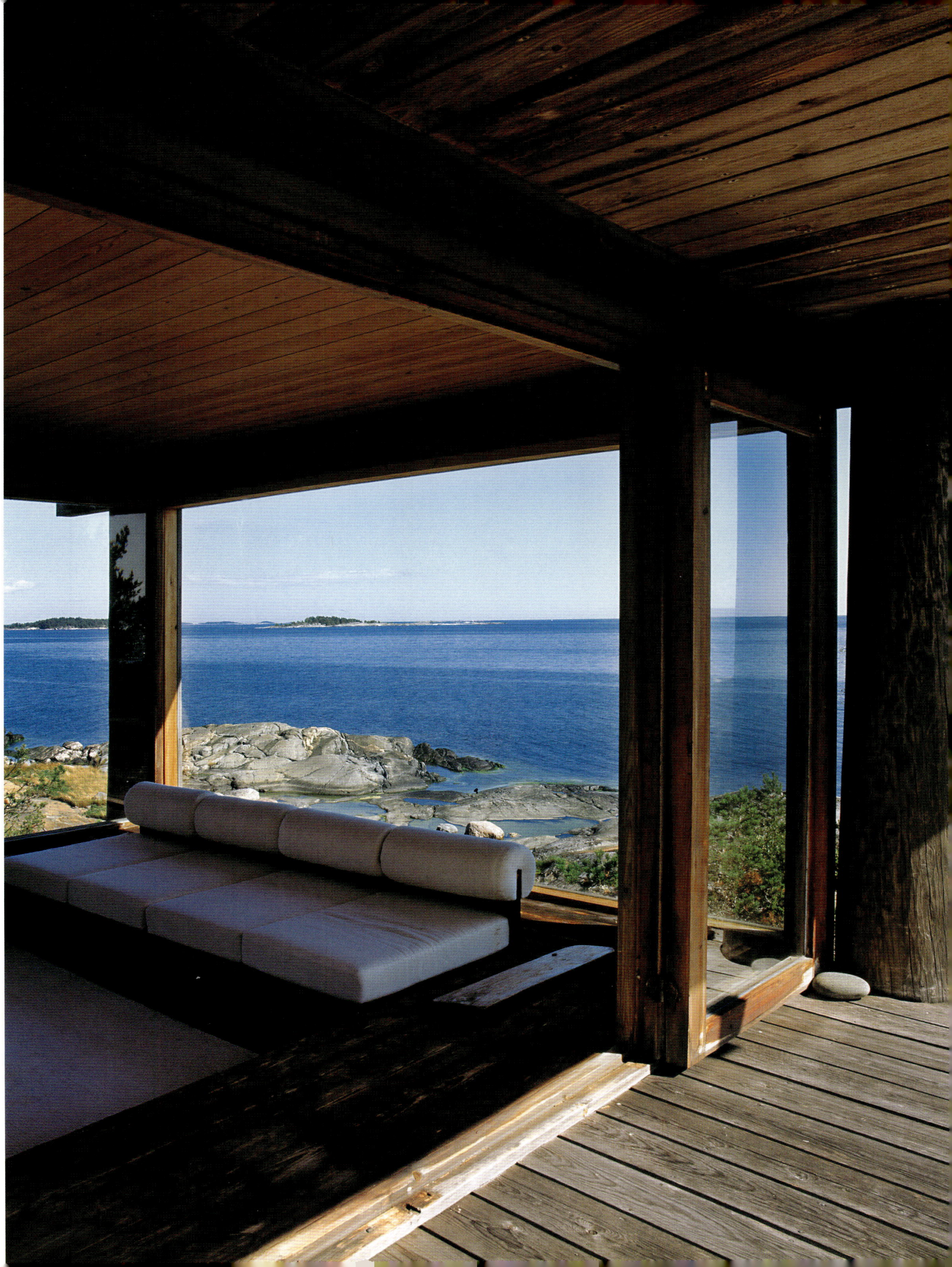

Ruusuvuori Cabin and Sauna

Kerimäki, 1968
Aarno Ruusuvuori

Aarno Ruusuvuori was one of the most influential figures in Finnish architecture during the 1960s. He was particularly known for his skillful and expressive use of concrete. Like many of his contemporaries he was also interested in systematization and prefabricated building. The clarity of the design of his cabin and sauna in the municipality of Kerimäki in central Finland is typical of the uncompromising nature and precision that characterizes Ruusuvuori's works from the 1960s.

The cabin and sauna are situated in the shade of alder and birch trees in the flat terrain around Lake Puruvesi. The oblong-shaped cabin, placed parallel to the shoreline, replicates the principles of traditional Finnish rural storehouses, which were also used for inhabitation in the summertime. It contains small, separate sleeping alcoves, whose size is determined by the dimensions of a bed. Natural light enters the alcoves through glass doors, and a narrow wooden terrace connects the individual spaces while forming a low platform for the building. A birch tree growing through the canopy ties the cabin to nature. A nearby old shoreline cottage was used for cooking.

The glazed front of the sauna faces the lake, offering an unhindered view of the landscape. Its close proximity to the lake allows reflections from the water surface to be projected all the way up to the sauna benches, adding to the meditative atmosphere of the space. The dimensions are as small as possible, and the use of space is maximized. Indeed, the building has the character of a piece of furniture. A few years before the sauna's construction, Ruusuvuori had developed the Marikylä village for the Marimekko company, which included buildings based on prefabricated room elements. The sauna of the village's prototype house was developed for mass production, and Ruusuvuori used the same tripartite glass-walled spatial division in his own sauna building.

The floors of the two low buildings are near ground level, seamlessly joining together the interior and exterior spaces. The simple form of the cabins, with their dark-painted plank walls, contrasts with the surrounding forest landscape. Ruusuvuori and his family usually stayed at the summer house from mid-June to the end of July. Life at the cabin was family-oriented and relaxed, and Ruusuvuori used to fish there enthusiastically.

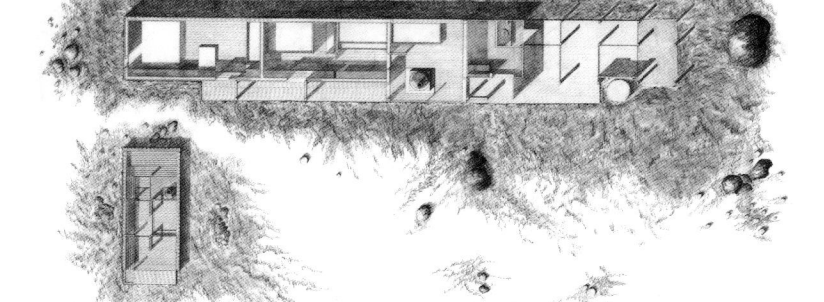

RIGHT
Plan

OPPOSITE
The Ruusuvuori Cabin

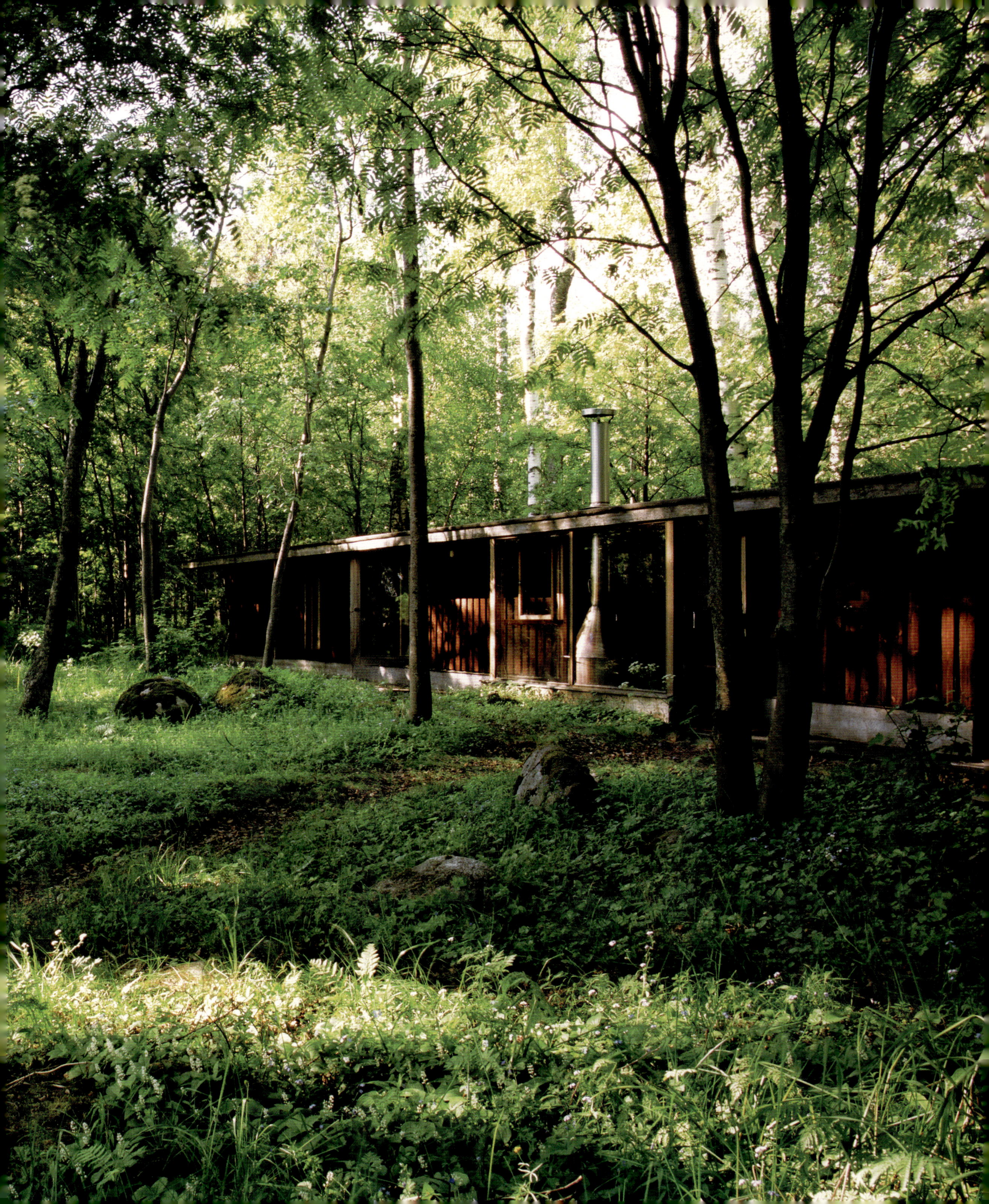

RIGHT
The Ruusuvuori Sauna

BOTTOM
The glass wall of the sauna faces the lake.

OPPOSITE, TOP
Section

OPPOSITE, BOTTOM
The horizontal, low building in the landscape

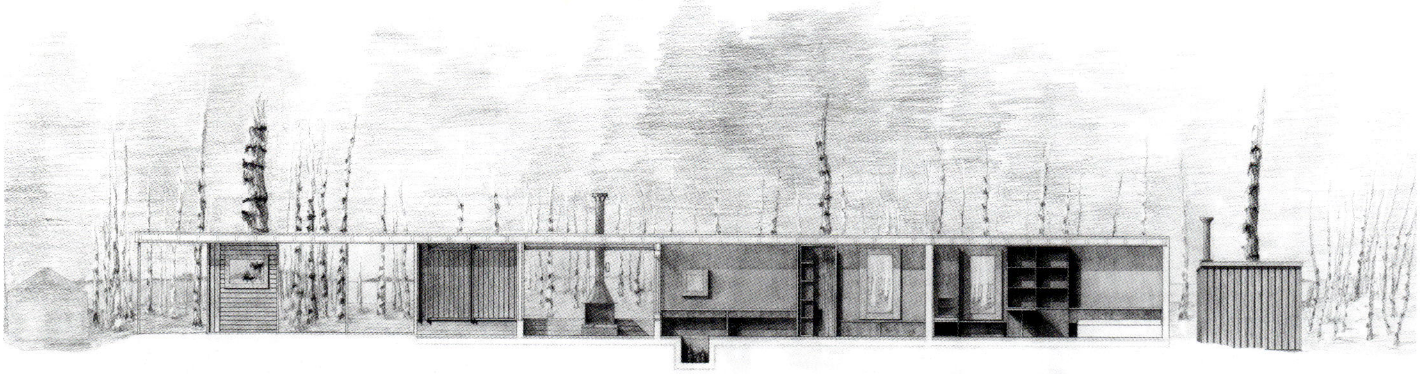

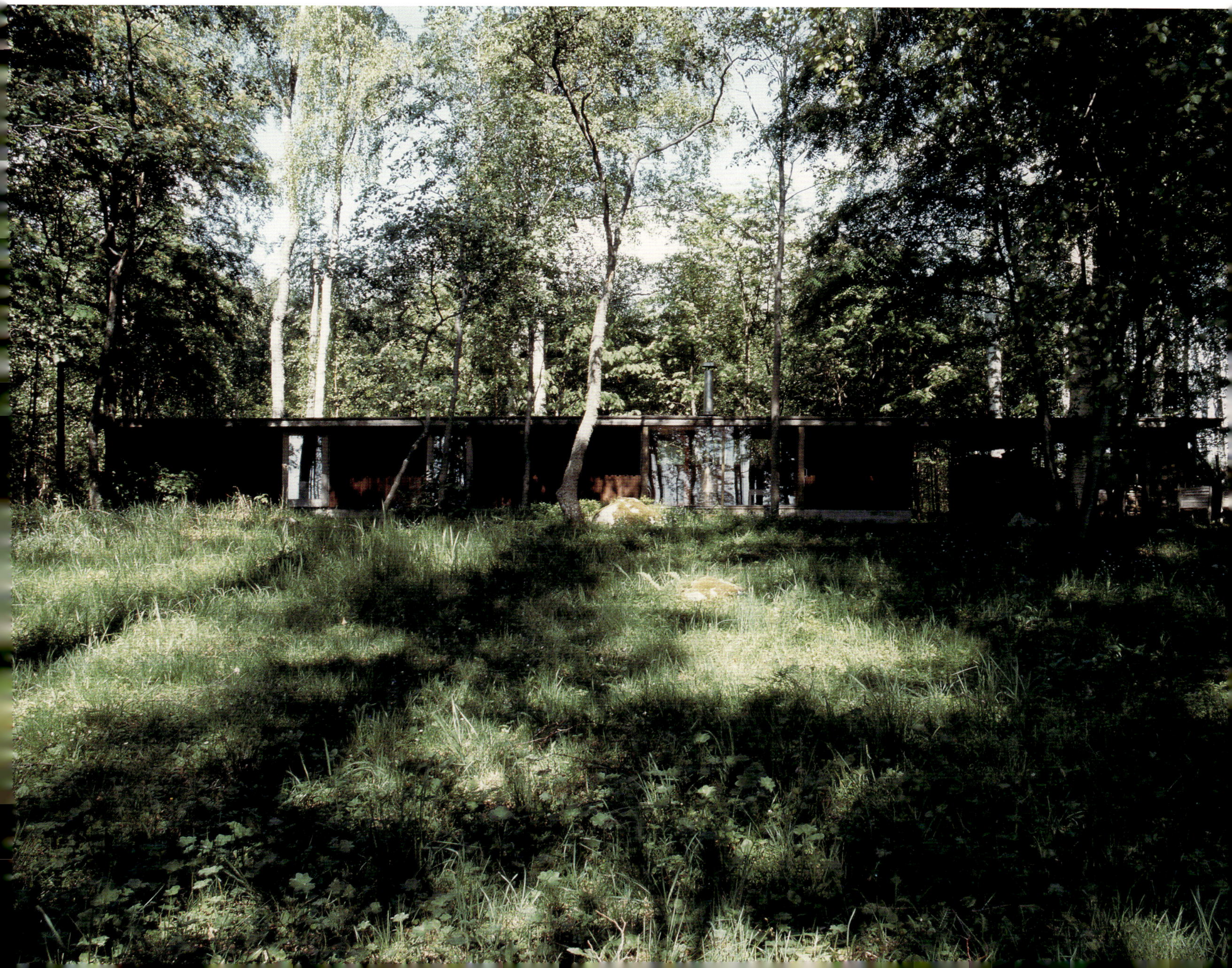

BELOW
Bedroom cabin interior

OPPOSITE
Sitting near the fireplace one can enjoy both the warmth of the fire and a broad view of the landscape.

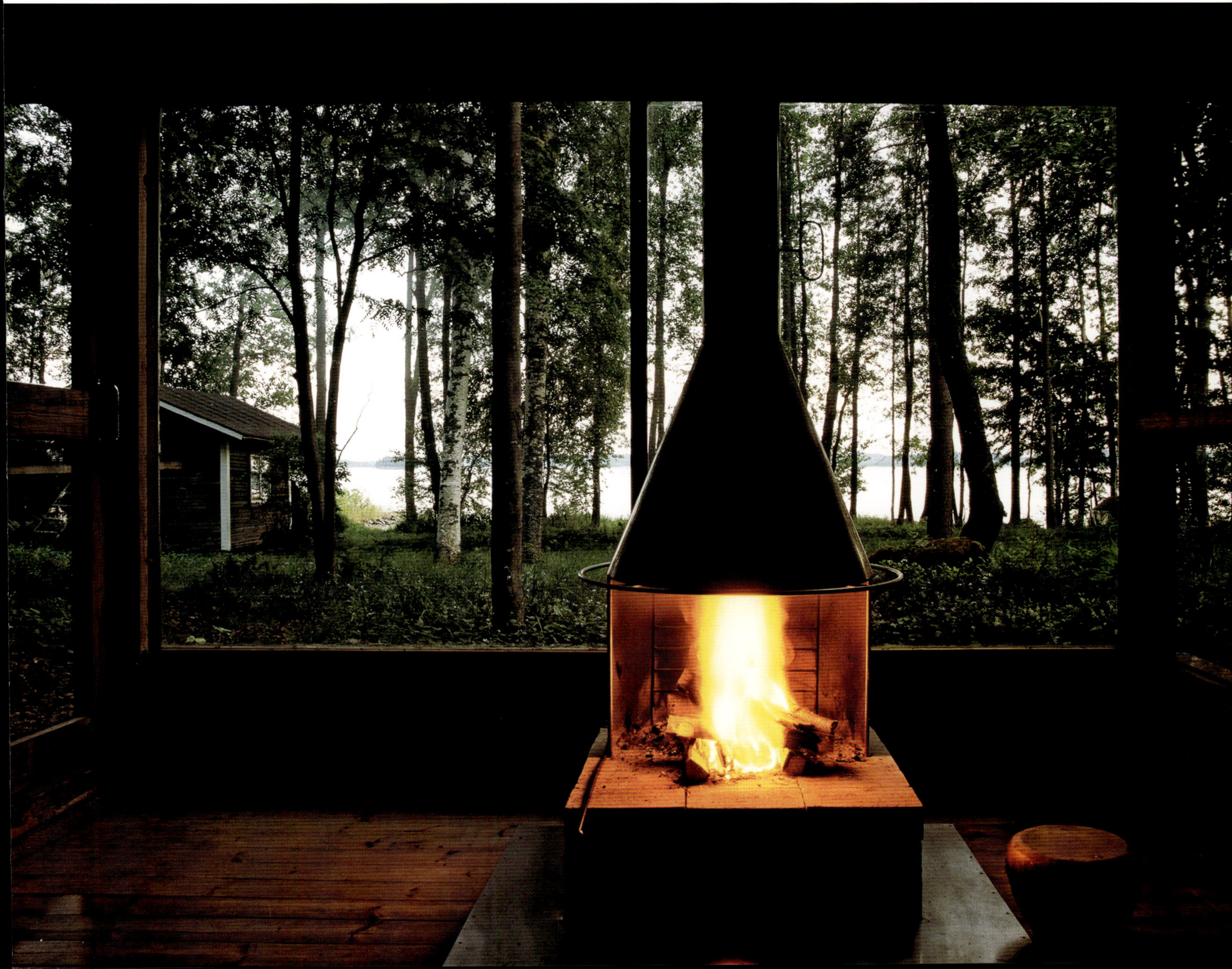

The Ilonen Cabin

Kiljava, 1970
Pirkko and Arvi Ilonen

The Ilonen Cabin was one of the last of approximately twenty-five summer cottages that were built starting in the mid-1940s in Vähä-Kiljava, an area belonging to the Finnish Association of Architects (SAFA). It follows the same principles of simplicity and modest comfort as the earlier houses, such as Kaj Englund's Villa Silla, even though architectural styles had changed since then.

The low, green-and-yellow-painted cabin is situated among trees on the shore of a lake that is part of Vähä-Kiljava. It turns its back on the road that cuts through the area, opening up instead toward the shore. An entrance canopy between the cabin's residential section and storage area can also be used as a carport. The cabin is characterized by its structural clarity and modularity. The main building frame is steel—as are the corrugated sheets used as the roof's load-bearing structure—while the external walls consist of prefabricated timber elements.

The uniform residential space is divided into kitchen, dining, and living areas. Two small bedrooms are hidden behind sliding doors decorated with supergraphics. The lakeside facade is completely glazed, and a small open terrace continues from the cabin toward the lake. The use of color in both the facades and the interior gives the building immediacy and a certain energy and emphasizes the relationship between its structure and surfaces.

The cabin's structural and material choices were related to the principles of buildings that Pirkko and Arvi Ilonen were designing at that time—steel structures, gas stations, and cafeterias. The industrially produced, prefabricated parts offered the opportunity for rapid and efficient construction. The similarity between the Ilonens' cabin and their service stations made some of their neighboring colleagues remark that the family spent their summers in a former gas station. The building's bright colors also evoked discussion. These comments reveal an aspect of life in Vähä-Kiljava: it is a very social place, and professional affinity creates a special atmosphere in the vacation area.

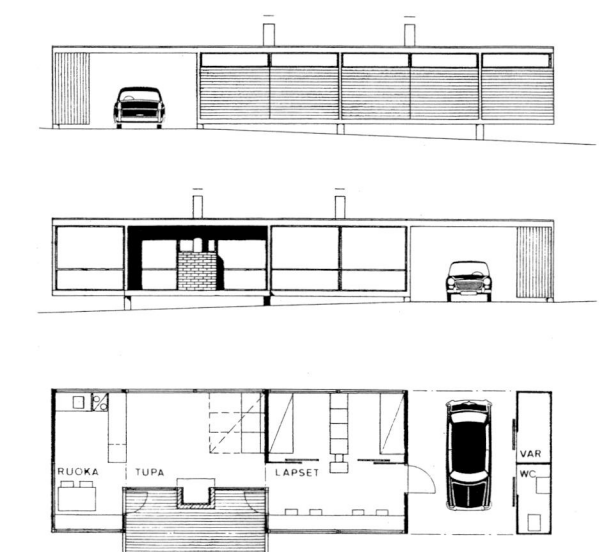

RIGHT
Plan and facade drawings

OPPOSITE
The cabin in the landscape

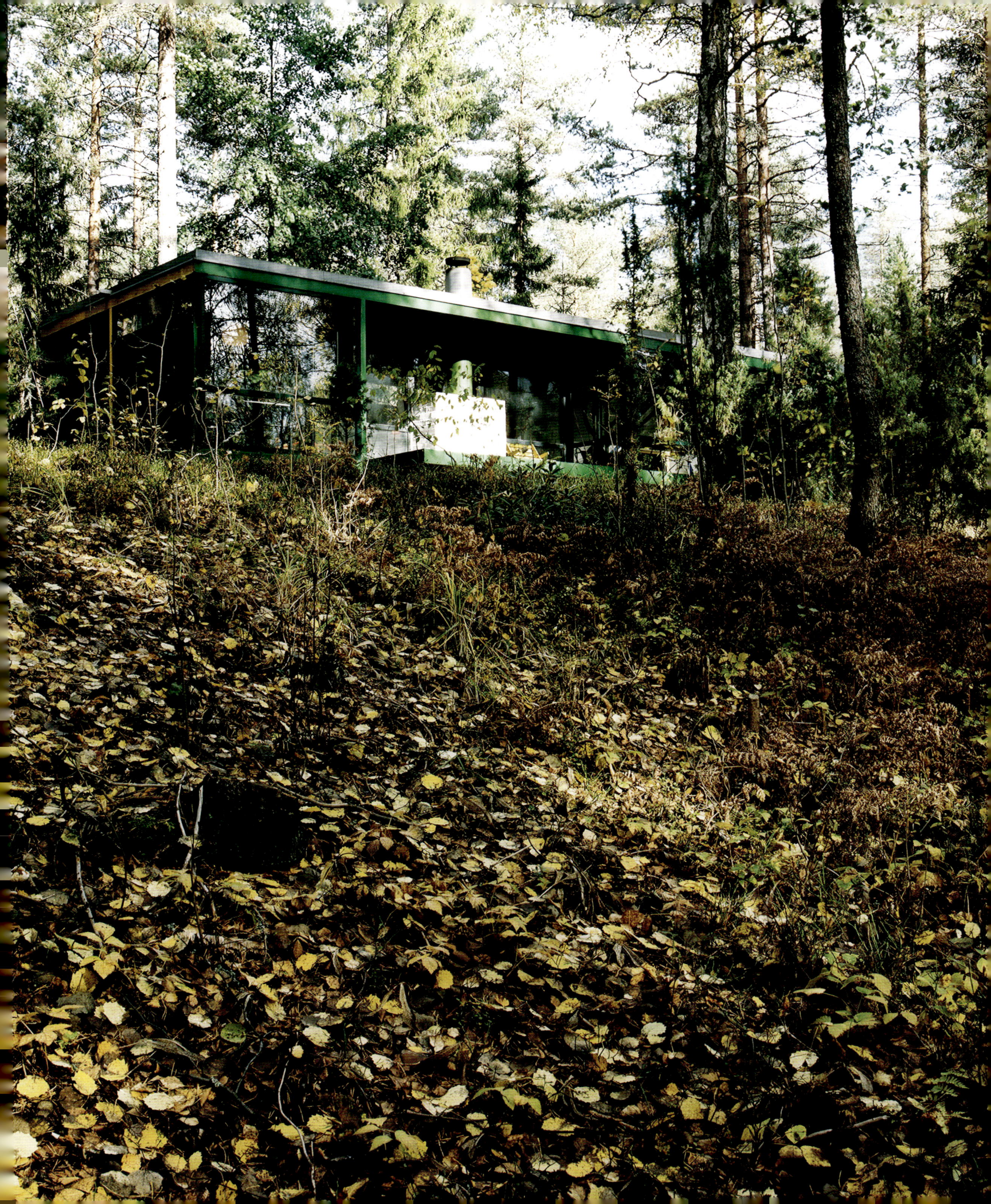

BELOW
The cabin's lakeside facade has large windows

OPPOSITE, TOP
The steel frame of the cabin

OPPOSITE, BOTTOM
The original colors of the cabin were bright yellow and green

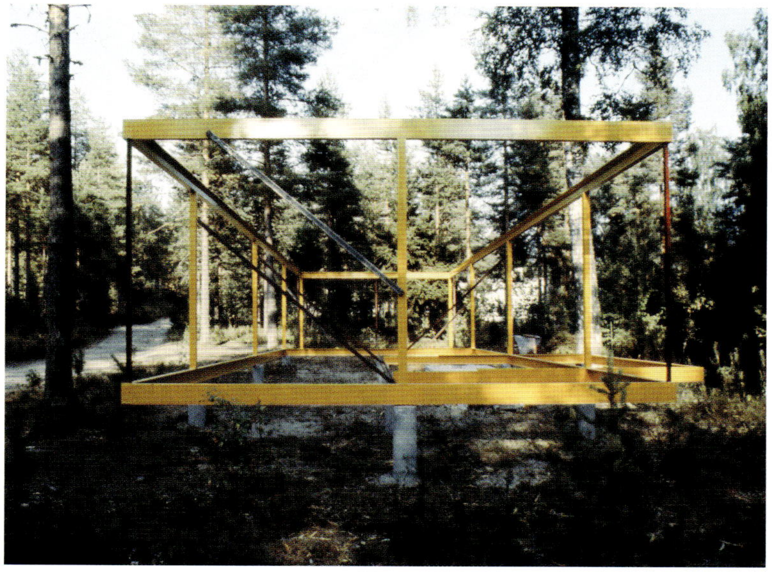

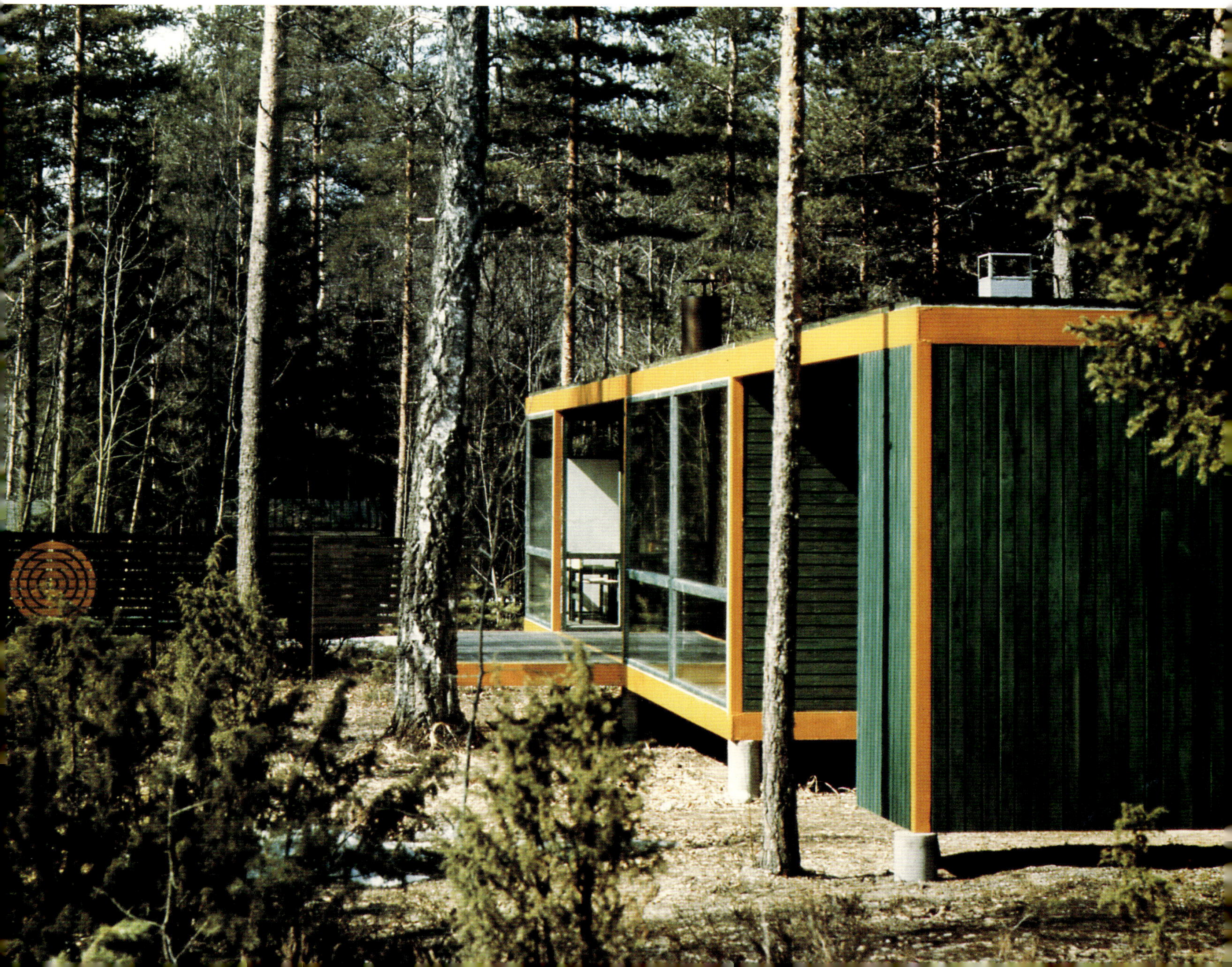

RIGHT:
Bubble window on the main door

BOTTOM
Children's bedroom

OPPOSITE
View through the cabin, with bedrooms on the right and working tables by the window

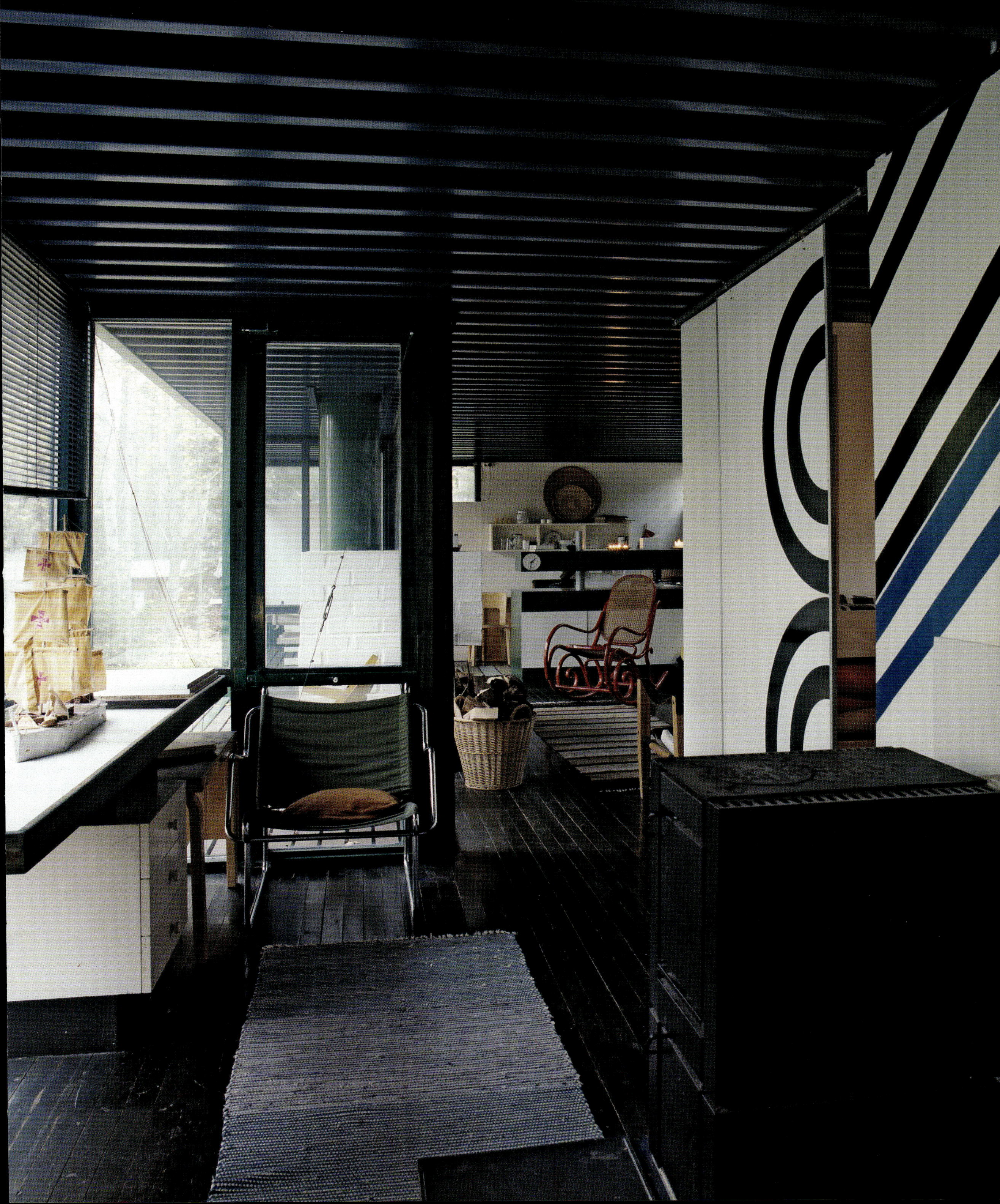

Living space

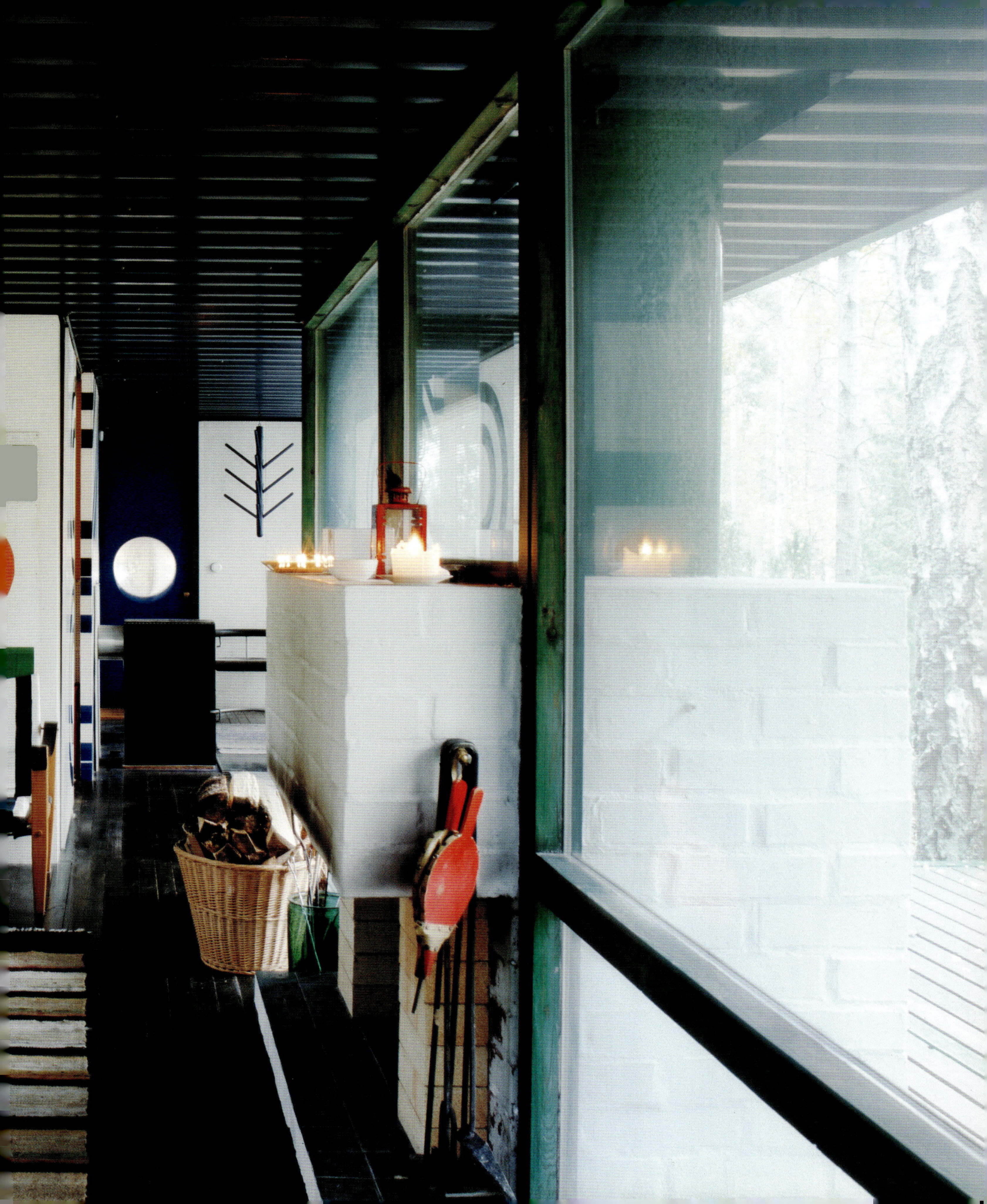

Two Saunas

Tenhola, 1985
Reima and Raili Pietilä

In the mid-1980s Reima and Raili Pietilä acquired an old, small farmhouse on the south coast of Finland for use as their summer residence. They called the place Mäyrämäki (Badger Hill) because of the badger tracks visible in the surrounding terrain. Near the old house Reima and Raili each designed their own sauna; the resulting buildings are—in shape and character—a reflection of their designers.

The saunas are situated on a slope covered with juniper trees. Though both of the saunas are built of dark logs, they each have their own distinct character. Raili's smoke sauna crouches in a hollow close to the forest edge, while Reima's sauna is higher on the slope looking out toward a sea bay. The works of the Pietiläs often contain changing angles and are complex and multilayered. A feature of central importance, however, is how the buildings grow from their locations and landscape.

The solid log walls and shallow-pitched roof of Reima's predominantly dark sauna give it a lively character. The chimney flue appears to grow from the roof. The round-edged eaves provide shelter both for the entrance and stacks of firewood. Unlike in a traditional log cabin, the interlocked logs are partly cut to an uneven length.

For Reima, the sauna cabin was a place for contemplation and writing. In contrast to the darkness of the external walls, light wood dominates the interior. A diagonally placed ceiling panel creates spatial tension. The windows, which are the height of a log, provide low, horizontal views of the landscape. Despite its simple form, the sauna feels multi-dimensional, with its carefully placed openings and customized furniture—such as small stools used both in the washing room and changing room—also designed by Reima.

Raili's smoke sauna is a small, low cabin built of round logs. Its low entrance door, requiring anyone entering to bow one's head, is reminiscent of a Japanese tearoom. Even the sauna stove is placed in a depression in the ground. The long, gabled eaves of the pitched roof provide some shelter for washing oneself outdoors. The lowest logs extend out from the wall and form a bench-like level. The building resembles a badger's cottage out of a fairy tale. Raili made specific reference to the badgers living in the area in the door hinges of her sauna, which are shaped like badger paws and seem like traces left behind by the animal.

Both saunas are personal statements: Reima's sauna is larger and more visible while Raili's is small and more hidden. This reflects the Pietiläs' public personas: Reima had a more extroverted role as a professor at Oulu University while Raili was more involved with office work.

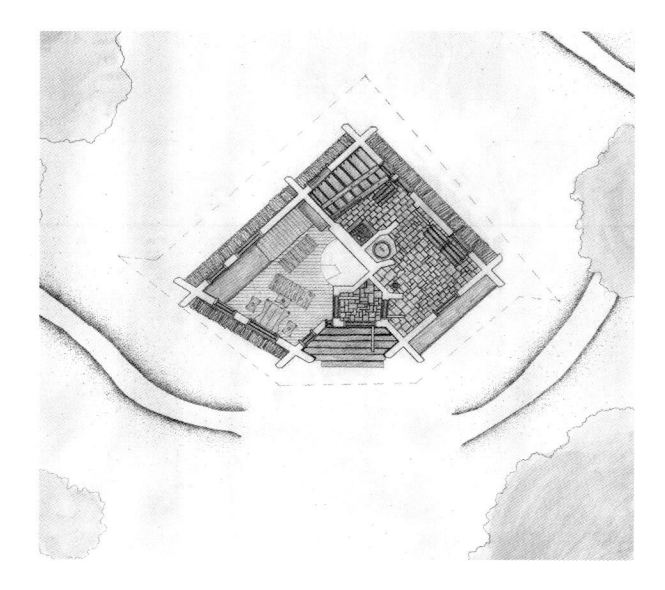

RIGHT
Site plan

OPPOSITE
Raili Pietilä outside Reima's sauna

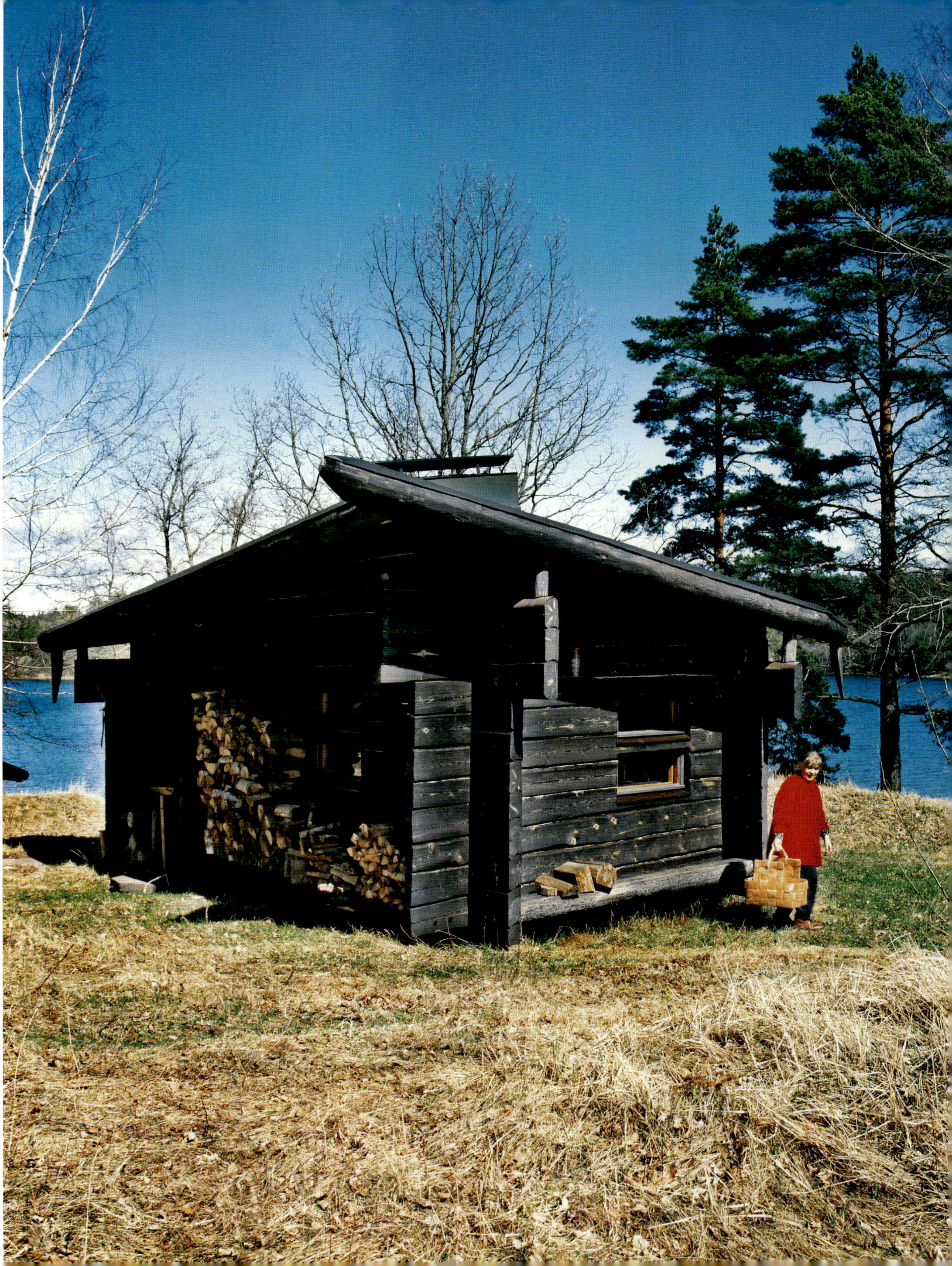

RIGHT
Reima's sauna, section and facade drawings

BOTTOM
Sauna room

OPPOSITE
The dressing room was also used as a small workroom.

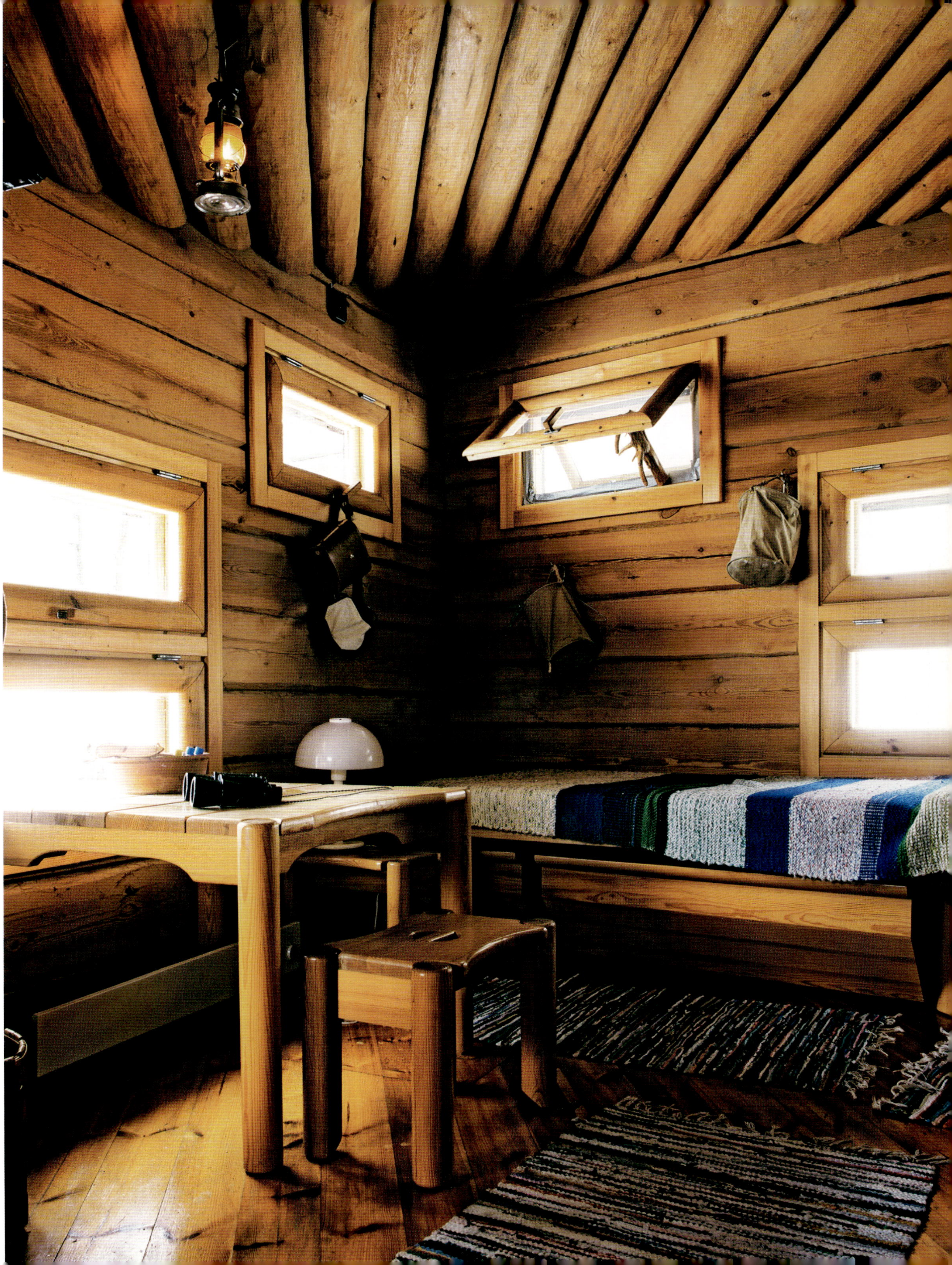

RIGHT
Raili's sauna, door with hinges in the form of badger paws

BOTTOM
Sauna guests

OPPOSITE
Raili's sauna

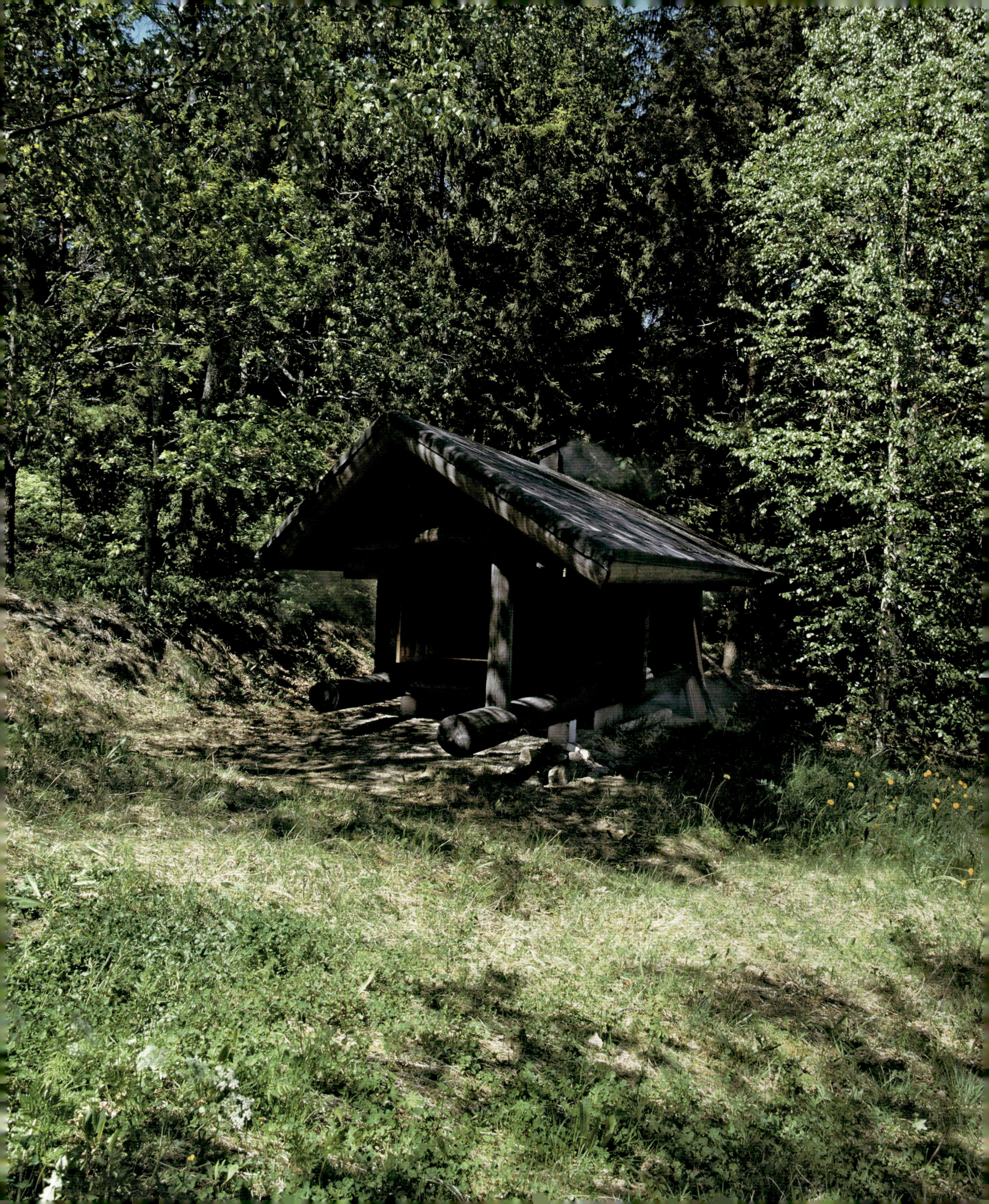

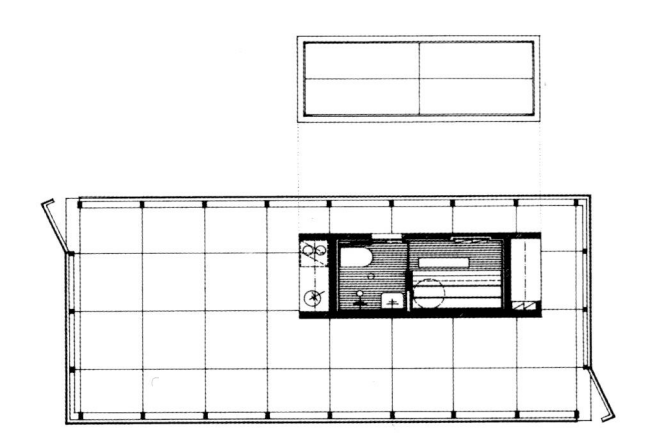

Weekend Atelier

Puolarmaari, 1991–92
Juha Kaakko, Ilkka Laine, Kimmo Liimatainen, and Jari Tirkkonen

The small Weekend Atelier designed by the four young architects Juha Kaakko, Ilkka Laine, Kimmo Liimatainen, and Jari Tirkkonen is located in the Puolarmaari allotment gardens. Allotment gardens have existed in Finland since the beginning of the twentieth century. This garden type originated in Germany in the nineteenth century with the intention to offer the working-class population an opportunity for a healthy outdoor pastime and to encourage diligence and self-reliance. Apart from the garden itself, an allotment sometimes contained a small cabin, though it was forbidden to live there permanently. The allotment garden area in Puolarmaari, in the city of Espoo, was established at the beginning of the 1990s, continuing the allotment garden tradition in a modern way. The area was divided into zones for different types of cabins. The Weekend Atelier was built in a zone reserved for more experimental cabins, providing a more free-form building environment than traditional allotments.

The young architects not only designed their cabin but also participated in the construction work. The principles behind the atelier's structural design are simple and clear: the timber frame of the pitch-roofed cabin is left exposed on the interior; the walls and roof are covered with translucent plastic sheeting, whose joints are fastened with tape. There are no ordinary doors or windows.

The atelier consists of a single adaptable space, with a freestanding dark-colored block containing a kitchen and sauna in its center, anchoring the space. All the technical installations are situated beneath the plywood floor, which also functions as a storage area. Flexibility and minimalism are also emphasized in a built-in table that can be raised from the floor.

Sunlight and shadows cast from the surrounding foliage filter through the translucent plastic sheets during the day. In the evening the lit atelier glows like a lamp. A feeling of lightness and experimentation with details were the central concepts in the design of the Weekend Atelier, which was used by its owners to think, socialize, and work.

ABOVE
Plan

OPPOSITE
Night view of the atelier

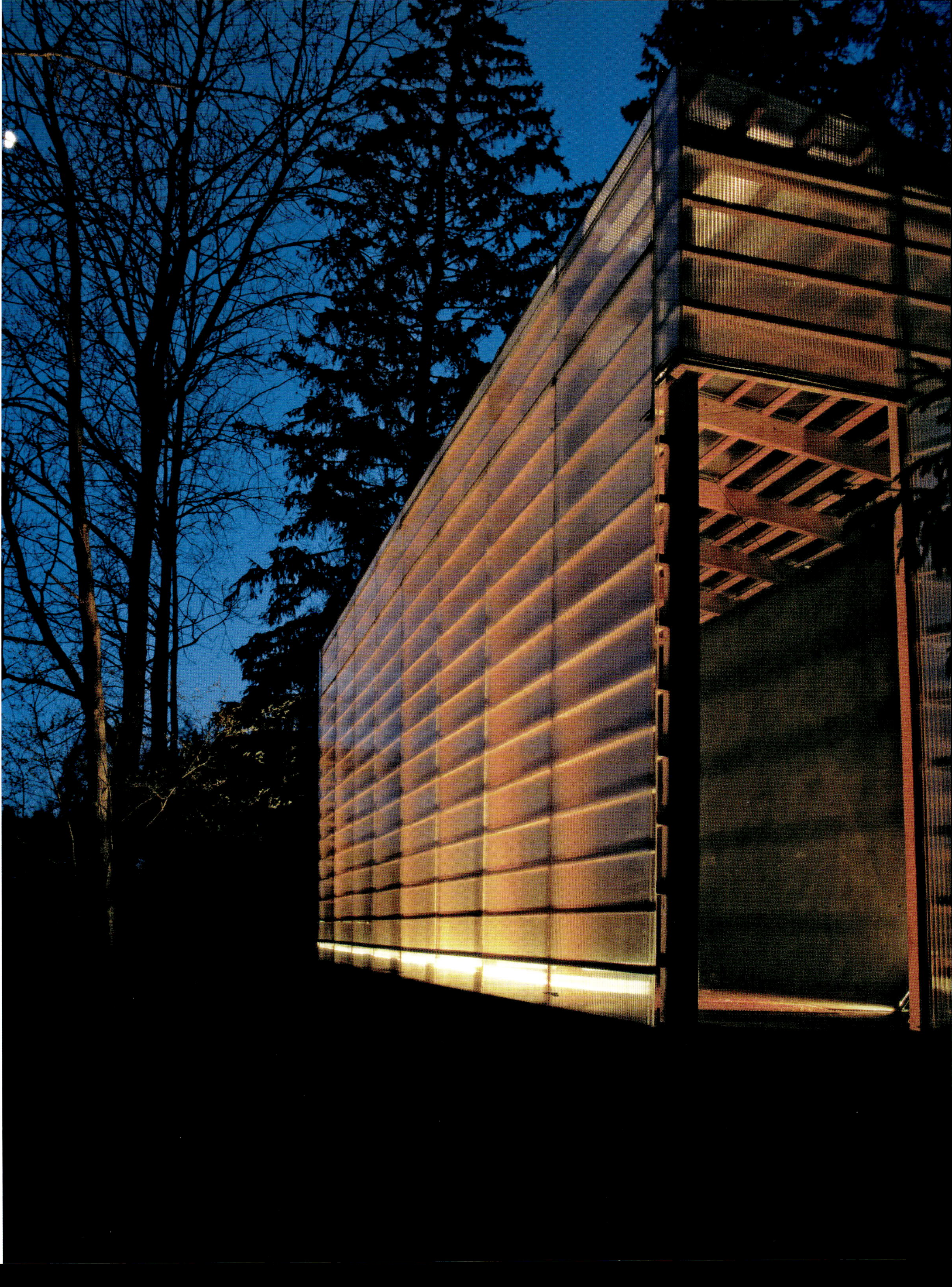

RIGHT
Sauna interior

BOTTOM
Springtime view of
the atelier

OPPOSITE
Interior

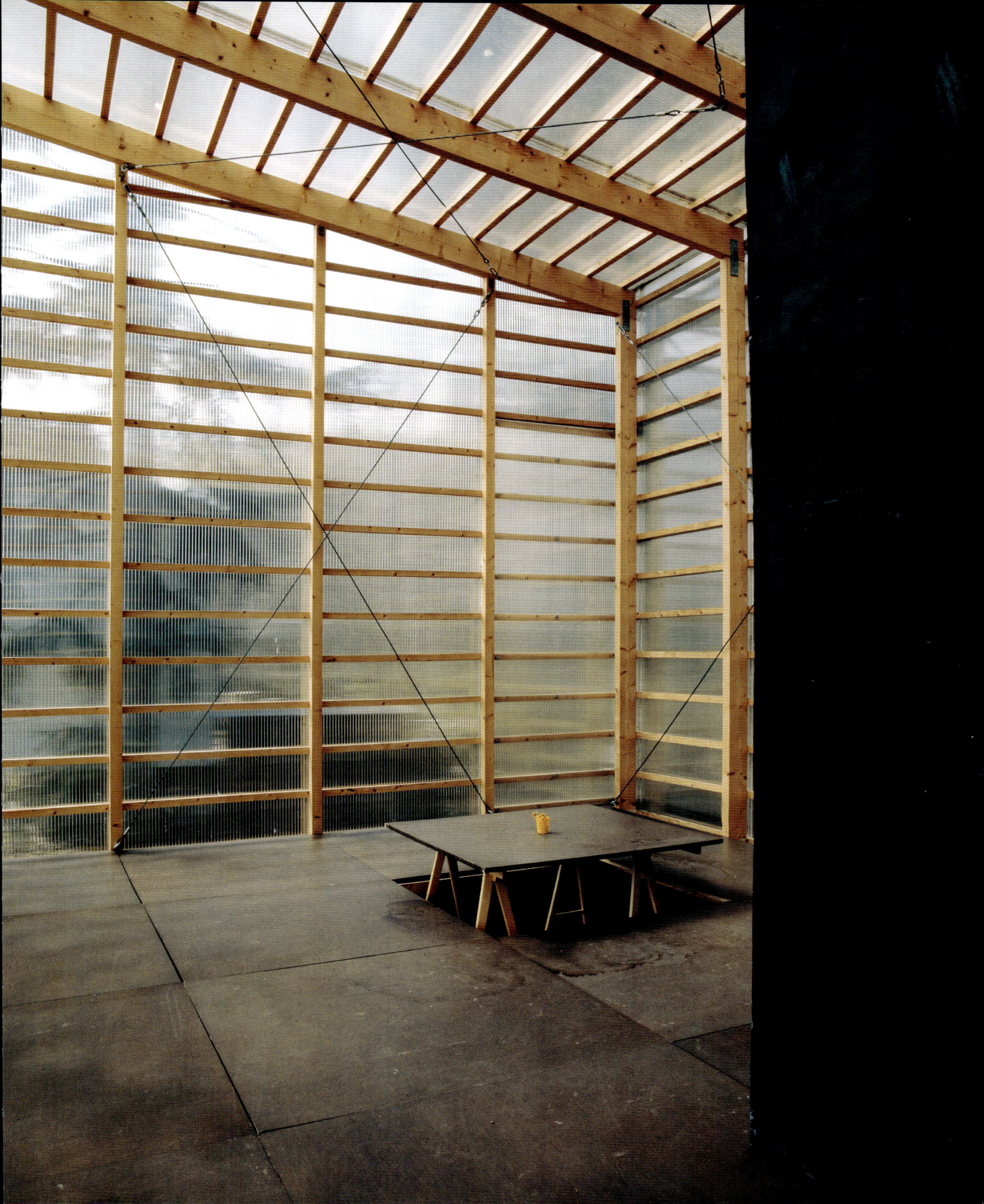

RIGHT
Perspective of the interior

BOTTOM
Atelier interior with the kitchen and sauna block

OPPOSITE
Lit from within, the atelier glows like a lantern.

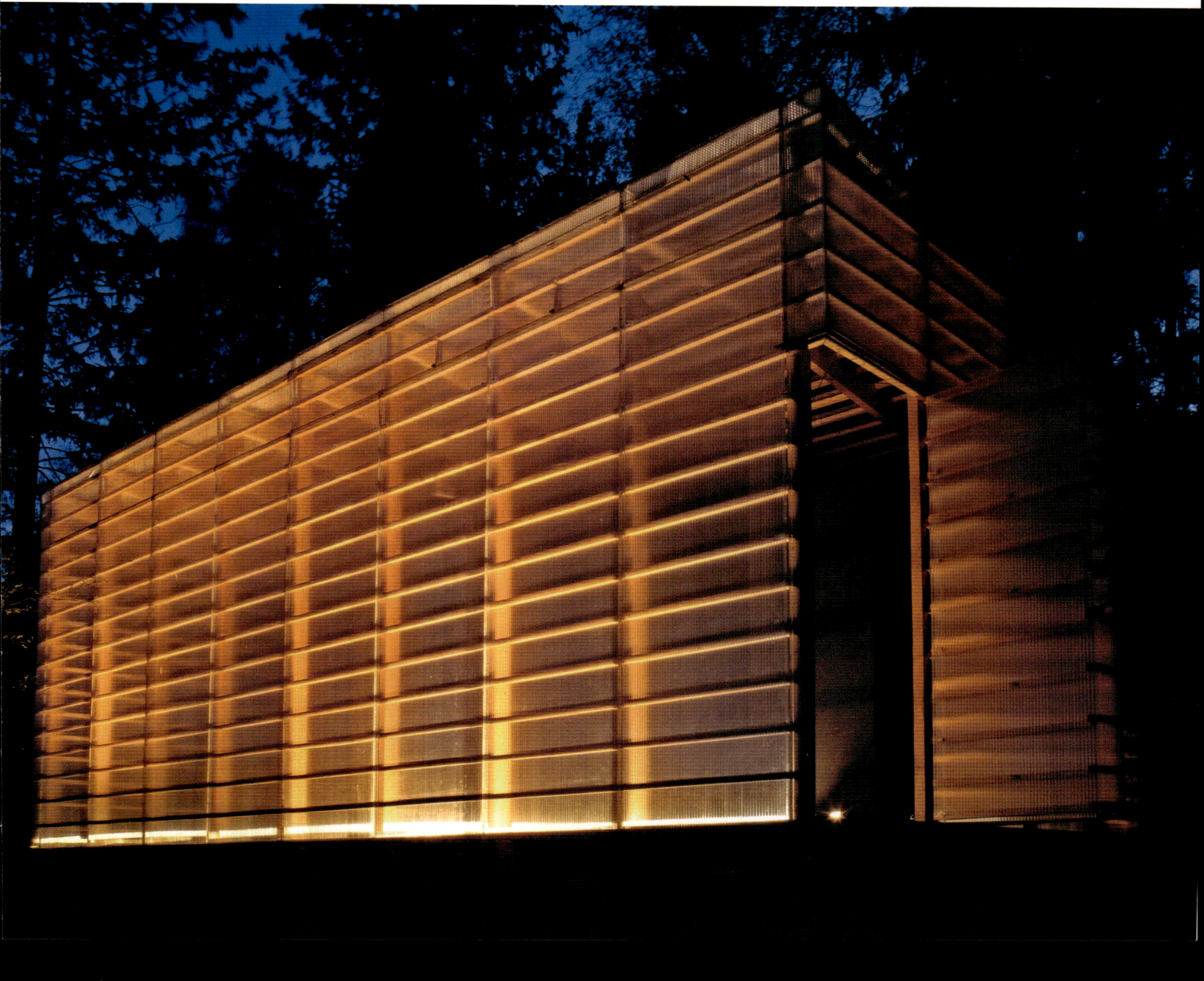

Villa Sara

Taivassalo, 1994
Pekka Pitkänen

Villa Sara is located in the Taivassalo municipality in the Turku archipelago in southwest Finland, on a sloping site amidst pine trees. A cultivated garden complements the natural forest terrain. Pitkänen first built a small cabin—called Villa Patilo—on this site in the 1960s, along with a sauna by the seashore, which is still in use. Similar to Villa Patilo, Villa Sara has a sheltered and enclosed courtyard, which functions as one of the rooms of the villa, offering a warm place even on windy days. The single tree growing in this space brings nature into the house. A workroom overlooks the yard, while the living room and dining space—as well as the terrace between them—are oriented toward the shoreline and the forest landscape. A window at the corner of the dining area offers a broad view of the nearby sea bay. The level of comfort in the villa is comparable to a city apartment, and unlike most summer houses in Finland, Villa Sara can be occupied throughout the entire year.

The light, unpainted wood surfaces are a central feature in the interior and form a contrast to the dark exterior walls, which tie the building, together with the cabin's low horizontal form, to the surrounding landscape. The details of Villa Sara are carefully executed and integrated into the whole. Balance and sensitivity, typical for all of Pitkänen's works, are strongly present in the house.

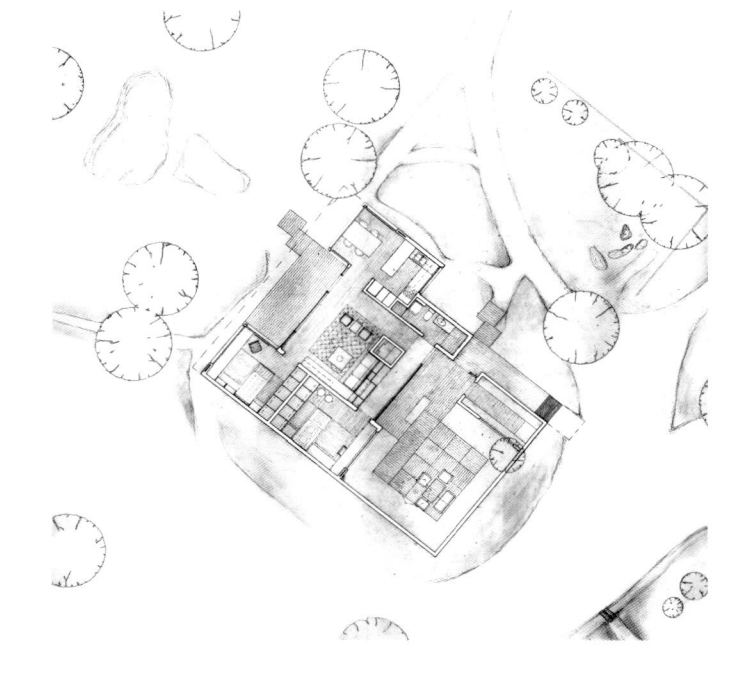

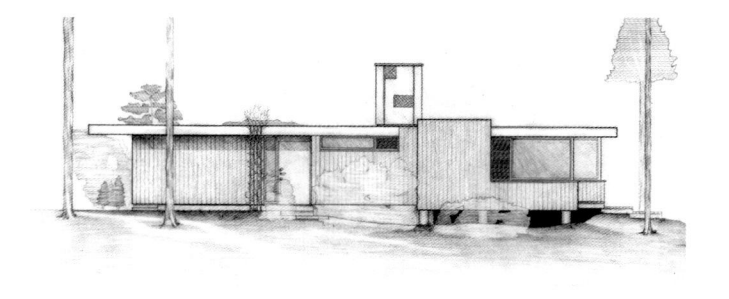

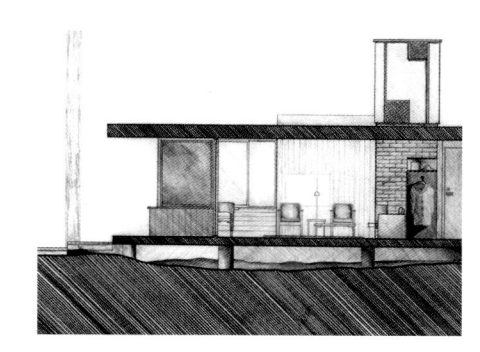

TOP
Plan

MIDDLE AND BOTTOM
Entrance facade and section detail

OPPOSITE
Entrance facade

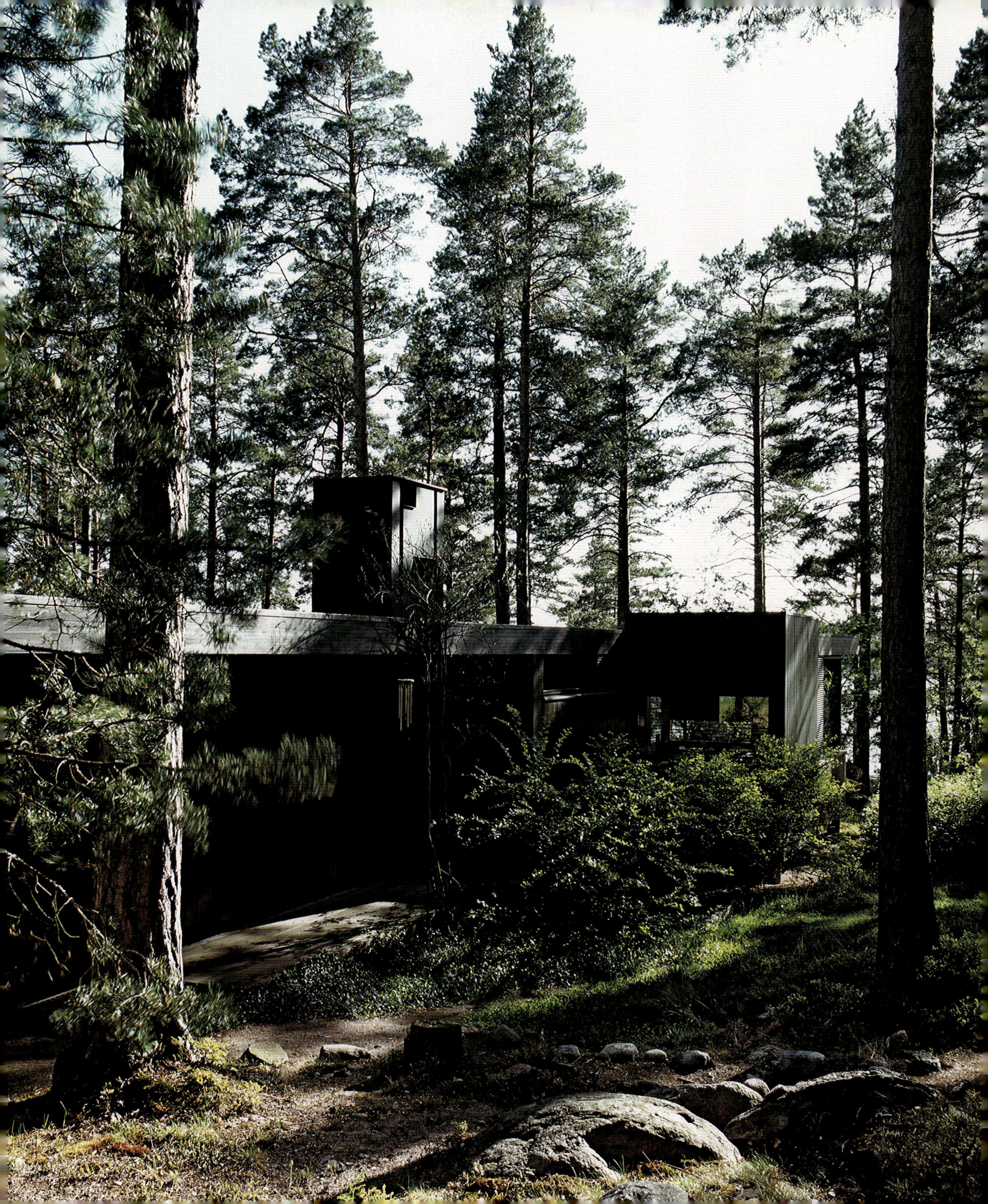

Dining-room corner and terrace

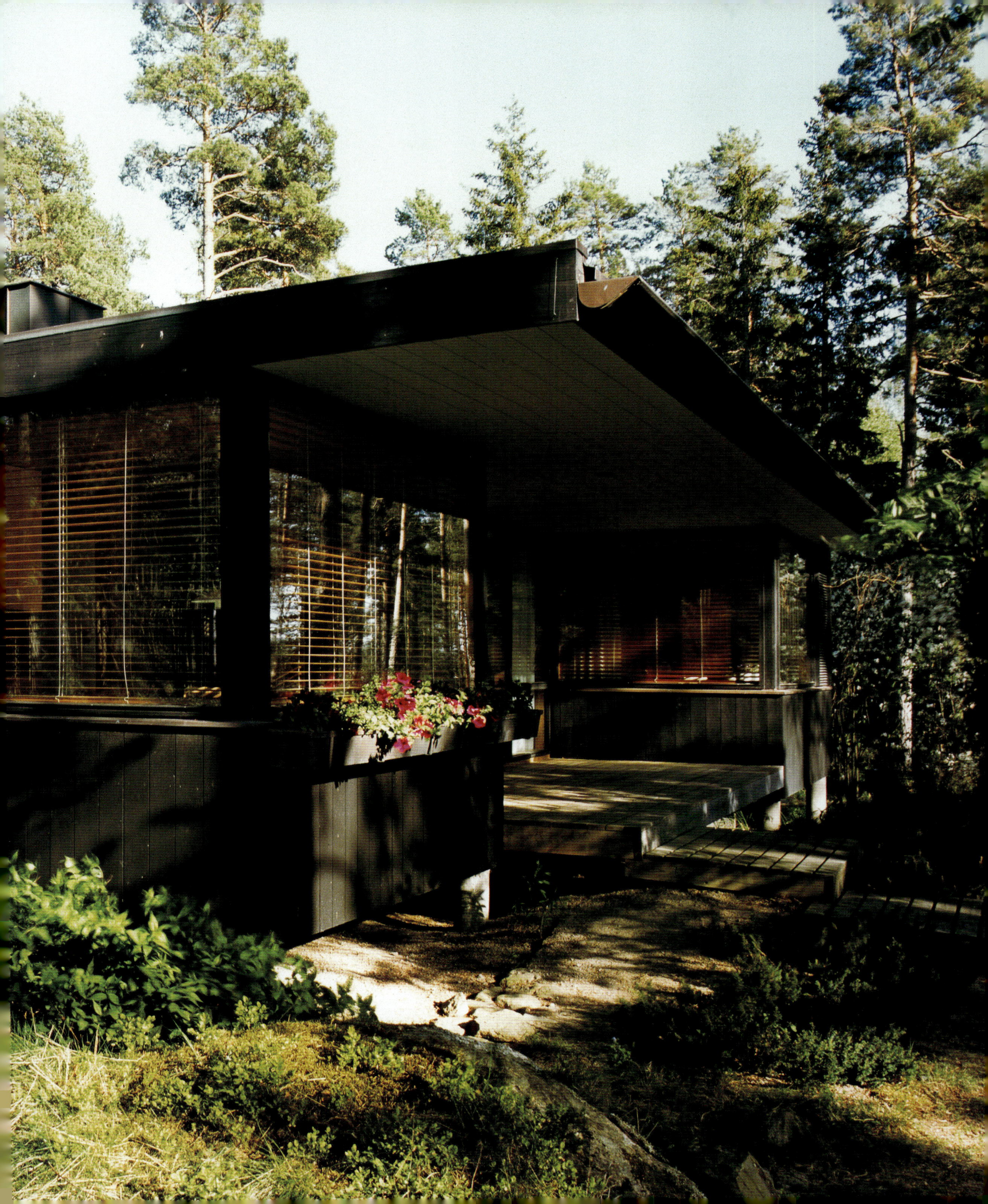

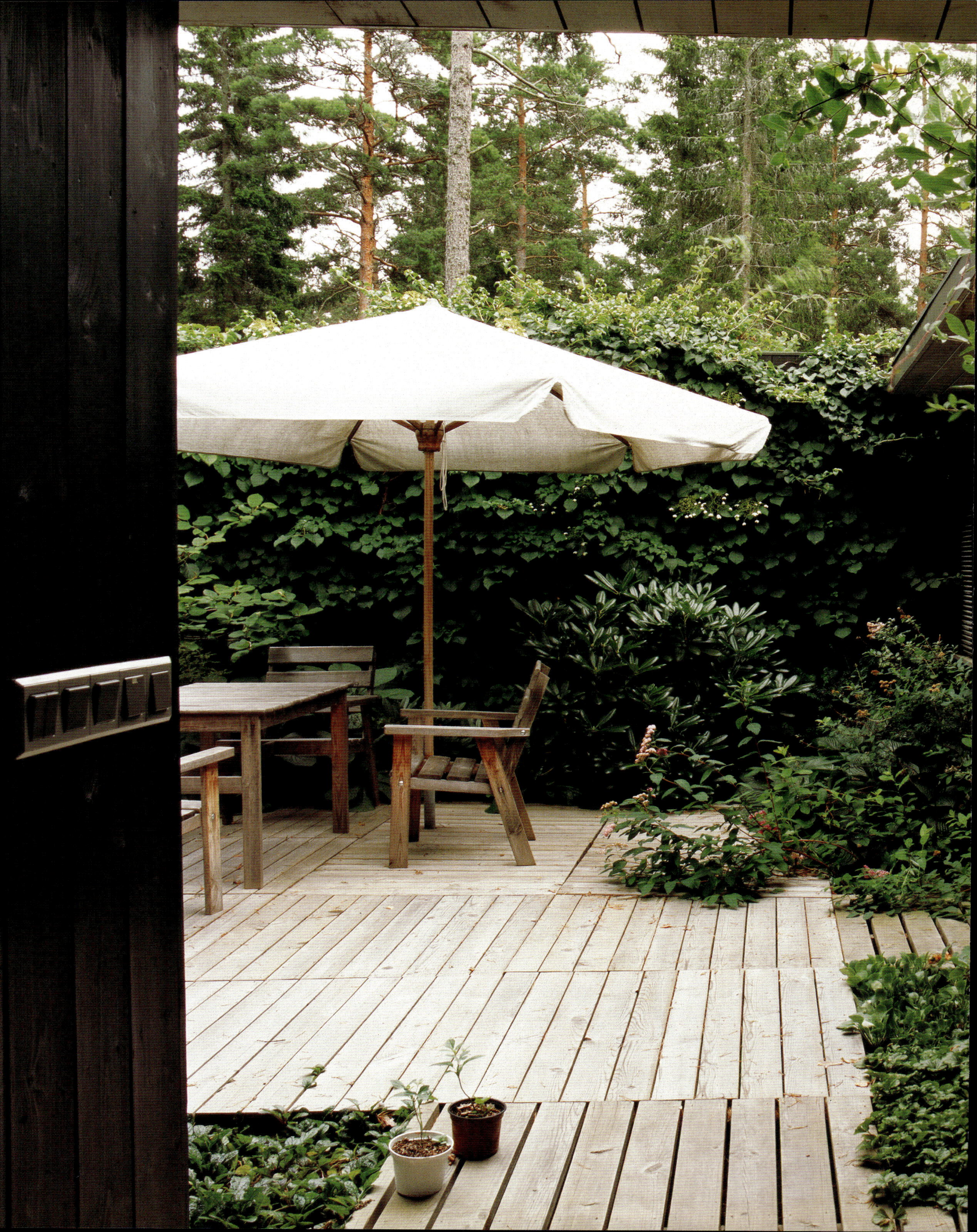

Inviting atmosphere of the atrium courtyard

RIGHT
Living room

BOTTOM
The windows in the dining room open to the seaside.

OPPOSITE
Living-room corner

UUSI ISO ATLAS
BARN BOOK
POHJOLAN KASVIT I
POHJOLAN KASVIT II
POHJOLAN KASVIT III

Summer Cabin

Stora Bergskär, 1991–95
Juhani Pallasmaa

Originally built by architect Aarno Ruusuvuori in the 1960s, the Summer Cabin on the island of Stora Bergskär in southwest Finland was extended by Juhani Pallasmaa in the 1990s. The cabin is located in a hollow, protected from the wind, from where one's view passes over a small rocky mound toward the open sea.

Pallasmaa's extension opened the cabin up toward the forested rock outcrop to the building's rear. Providing additional space for everyday activities, the extension also gave the building, which had been oriented toward the east, a new direction and a view toward the evening sun, allowing it to respond more closely to its environment and the cycle of the day. Despite its small size—only 140 square feet—the cabin has various uses as a place for relaxing, socializing, eating, and working. It also contains a sleeping alcove, which is closed off as a separate space.

The building has a minimal structure, and even the window frames help to support the facade. Through the glazed roof of the living space natural light streams in and the treetops and the ever-changing light and colors of the sky become a part of the room. The surrounding "miniature landscape" of the harsh archipelago climate has a Japanese spirit—with lichen and dwarfed, gnarled pine trees—and the view from the two small windows above the worktable is calmingly harmonious and balanced. The family often spends several summer weeks on Stora Bergskär. Pallasmaa has stated that the first week is for sleeping, the second for reading, the third for writing, and the fourth for drawing. He emphasized that it takes time before one's senses are cleansed from urban life, before one can see and hear the surrounding nature.

Pallasmaa also surrounded the existing cabin with a narrow terrace that wraps around three sides of the building, opening it up to the landscape. The side terrace is reserved for a summer kitchen, storage, water heating, and an outdoor shower, while the terrace in front of the building is used as an outdoor living space. The curved shape of the third rear terrace provides additional space while still respecting the existing terrain through its delicate placement.

The untreated wooden boarding on the facades has acquired a grey patina, matching the color palette of the surrounding landscape. Pallasmaa has used the arc shape—seen here in the cabin's curved rear terrace—in many of his works, both in buildings and designs for public squares. In architecture the arc expresses a gesture outward and demarcates integrity. It implies a totality that is complete and precisely defined. As Pallasmaa has stated, our imagination completes the arc to become a full circle. In the summer cabin extension the arc defines the sphere of man and the home.

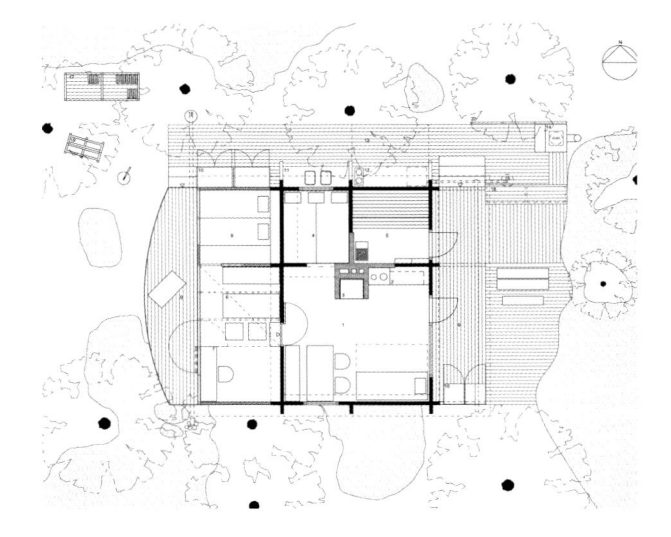

RIGHT
Plan

OPPOSITE
Rear terrace

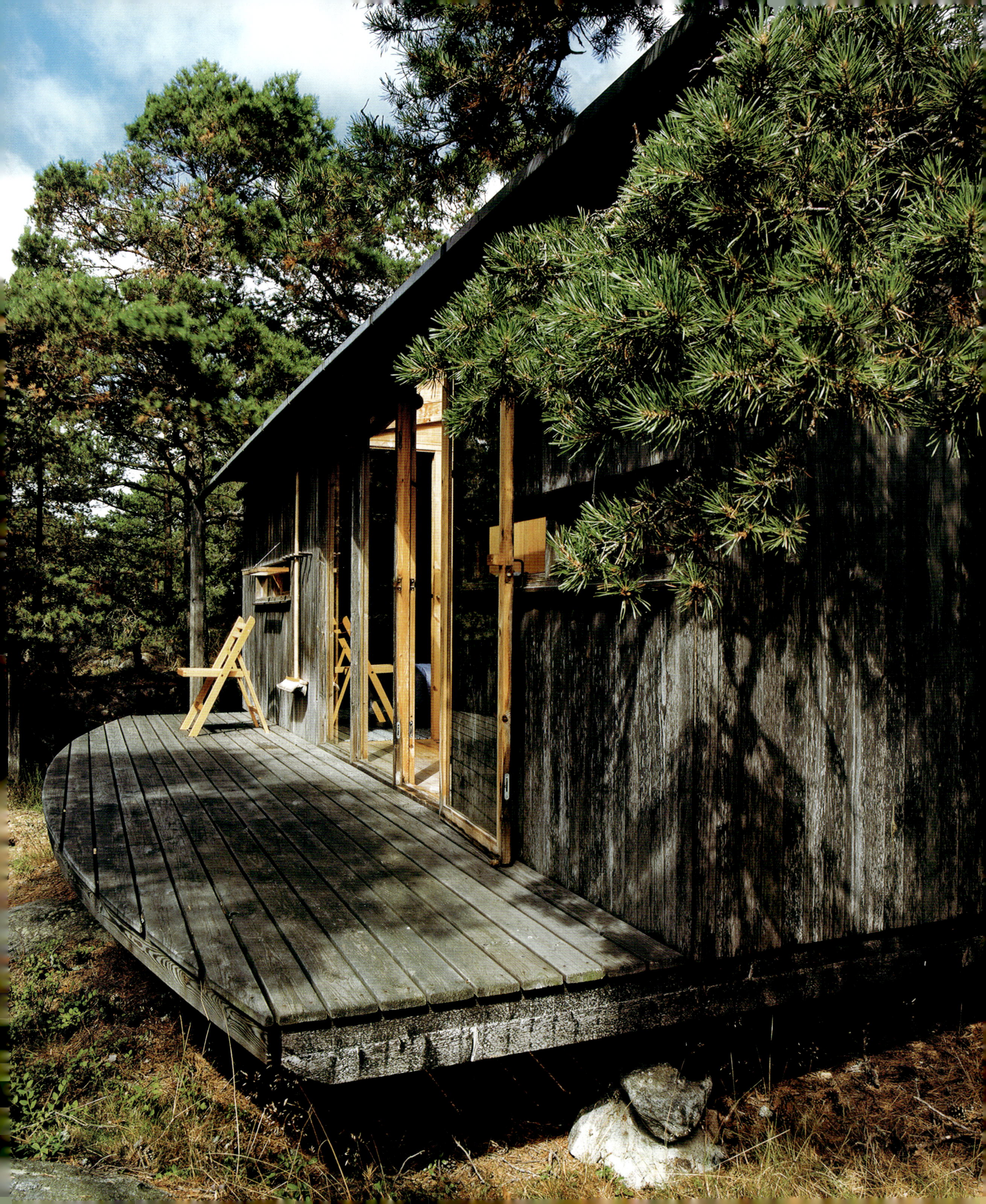

RIGHT
Section

BOTTOM
Seaside facade and terrace

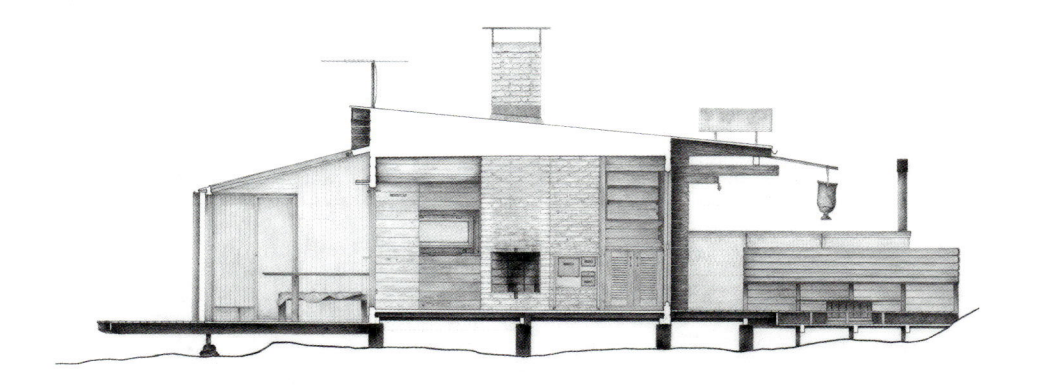

RIGHT
Work corner. The lures hanging on the wall are used for fishing, Pallasmaa's summer hobby.

BOTTOM
The grey exterior contrasts with the light colors inside.

The extension provides additional space for living, dining, and working.

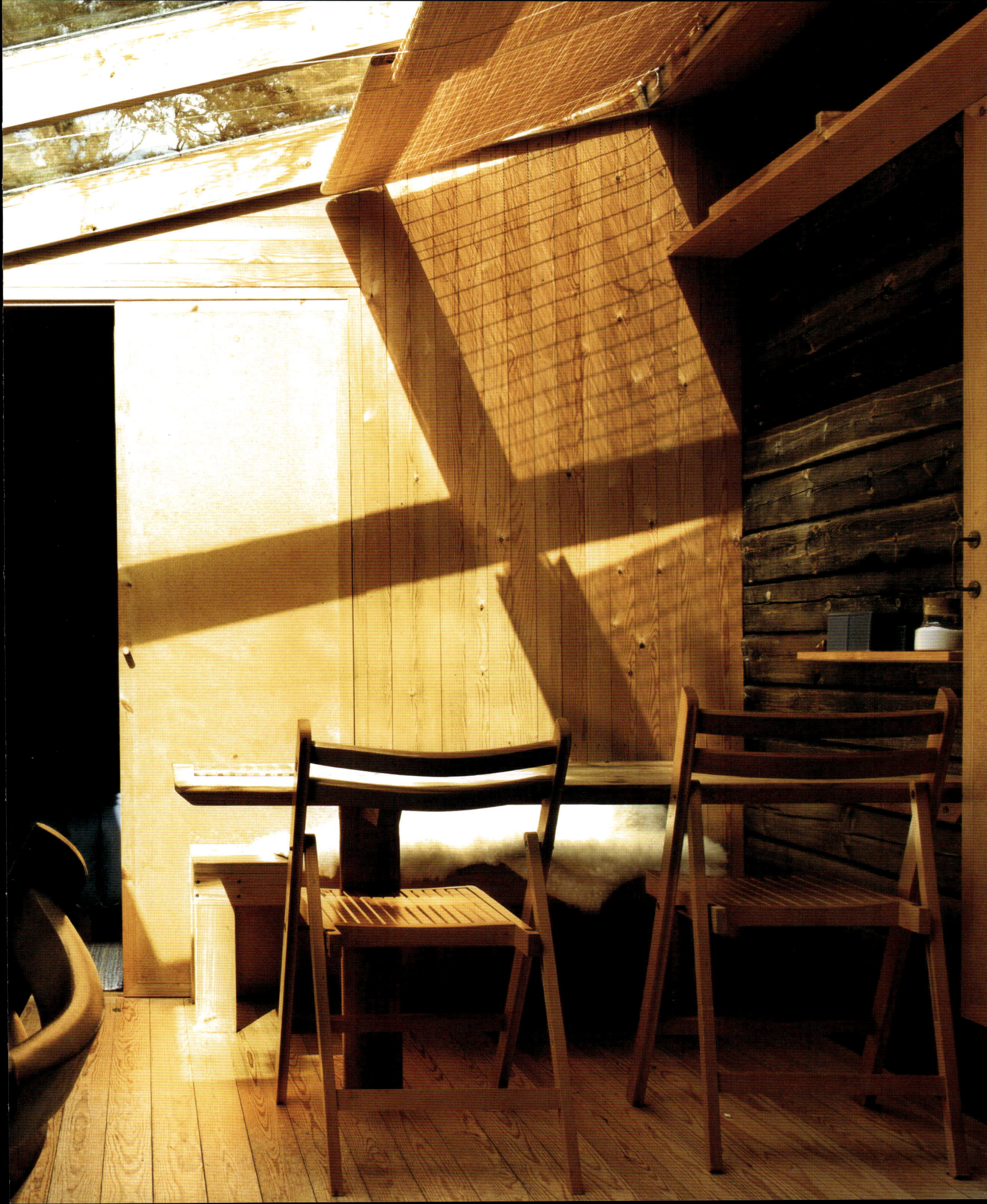

Holiday Home

Hiittinen, 1996
Kristian Gullichsen

The summer house of Kristian Gullichsen and his family is situated in a bay in the southwest archipelago. Gullichsen had previously built a cabin and two sheds on the same island—and even transferred an old fisherman's cabin there—but also wanted to have a house solely for summer use. The architect carefully sited and designed the new building to give the impression of it having always been there. Its grey, weathered plank walls and roof merge into the surrounding natural landscape.

Life in the villa varies according to the time of day and weather. The family performs daily chores on the east side in the morning sun, and in the evening sits together on the west side to enjoy the setting sun. The house's long, sliding glass walls are opened or closed depending on the wind. The interior space can be completely exposed to the summer breeze by opening wide doors on opposite sides of the building's central section. In sunny weather the living area is almost like a spacious veranda. At the end of the long main room is a closed-off bedroom with a small loft space above this alcove.

Gullichsen's summer house is a sensitive crystallization of the essential themes of his long career. From his earliest works, he combined modernist themes with local or historical motifs. Later in his career he made references to the works of masters of modern architecture such as Le Corbusier or Alvar Aalto and tied them to the landscape in a controlled way. Gullichsen's architectural thinking was also profoundly influenced by his childhood home, Villa Mairea. His own summer house is a shelter that opens and closes following the course of the day, becoming a natural part of the landscape.

RIGHT
Plan

OPPOSITE
The Holiday Home is located near a sea bay.

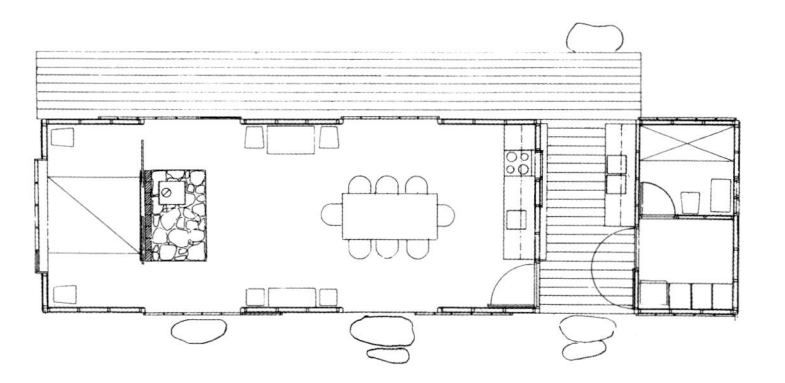

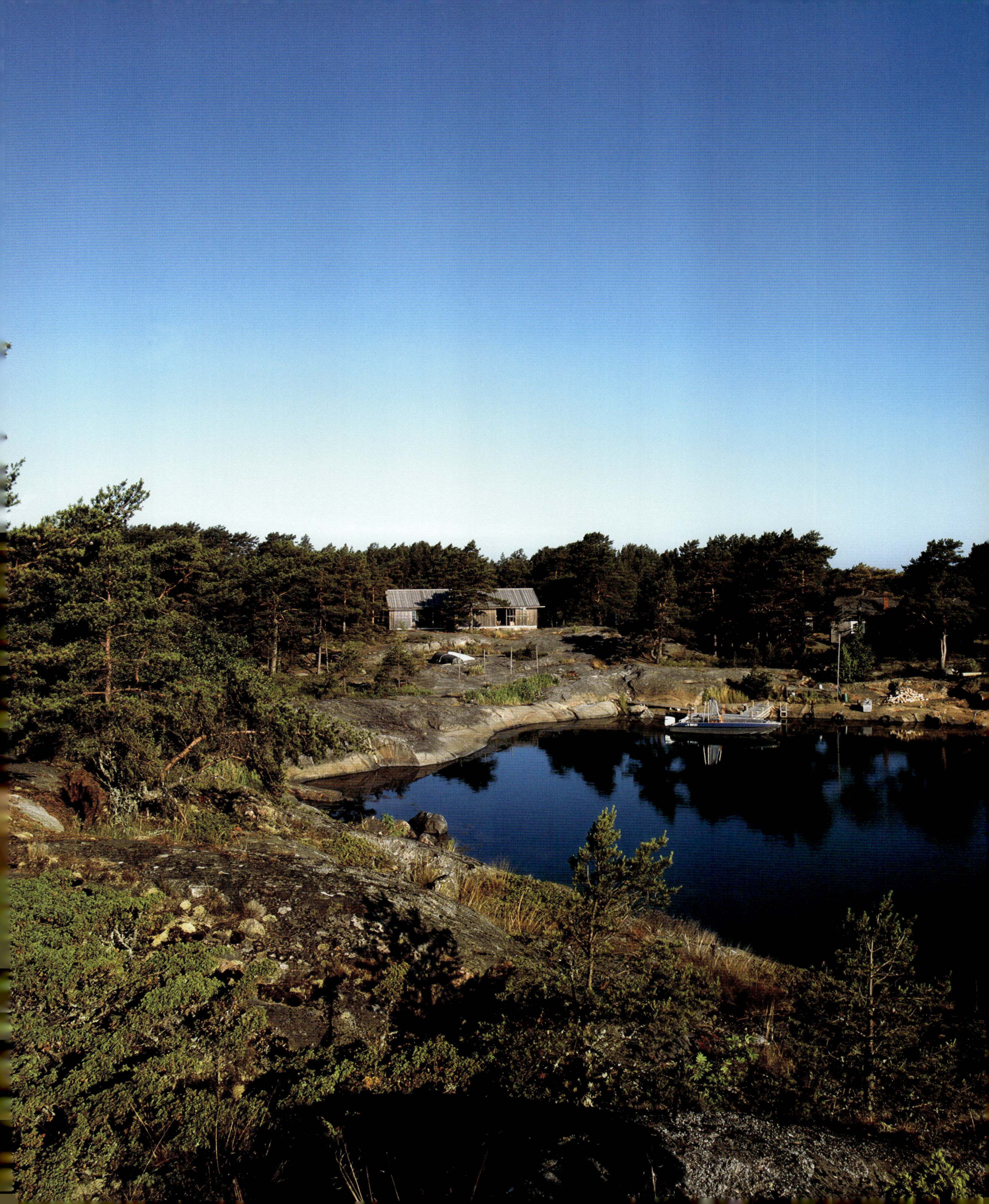

RIGHT
The house in the archipelago landscape

BOTTOM
The grey, weathered building merges into its surroundings.

OPPOSITE
Sliding-glass walls are essential in this summer house.

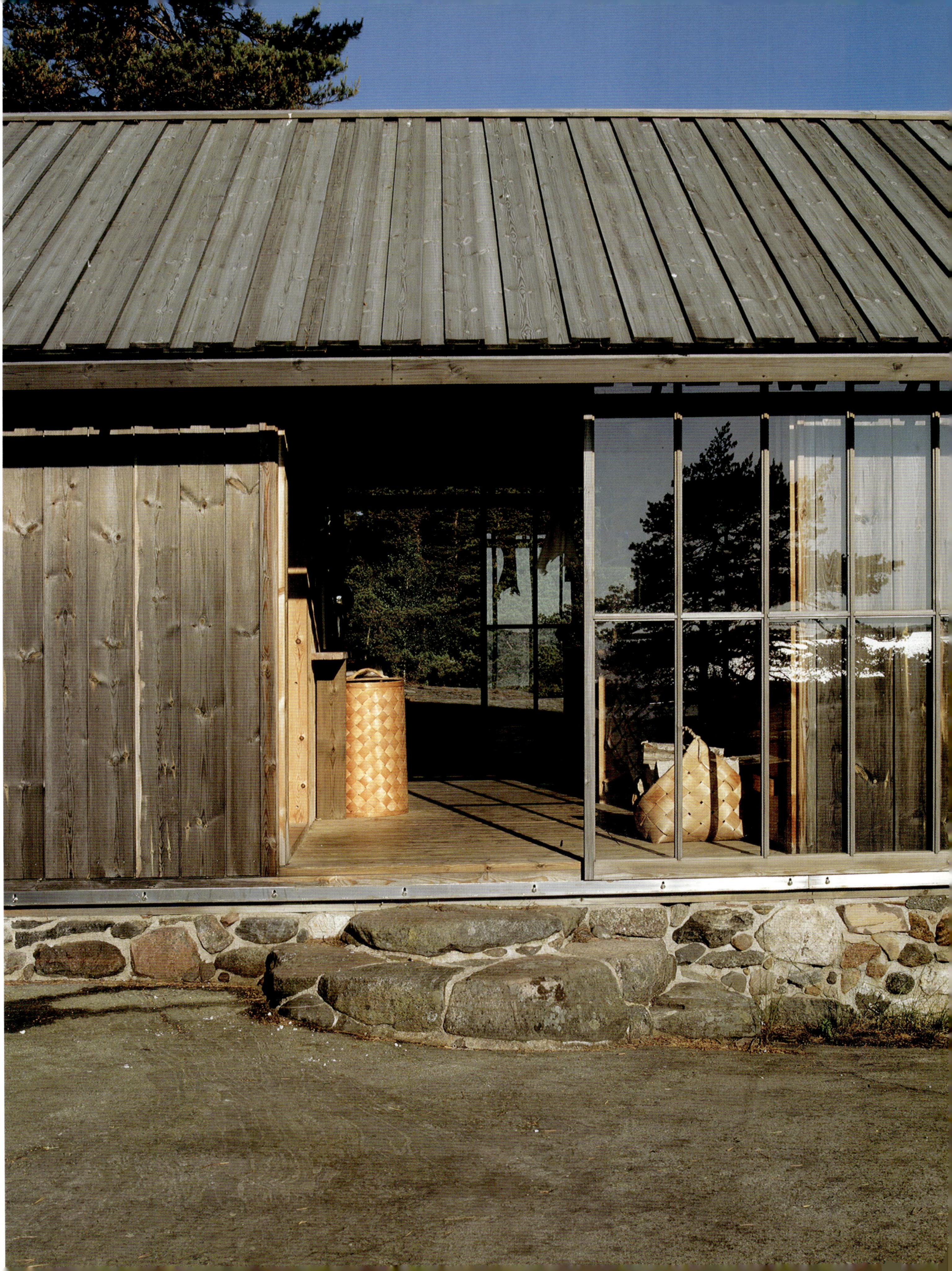

RIGHT
Southfacing window at the gable end

BOTTOM
The open space is used for many everyday activities.

OPPOSITE
The late-afternoon sun shines into the house.

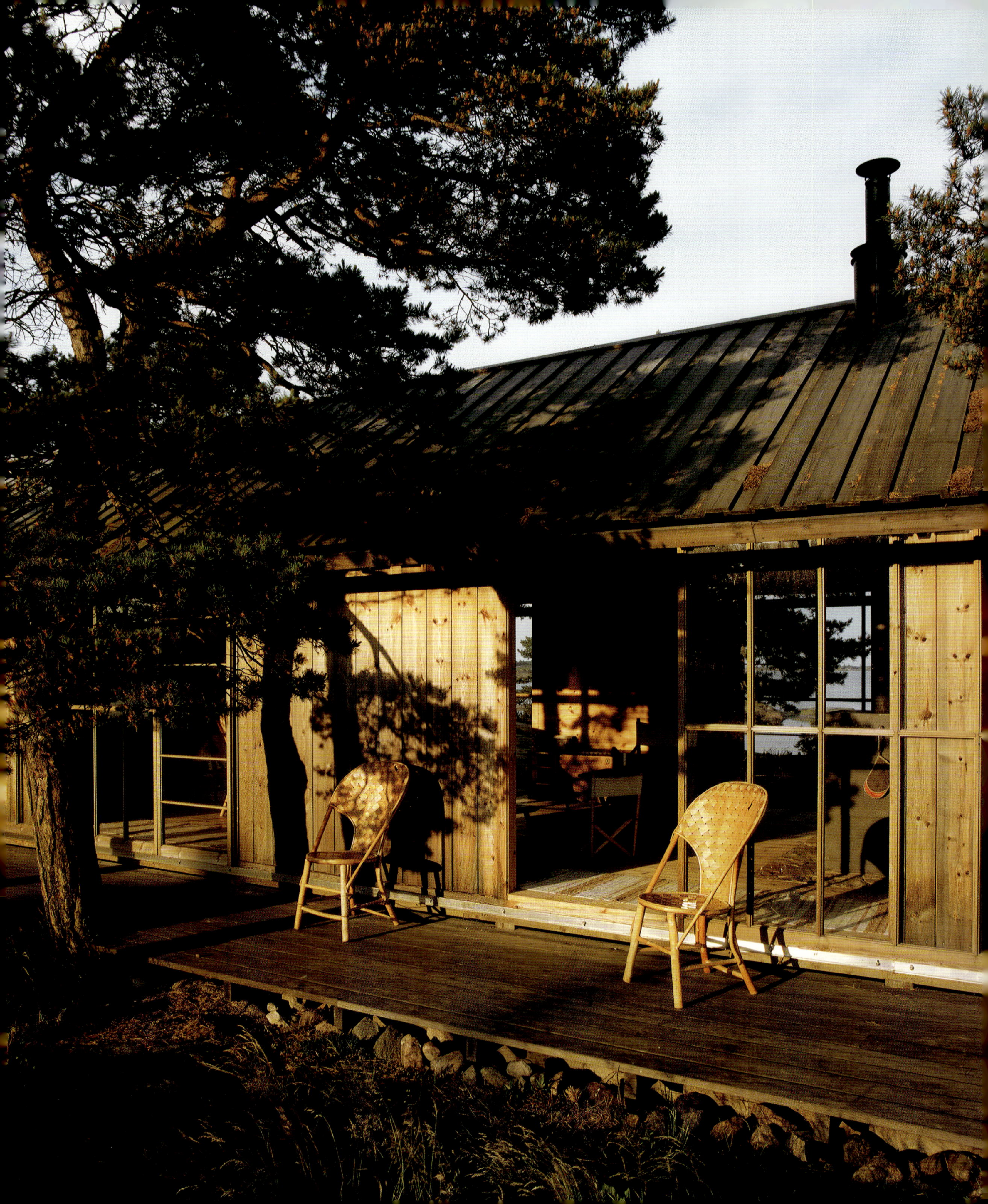

BELOW
The interior has the atmosphere of a veranda.

OPPOSITE
The exposed roof structure in the central living space

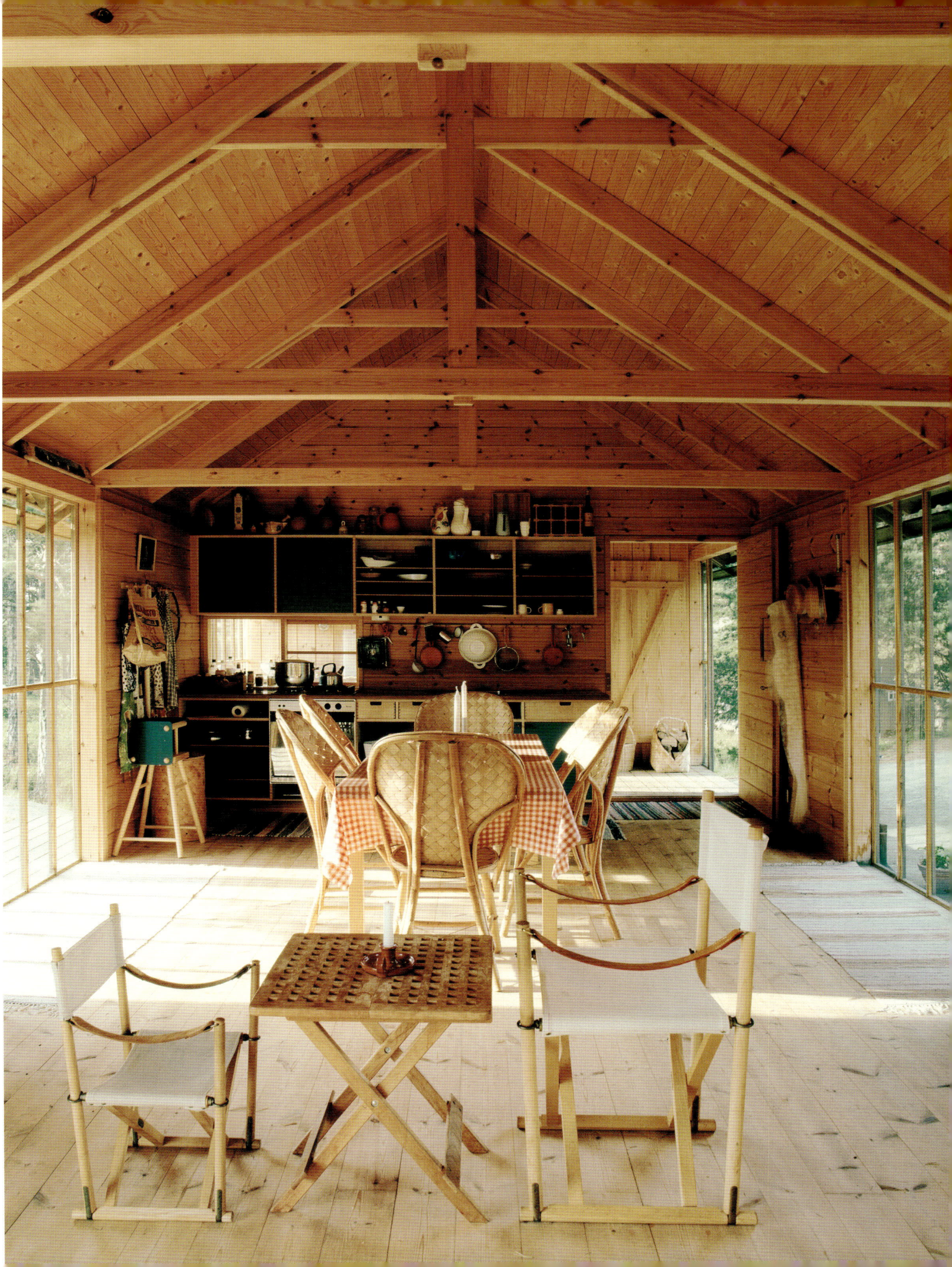

Villa Aulikki

Halskär, designed 1986–94, built 1995–2003
Erkki Kairamo and Aulikki Jylhä

Halskär, a treeless island in the open sea, offers a minimum amount of shelter. Spending the summer here means living at the mercy of nature. Erkki Kairamo and Aulikki Jylhä's summer house—consisting of an old fisherman's cottage and a new building—hides behind a stage-set-like wall of timber planks in the most protected part of the island, at the edge of exposed rocks and amidst a low carpet of juniper bushes. As a trace of man, a wooden horizontal beam traverses past the buildings and beyond to the exposed rocks. A pennant mast at the end of the villa on the shoreline side draws a vertical line as a counterpart to the horizontal beam. Erkki Kairamo once stated: "I am ultimately a realist. I proceed from the concrete situation that exists. This does not have to pose an obstacle to creating architecture. If one invests every-thing, like a gambler, the impossible may become possible. The objective is unquestionable, a building or milieu must resound clearly like a cut of pain."[1]

Space in the house is reduced to the bare essentials: just like on a boat, it comprises sleeping areas and a small living room. As a keen yachtsman, Kairamo knew how to solve the need for shelter in a harsh environment and how to utilize the possibilities offered by nature and the location. At first the old 65-square-foot one-room fisherman's cabin was sufficient for a couple. However, additional space was eventually required: for their children's families, for other guests, and to enable visits to the island in the spring and fall. The old cabin—which was situated in the most sheltered part of the island—was moved slightly so that a new 161-square-foot house could be built. The new building, the old cabin, and the small yard between them—as well as an outdoor toilet—are arranged in a straight line along a depression in the rock. Kairamo carefully placed the new cabin to leave a narrow space between the building and the rock, which functions as a natural cooling area. In the yard between the two cabins, a sail canopy offers both shade at midday during the hot summer and shelter from the rain. Everything the sea brings to the island—pieces of wood or boxes—is utilized. The building itself is like a piece of driftwood that has washed ashore, and—turning grey with the passing years—it is gradually becoming a part of the rock landscape. The surrounding unimpeded view of the horizon offers space for one's thoughts.

ABOVE
Sketch by Kairamo

OPPOSITE
Vertical pennant mast at the end of the cottage

1 Marja-Riitta Norri and Virpi Kumpulainen, eds., *Erkki Kairamo: Luonnoksia* [Erkki Kairamo: Sketches] (Helsinki: Suomen rakennustaiteen museo, 1997), 10.

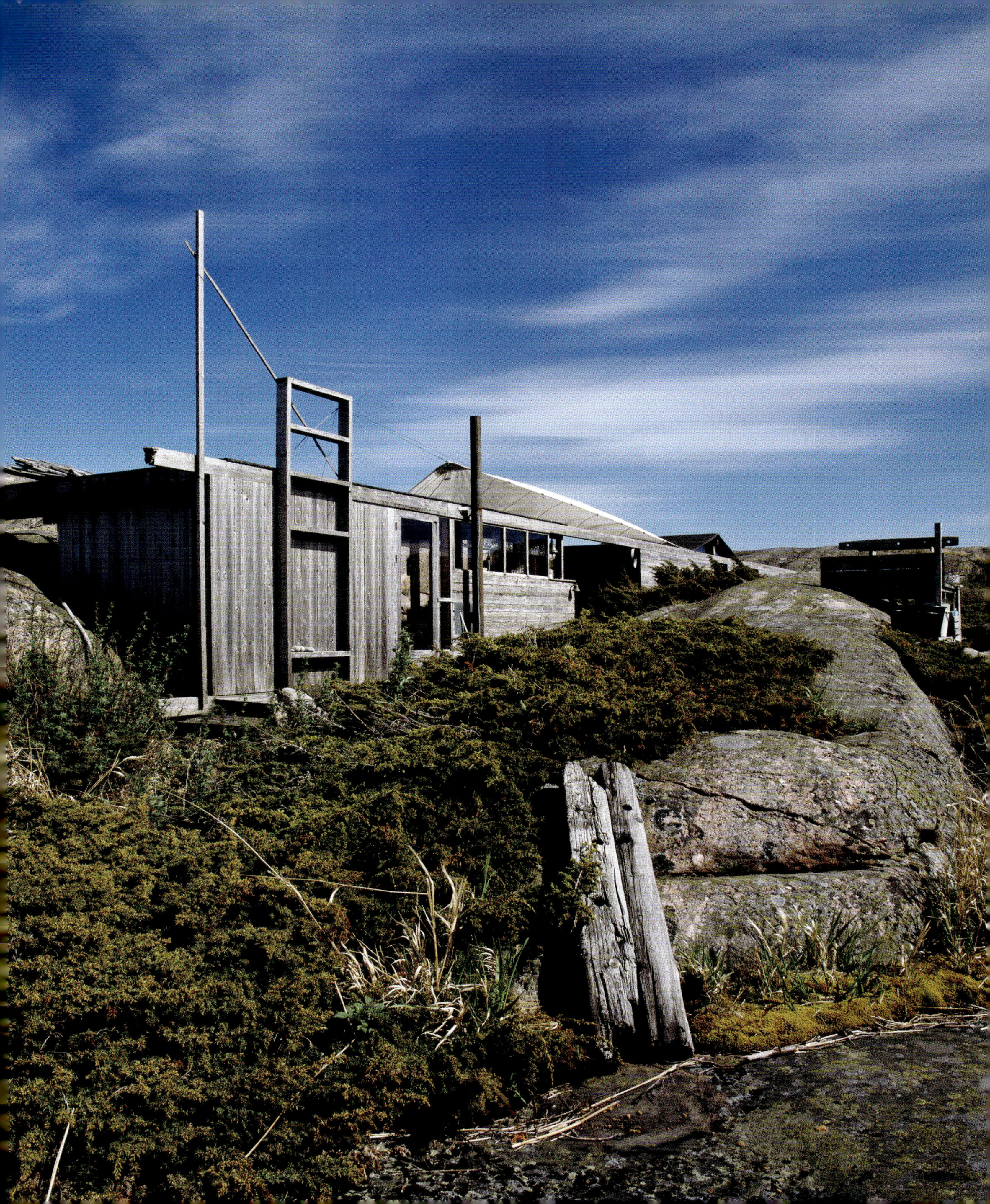

TOP AND MIDDLE
Site section and site plan

BOTTOM, LEFT
The barren island landscape

BOTTOM, RIGHT
View of the building and sail canopy from above

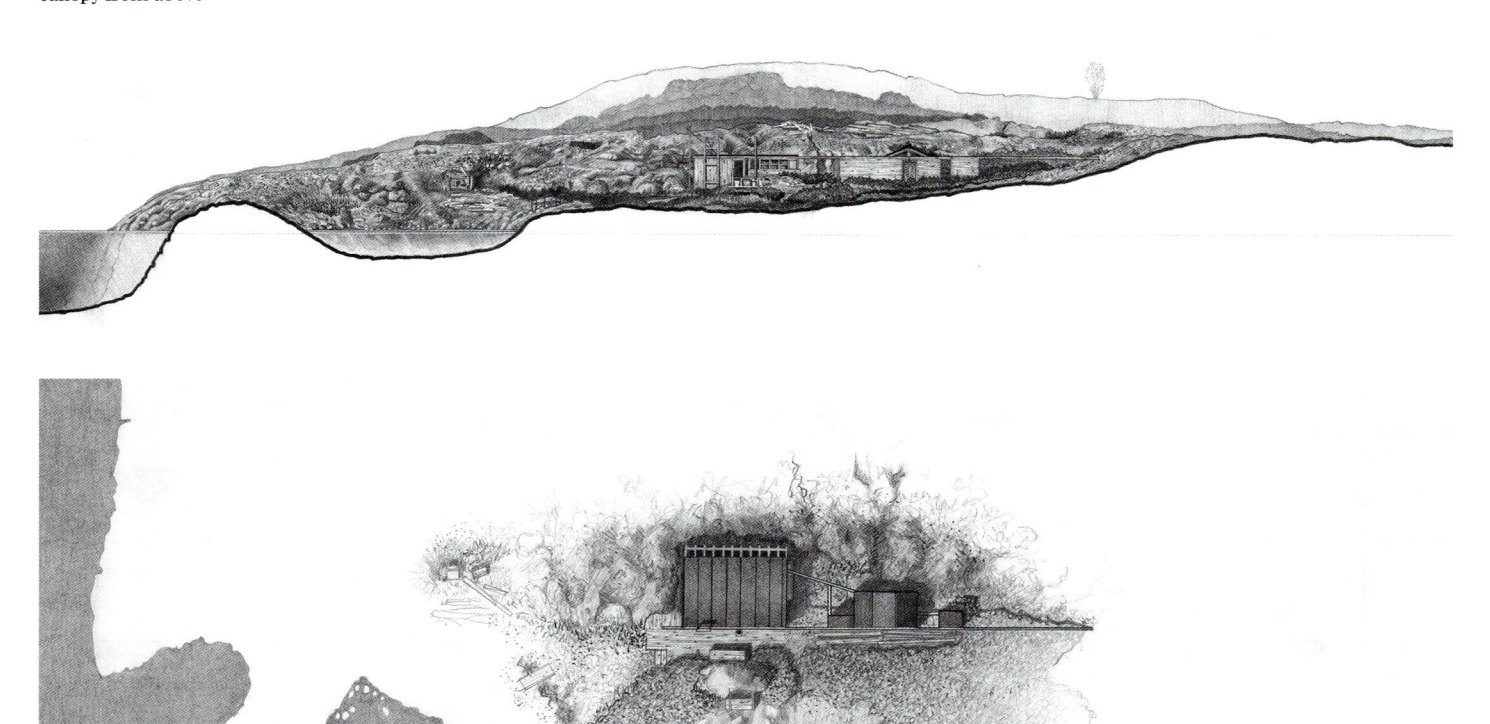

RIGHT
Sections

BOTTOM
A small natural pond in the middle of the island

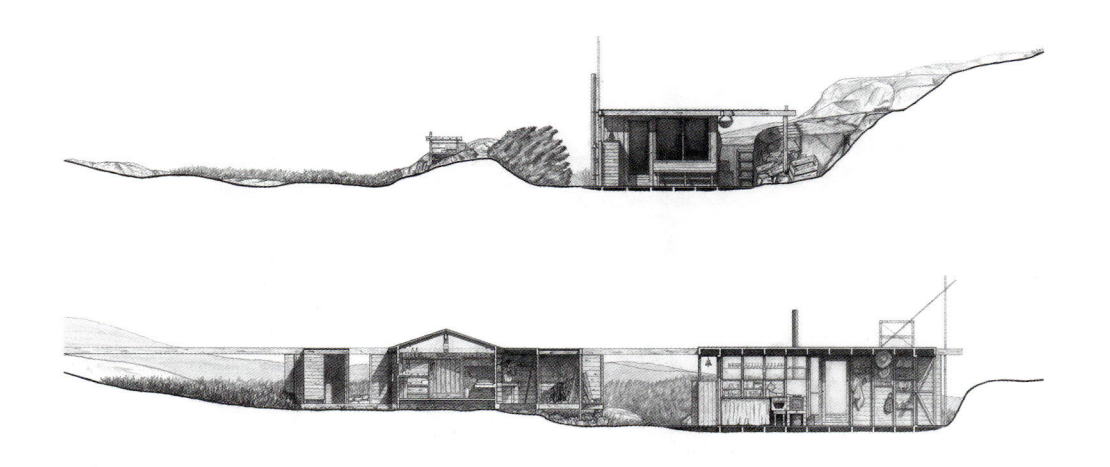

RIGHT
The Kairamo family utilizes pieces of driftwood or boxes washed up by the sea.

BOTTOM
The terrace faces south to capture the sun.

OPPOSITE
The stage-set wall provides shelter from the wind.

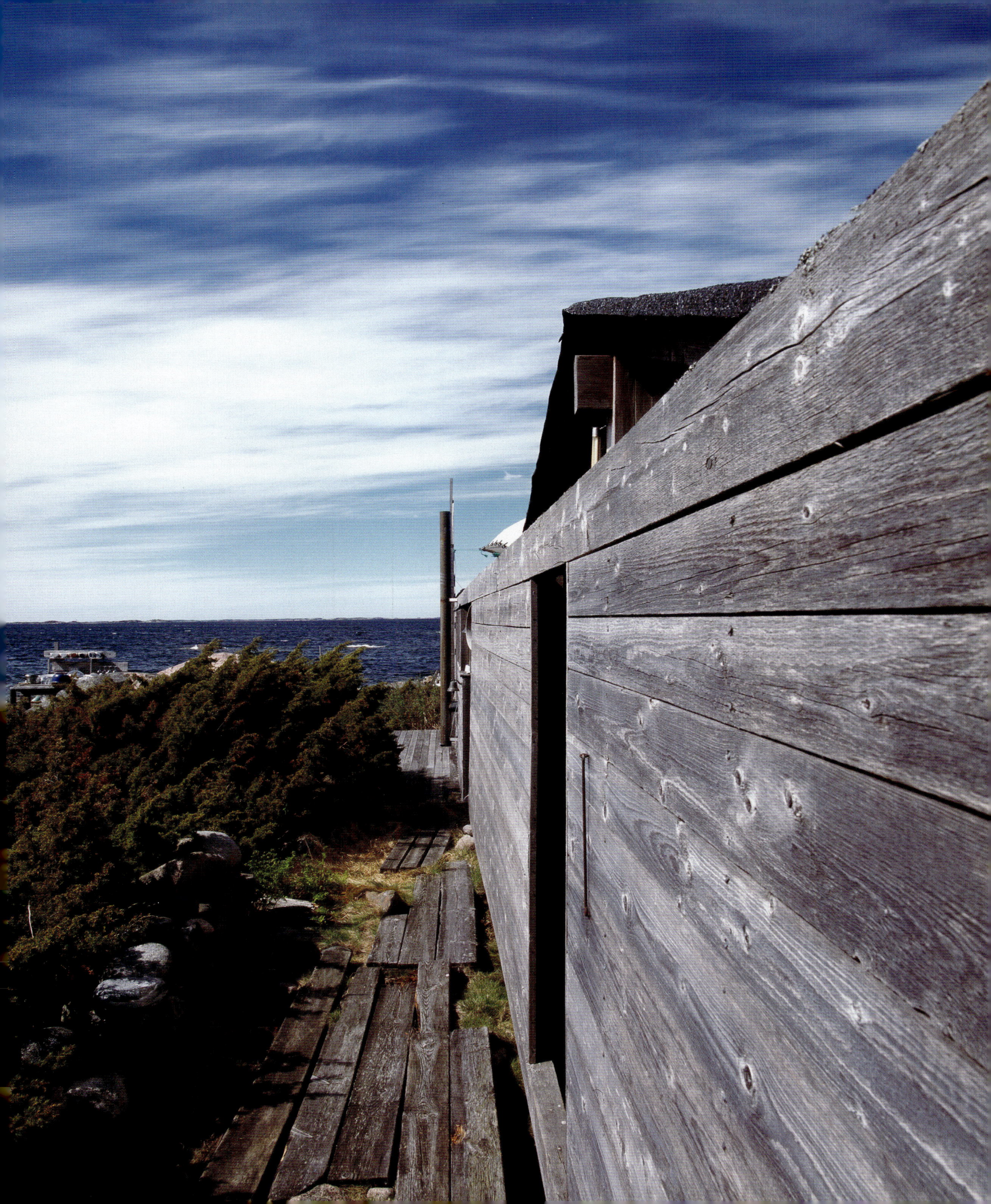

BELOW
Interior of the main cabin

OPPOSITE, TOP
Kairamo incorporated an old fisherman's hut into the new cabin.

OPPOSITE, BOTTOM
Kitchen corner

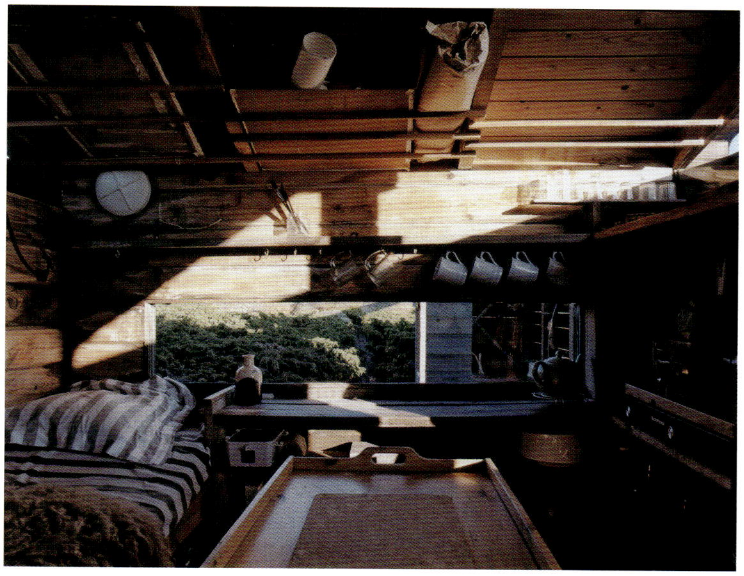

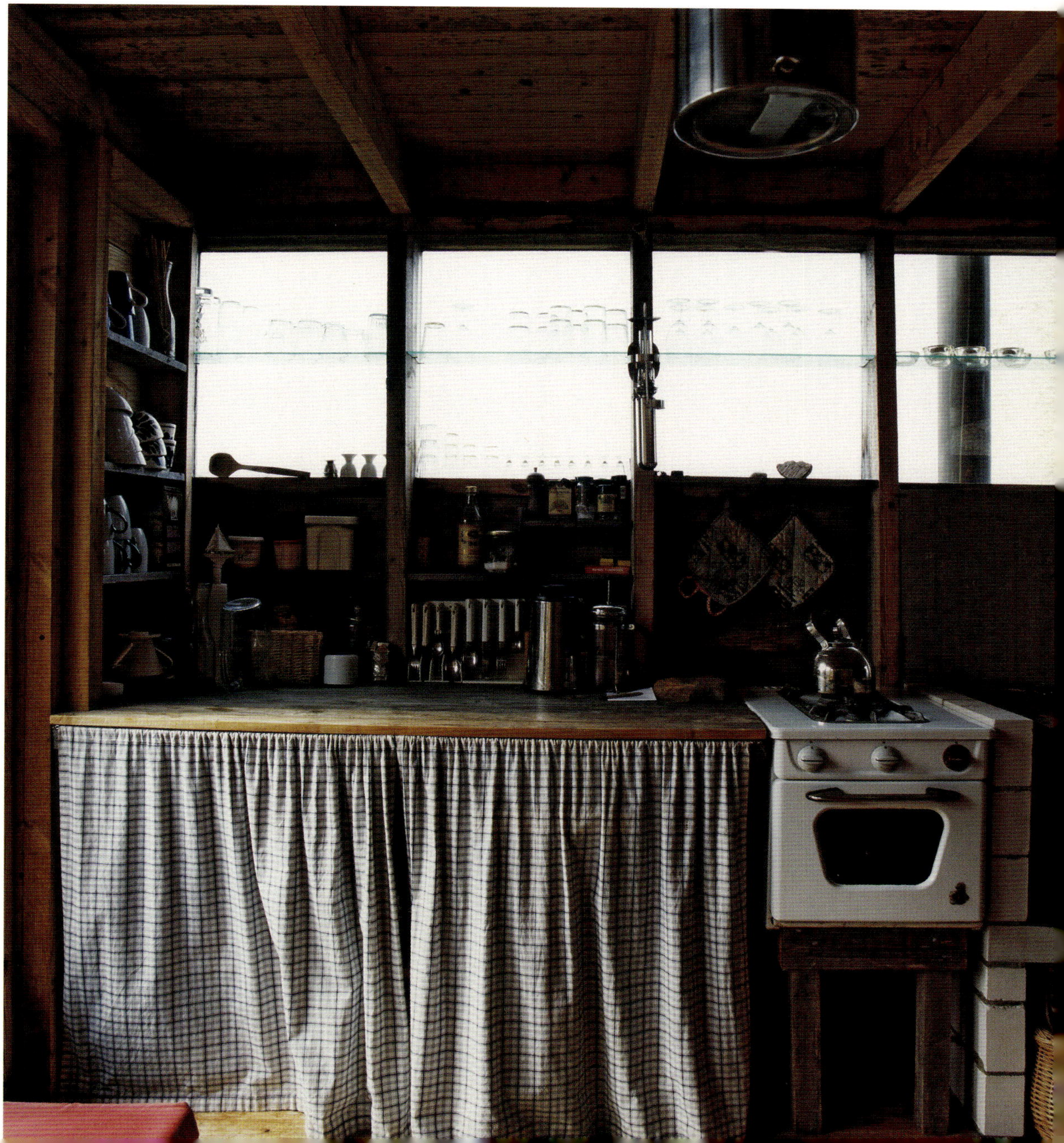

The unimpeded horizon

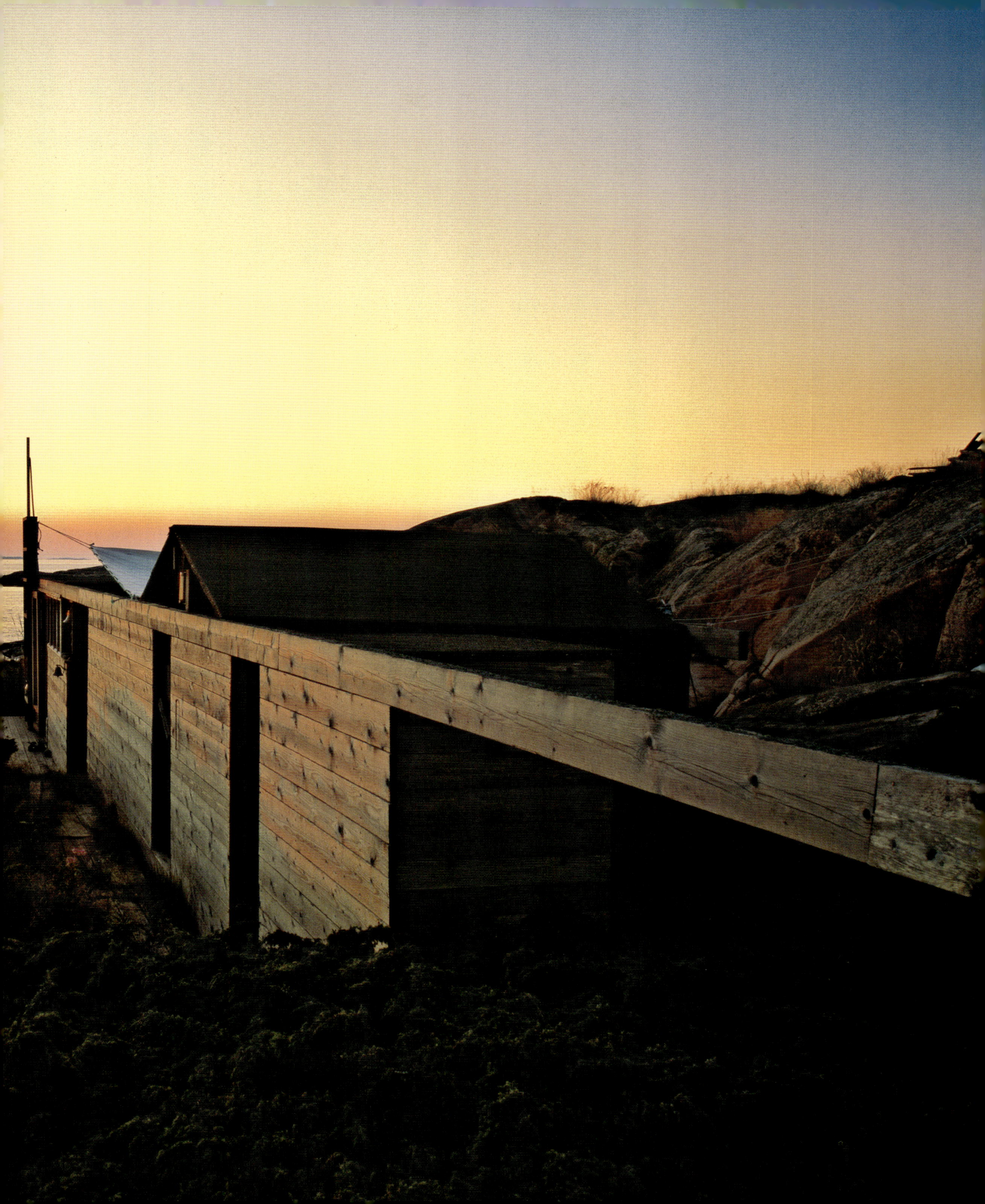

The Architects: Selected Works

Lars Sonck (1870–1956)
Architect, Polytechnical Institute,
Helsinki, 1894

SELECTED WORKS:
St. Michael's Church, Turku, 1894–1905
Lasses Villa, Finström, Åland, 1895
St. John's Cathedral, Tampere,
    1899–1907
Town plan for the Töölö district of
    Helsinki, 1899–1906
Ainola, Tuusula, 1904
Helsinki Telephone Company Building,
    Helsinki, 1905
Eira Hospital, Helsinki, 1905
Kallio Church, Helsinki, 1906–12
Mortgage Society Building, Helsinki,
    1908
Stock Exchange, Helsinki, 1911
Harbor Warehouse, Katajanokka,
    Helsinki, 1911–13
Villa Kultaranta, Naantali, 1916
Mikael Agricola Church, Helsinki,
    1932–35
Town Hall, Mariehamn, Åland, 1939

Eliel Saarinen (1873–1950)
Architect, Polytechnical Institute,
Helsinki, 1897

SELECTED WORKS:
Finnish Pavilion, Paris World Fair,
    1898–1900 (Gesellius, Lindgren,
    and Saarinen)
Pohjola Building, Helsinki, 1899–1901
    (Gesellius, Lindgren, and Saarinen)
Olofsborg, Helsinki, 1900–1902
    (Gesellius, Lindgren, and Saarinen)
Villa Pulkanranta, Mäntyharju, 1900–1901
Atelier House, Hvitträsk, Kirkkonummi,
    1902–03 (Gesellius, Lindgren, and
    Saarinen)
Suur-Merijoki, Viipuri rural commune,
    1901–03 (Gesellius, Lindgren, and
    Saarinen)
National Museum, Helsinki, 1902–11
    (Gesellius, Lindgren, and Saarinen)
Helsinki Railway Station, Helsinki,
    1904–14, 1919
Munkkiniemi-Haaga plan, Helsinki,
    1910–15
Lahti Town Hall, Lahti, 1911–12
Pro Helsingfors plan, 1918
Cranbrook Academy of Art, Bloomfield
    Hills, Michigan, 1925–43
Cranbrook School for Boys, 1925–30
Kingswood School Cranbrook, 1929–31
Cranbrook Academy of Art Library and
    Museum, 1939–42

Oiva Kallio (1884–1964)
Architect, Polytechnical Institute,
Helsinki, 1908

SELECTED WORKS:
Karkku Church, Karkku, 1911–13
SOK headquarters, Helsinki, 1919–21
    (with Kauno S. Kallio)
Aurejärvi Church, Aurejärvi, 1921–24
Villa Oivala, Villinge, 1924
Imatra Power Station, Imatra, 1926–29
    (with Kauno S. Kallio)
Hämeenlinna Savings Bank,
    Hämeenlinna, 1928–29
Pohja Office Building, Helsinki, 1928–30
Yrjönkatu 17 (residential building),
    Helsinki, 1935–36

Aino Aalto (1894–1949)
Architect, Helsinki University of Technology, 1920

SELECTED WORKS:

Villa Flora, Alajärvi, 1926, alterations 1938
Pöytyä Parish Hall, Pöytyä, 1930
Noormarkku Children's Welfare and Health Center, Noormarkku, 1945
Selected projects of the Aalto office in which Aino Aalto participated:
Paimio Sanatorium, Paimio, 1929–33
Viipuri Library, Viipuri, 1927–35
Aalto House, Helsinki, 1935
The interior of the Savoy restaurant, Helsinki, 1936
Sunila Pulp Mill Office, Kotka, 1936–37
Villa Mairea, Noormarkku, 1938–39
Baker House Dormitory, Massachusetts Institute of Technology, Cambridge, Massachusetts, 1946–49

Erkki Huttunen (1901–1956)
Architect, Helsinki University of Technology, 1927

SELECTED WORKS:

SOK Office and Warehouse Building, Rauma, 1930–31
SOK Mill and Grainstore, Viipuri, 1930–32
Kotka Town Hall, Kotka, 1931–34
Alko Rajamäki Factory, Nurmijärvi, 1933–38
Nakkila Church, Nakkila, 1935–37
Villa Huttunen, Nuuksio, 1937–38
SOK Office and Warehouse Building, Oulu, 1937–38
Rajamäki Church, Rajamäki, 1937–38
Sokos Commercial Building, Helsinki, 1938–52
French Embassy, Helsinki, 1949–52

J. S. Sirén (1889–1961)
Architect, Helsinki University of Technology, 1913, Professor

---

SELECTED WORKS:

Finnish Parliament House, Helsinki, 1924–31
Helsinki University Main Building extension, Helsinki, 1931–37
Lassila & Tikanoja Office Building, Helsinki, 1934–35
The Blue House (La Maison Bleue), Borgholm, 1938–39
Bank of Finland Vaasa offices, Vaasa, 1943–45, 1952

Kaj Englund (1905–1976)
Architect, Helsinki University of
Technology, 1931

———

SELECTED WORKS:

Villa Bjerges, Helsinki, 1938 (with Dag
    Englund)
Standardized houses for the Ministry of
    Social Affairs, 1941–45
Villa Silla, Kiljava, 1947
Mäntylä Residential Area, Kemi, 1940s
Housing in Karihaara, Kemi, 1940s
Männikkötie 5, Helsinki, 1959

Alvar Aalto (1898–1976)
Architect, Helsinki University of
Technology, 1921
Academician of Art, 1955

———

SELECTED WORKS:

Workers' Club, Jyväskylä, 1924
Muurame Church, Muurame, 1926–29
Paimio Sanatorium, Paimio, 1929–33
Viipuri City Library, Viipuri (now Russia),
    1927–35
Sunila Pulp Mill and Housing Area,
    Kotka, 1936–39, 1945–47, 1951–54
Villa Mairea, Noormarkku, 1938–39
Baker House Dormitory, Massachusetts
    Institute of Technology, Cambridge,
    Massachusetts, 1946–49
Muuratsalo Experimental House,
    Muuratsalo, 1952–54
Säynätsalo Town Hall, Säynätsalo,
    1950–52
National Pensions Institute, Helsinki,
    1948–57
House of Culture, Helsinki, 1952–58
Vuoksenniska Church, Imatra, 1956–58
Seinäjoki Town Center, 1956–88
Helsinki University of Technology,
    Otaniemi, Espoo, 1949–74
Finlandia Hall, Helsinki, 1962–75

Bertel Saarnio (1912–1969)
Architect, Helsinki University of
Technology, 1940

———

SELECTED WORKS:

Summer Villa, Bökars, 1955
Heinola School, Heinola, 1957
Villa Malmsten, Helsinki, 1957
Rauma Water Tower, Rauma, 1964
Vasa Sparbanken Building, Vaasa, 1970
Helsinki Water (water treatment facility),
    Helsinki, 1959
Kouvola Town Hall, Kouvola, 1968 (with
    Juha Leiviskä)

Heikki Castrén (1929–1980)
Architect, Helsinki University of Technology, 1956

Mirja Castrén (1930–)
Architect, Helsinki University of Technology, 1956

SELECTED WORKS:
Villa Skata, Löparö, 1953–55, 1962–67
Espoo Town Hall, Espoo, 1971 (Castrén-Jauhiainen-Nuuttila Architects)
Seinäjoki Railway and Bus Station, Seinäjoki, 1971 (Castrén-Jauhiainen-Nuuttila Architects)
Oulunkylä Church, Helsinki, 1972 (Castrén-Jauhiainen-Nuuttila Architects)
Pohjola Head Office, Helsinki, 1967–69 (Castrén-Jauhiainen-Nuuttila Architects)
Keskuskatu 7 (office building), Helsinki, 1968 (Castrén-Jauhiainen-Nuuttila Architects)
Neste Head Office, Espoo, 1971–76 (Castrén-Jauhiainen-Nuuttila Architects)
Pasila Office Building, Helsinki, 1981 (Castrén-Jauhiainen-Nuuttila Architects)

Mikko Pulkkinen (1940–)
Architect, Helsinki University of Technology, 1971

SELECTED WORKS:
The Pulkkinen Cabin, Kustavi, 1967
Ateneum Art Museum, renovation, Helsinki, 1979–91 (LPR Architects)
Turku Art Academy and Conservatory, Turku, 1993–97 (LPR Architects)
Forum Marinum, Turku, 1999–2005 (LPR Architects)
Suomenlinna Visitor Center, Helsinki, 1995–98 (LPR Architects)
G. A. Serlachius Museum, renovation, Mänttä, 2000–2003 (LPR Architects)
Helsinki Music Center, Helsinki, 2000– (LPR Architects)

Kaija Siren (1920–2001)
Architect, Helsinki University of Technology, 1948

Heikki Siren (1918–)
Architect, Helsinki University of Technology, 1946, Professor honoris causa, 1970

SELECTED WORKS:
Otaniemi Chapel, Espoo, 1953–57
National Theater, small stage, Helsinki, 1954
Kontiontie Houses, Espoo, 1955
Orivesi Church, Orivesi, 1961
Helsinki Cathedral, restoration, 1961–63 (with J. S. Sirén)
Lingonsö Holiday Island, Barösund, 1966–69
Pirkkola Sports Park, Helsinki, 1968–74
Ympyrätalo Office and Commercial Building, Helsinki, 1968
Housing Area, Boussy St. Antoine, Paris, France, 1970
Brucknerhaus Concert Hall, Linz, Austria, 1974
Golf-center, Onuma, Japan, 1976
Conference Palace, Baghdad, Iraq, 1982

Aarno Ruusuvuori (1925–1992)
Architect, Helsinki University of Technology, 1951, Professor

---

SELECTED WORKS:
Hyvinkää Church, Hyvinkää, 1958–61
Tapiola Church, Espoo, 1963–65
Weilin & Göös Printing Company, Espoo, 1964–66
Roihuvuori Primary School, Helsinki, 1964–67
Marimekko Printing Company, Helsinki, 1967
Police Headquarters, Mikkeli, 1968
Ruusuvuori Cabin and Sauna, Kerimäki, 1968
Helsinki City Hall, renovation and extension, 1960–70, 1988

Pirkko Ilonen (1934–)
Architect, Helsinki University of Technology, 1962

Arvi Ilonen (1933–)
Architect, Helsinki University of Technology, 1961

SELECTED WORKS:
Kelkkamäki Funeral Chapel, Laukaa, 1964–66
Järvenpää Water Tower, Järvenpää, 1964–66
The Ilonen Cabin, Kiljava, 1970
Vuosaari Church, Helsinki, 1976–80
Ministry of Labor, office building, renovation, Helsinki, 1980–84
Lepaa Horticulture and Landscape Design Institute, renovation, Hattula, 1987–94

Reima Pietilä (1923–1993)
Architect, Helsinki University of Technology, 1953, Professor
Academician of Art, 1982

Raili Pietilä (1926–)
Architect, Helsinki University of Technology, 1956

SELECTED WORKS:
Finnish Pavilion, Brussels World Fair, 1956–58
Kaleva Church, Tampere, 1959–66
Dipoli Student Union Building, Espoo, 1961–66
Suvikumpu Housing Area, Espoo, 1962–69, 1979–83
Finnish Embassy, New Delhi, India, 1963, 1980–85
Sief Palace Area, Kuwait, 1973–82
Metso, Tampere Main Library, 1978–85
Lieksa Church, Lieksa, 1979–84
Two Saunas, Tenhola, 1985
Mäntyniemi, Official Residence of the President of Finland, Helsinki, 1984–93

Juha Kaakko (1964–)
Architect, Helsinki University of
Technology, 2001

Ilkka Laine (1964–)
Architect, Helsinki University of
Technology, 1993

Kimmo Liimatainen (1965–)
Architect, Helsinki University of
Technology, 1993

Jari Tirkkonen (1965–)
Architect, Helsinki University of
Technology, 1999

SELECTED WORKS:
Finnish Pavilion, Seville World Fair, 1992
 (Monark: Jääskeläinen-Kaakko-
 Rouhiainen-Sanaksenaho-
 Tirkkonen)
Weekend Atelier, Puolarmaari, Espoo,
 1991–92

Pekka Pitkänen (1927–)
Architect, Helsinki University of
Technology, 1953, Professor honoris
causa, 1988

SELECTED WORKS:
The Chapel of the Holy Cross, Turku,
 1965–67
Parish Center, Säkylä, 1968
Parish Center, Kurikka, 1969
Finnish Parliament House, extension,
 Helsinki, 1970–85 (Pitkänen-Laiho-
 Raunio Architects)
Turku Cathedral, renovation, Turku, 1979
 (Pitkänen-Laiho-Pulkkinen Archi-
 tects)
Harjavalta Church, Harjavalta, 1984
Villa Sara, Taivassalo, 1994
Turku Court House, Turku, 1997

Juhani Pallasmaa (1936–)
Architect, Helsinki University of
Technology, 1966, Professor

SELECTED WORKS:
Moduli 225, holiday house prefabrication
 system, 1968–72 (with Kristian
 Gullichsen)
Summer atelier of artist Tor Arne, Vänö
 Island, 1970
Art Museum, Rovaniemi, renovation,
 1984–86
Institut Finlandais, Paris, 1986–91 (with
 Roland Schweitzer and Sami Tabet)
Itäkeskus Shopping Center, major
 extension, Helsinki, 1989–92
Ruoholahti Residential Area, outdoor
 spaces, Helsinki, 1990–91
Siida Sámi Museum and the Northern
 Lapland Nature Center, Inari,
 1990–97
Summer Cabin, Stora Bergskär, 1991–95
Cranbrook Academy of Art Arrival
 Feature, Bloomfield Hills, Michigan,
 1993–94 (with Dan Hoffman)
Bank of Finland Museum, Helsinki,
 2002–03
Kamppi Center, Helsinki, 2003–06

Kristian Gullichsen (1932–)
Architect, Helsinki University of Technology, 1960, Professor honoris causa, 1986

———

SELECTED WORKS:
Moduli 225, holiday house prefabrication system, 1968–72 (with Juhani Pallasmaa)
La Petite Maison, Grasse, France, 1972
Art Museum, Pori, 1981 (Gullichsen-Kairamo-Vormala Architects)
Malmi Church, Helsinki, 1981 (Gullichsen-Kairamo-Vormala Architects)
Kauniainen Church, Kauniainen, 1983 (Gullichsen-Kairamo-Vormala Architects)
Cultural Center, Pieksämäki, 1983–89 (Gullichsen-Kairamo-Vormala Architects)
Stockmann Department Store annex, Helsinki, 1989 (Gullichsen-Kairamo-Vormala Architects)
Olympos Condominium, Helsinki, 1993–95 (Gullichsen-Vormala Architects)
Holiday Home, Hiittinen, 1996
Finnish Embassy, Stockholm, Sweden, 2002 (Gullichsen-Vormala Architects)
University Library, Lleida, Spain, 2003 (Gullichsen-Vormala Architects)

Erkki Kairamo (1936–1994)
Architect, Helsinki University of Technology, 1963

———

Aulikki Jylhä (1941–)
Interior Designer, University of Art and Design Helsinki, 1966

———

SELECTED WORKS:
Marimekko Textile Plant, Helsinki, 1971–78 (Gullichsen-Kairamo-Vormala Architects)
Paper Mill, Varkaus, 1975–85 (Gullichsen-Kairamo-Vormala Architects)
Power Station, Varkaus, 1989–90 (Gullichsen-Kairamo-Vormala Architects)
Niittykumpu Fire Station, Espoo, 1986–91 (Gullichsen-Kairamo-Vormala Architects)
Itäkeskus Shopping Center, Helsinki, 1980–83 (Gullichsen-Kairamo-Vormala Architects)
Itäkeskus Office Tower, Helsinki, 1978, 1984–89 (Gullichsen-Kairamo-Vormala Architects)
Liinasaarenkuja Semi-Detached Houses, Espoo, 1980 (Gullichsen-Kairamo-Vormala Architects)
Stockmann Department Store annex, Helsinki, 1989 (Gullichsen-Kairamo-Vormala Architects)
Villa Aulikki, Halskär, designed 1986–94, realized 1995–2003
Lyökkiniemi Semi-Detached Houses, Espoo, 1989–90 (Gullichsen-Kairamo-Vormala Architects)

Selected Bibliography

Ahmavaara, Anna-Liisa, ed. *Asumme lähellä luontoa: Suomalaisia pientaloja ja saunoja* [We live close to nature: Finnish private houses and saunas]. Helsinki: Otava, 1966.

Blomstedt, Severi, Kari Kuosma, Eija Merenmies, Riitta Nikula, and Pia Strandman, eds. *J. S. Sirén: Arkkitehti—Architect 1889–1961*. Helsinki: Suomen rakennustaiteen museo [Museum of Finnish architecture], 1989.

Brandolini, Sebastiano. *Kristian Gullichsen, Erkki Kairamo, Timo Vormala: Architecture 1969–2000*. Milano: Skira, 2000.

Bruun, Erik, and Sara Popovits, eds. *Kaija + Heikki Siren: Arkkitehdit—Arkitekter*. Helsinki: Otava, 1976.

"Dipoli: Teknillisen Korkeakoulun Ylioppilaskunnan rakennus" [Dipoli: The Institute of Technology students' union building]. Reima Pietilä and Raili Paatelainen. *Arkkitehti* [The Finnish architectural review] 9 (1967): 14–20.

"Eduskuntatalo" [Parliament House]. J. S. Sirén. *Arkkitehti* 5 (1931): 66–85.

Enckell, Ulla. *Alvar Aalto Taiteilija—Konstnären—The Artist 1898–1976*. Helsinki: Amos Anderson Art Museum, 1998.

Exhibition of Finnish architecture. Exhibition catalogue. Helsinki: Suomen rakennustaiteen museo, 1979.

"Grankulla kyrka / Kauniaisten kirkko" [Kauniainen church]. Arkkitehdit Ky Gullichsen, Kairamo, Vormala. *Arkkitehti* 7 (1984): 52–59.

Harmia, Hugo. "Suomen Arkkitehtiliiton (S.A.F.A.) Vähä-Kiljava" [The Finnish Association of Architects' Vähä-Kiljava]. *Arkkitehti* 7 (1939): 95–102.

Hausen, Marika, Anna-Lisa Amberg, Kirmo Mikkola, and Tytti Valto. *Eliel Saarinen: Projects 1896–1923*. Helsinki: Suomen rakennustaiteen museo, 1990.

"Helvetinkolu: Suomen paviljonki Sevillan maailmannäyttelyssä" [Hell's Gorge]. Arkkitehtuuritoimisto 92 Oy (MONARK) / Jääskeläinen, Juha, Juha Kaakko, Petri Rouhiainen, Matti Sanaksenaho, and Jari Tirkkonen. *Arkkitehti* 4–5 (1992): 40–51.

"Huvila Nouksin-Pitkäjärven rannalla" [Villa by Lake Pitkäjärvi]. Erkki Huttunen. *Arkkitehti* 5 (1938): 77–78.

Jeskanen, Timo. *Kansanomaisuus ja rationalismi*. [Vernacularism and rationalism]. Espoo: Teknillinen korkeakoulu [Helsinki University of Technology], 1998.

Jetsonen, Jari and Sirkkaliisa Jetsonen. *Sacral Space: Finnish Modern Churches*. Helsinki: Building Information Ltd., 2003.

Jokinen, Teppo (Nikula, Riitta, and Kristiina Paatero, eds.). *Erkki Huttunen 1901–1956: arkkitehti* [Erkki Huttunen 1901–1956: Architect]. Helsinki: Suomen rakennustaiteen museo, 1993.

Keinänen, Timo. "Asuntosuunnittelun uranuurtaja" [A pioneer of housing design]. *Arkkitehti* 3 (2005): 72–74.

"Kesämaja Porvoon Hauenkoukussa" [Summer House]. Bertel Saarnio. *Arkkitehti* 4 (1963): 70–72.

"Kesätalo ulkosaaristossa. Summer cottage in the outer archipelago." Kristian Gullichsen. *Arkkitehti* 3 (2003): 42–47.

Kinnunen, Ulla, ed. *Aino Aalto*. Jyväskylä: Alvar Aalto Säätiö, Alvar Aalto-museo [Alvar Aalto Foundation, Alvar Aalto Museum], 2004.

"Koetalo, Muuratsalo" [Experimental house, Muuratsalo]. Alvar Aalto. *Arkkitehti* 9–10 (1953): 159–63.

"Kouvolan kaupungintalo, Kouvola" [Kouvola Town Hall]. Bertel Saarnio and Juha Leiviskä. *Arkkitehti* 6 (1969): 38–44.

"Kunnantalo, Säynätsalo" [The village hall, Säynätsalo]. Alvar Aalto. *Arkkitehti* 9–10 (1953): 149–62.

Lars Sonck 1870–1956 arkkitehti, architect. Exhibition catalogue. Helsinki: Suomen rakennustaiteen museo, 1981.

Leskelä, Pekka. *Arkkitehti Oiva Kallio: 1884–1964* [Architect Oiva Kallio: 1884–1964]. Espoo: Teknillinen korkeakoulu [Helsinki University of Technology], 1998.

"Mairea." Aino Aalto and Alvar Aalto. *Arkkitehti* 9 (1939): 134–37.

Maunula, Jarmo, ed. *Suomi rakentaa: 1965–1970* [Finland Builds: 1965–1970]. Helsinki: Suomen Arkkitehtiliitto, 1970.

———, ed. *Suomi rakentaa. Finland bygger 5* [Finland Builds 5]. Exhibition catalogue. Helsinki: Taidehalli [Art Hall], 1976.

Nakamura, Toshio. "The Leisure Studio." Group Kaakko, Laine, Liimatainen, Tirkkonen. *A+U* (August 1994): 20–27.

Norri, Marja-Riitta, ed. *Architecture in Miniature. Juhani Pallasmaa*. Helsinki: Raccolta Alvar Aalto alla Biennale di Venezia and the Museum of Finnish Architecture, 1991.

Norri, Marja-Riitta, and Maija Kärkkäinen, eds. *Aarno Ruusuvuori: Järjestys on kauneuden avain* [Aarno Ruusuvuori: Structure is the key to beauty]. Helsinki: Suomen rakennustaiteen museo, 1992.

Norri, Marja-Riitta, and Virpi Kumpulainen, eds. *Erkki Kairamo: Luonnoksia Sketches*. Helsinki: Suomen rakennustaiteen museo, 1997.

Norri, Marja-Riitta, Elina Standertskjöld, and Wilfried Wang, eds. *20th Century Architecture: Finland*. Helsinki and Frankfurt am Main: Museum of Finnish Architecture and the Deutsches Architektur Museum, 2000.

Norrmén, Pehr. "Oivala: Oiva Kallion kesäkoti" [Oivala: Oiva Kallio's summer home]. *Arkkitehti* 3 (1927): 29–30.

Pallasmaa, Juhani, ed. *Hvitträsk—koti taideteoksena* [The home as a work of art]. Helsinki: Suomen rakennustaiteen museo, 1987.

"Purjehtijan piilo" [Sailors' hideaway]. Aulikki Jylhä. *Arkkitehti* 3 (2003): 48–51.

"Pyhän Ristin kappeli, Turku" [Chapel of the Holy Cross, Turku]. Pekka Pitkänen. *Arkkitehti* 2 (1969): 52–55.

Quantrill, Malcolm. *One Man's Odyssey in Search of Finnish Architecture: An Anthology in Honour of Reima Pietilä. Suomalaisen arkkitehtuurin etsijä: Omistettu Reima Pietilälle*. Helsinki: Rakennustietosäätiö [Building Information Institute], 1988.

"Saunarakennus" [Sauna building]. Oiva Kallio. *Arkkitehti* 5 (1930): 72.

Schildt, Göran. *Inhimillinen tekijä* [The human factor]. Helsinki: Otava, 1990.

"Sininen talo: viikonloppu-ja kesämaja Barönsalmessa" [The Blue House: a weekend and summer cottage in Barösund]. J. S. Sirén. *Arkkitehti* 7–8 (1941): 99–100.

Sippo, Hanni, ed. *Alvar Aalto: The Brick.* Helsinki: Alvar Aalto Foundation, 2001.

Soiri-Snellman, Helena. *Ruissalon huvilat* [Ruissalo villas]. Turku: Turun maakuntamuseo, 1985.

"SOKOS Oy, Helsinki." Erkki Huttunen. *Arkkitehti* 4 (1949): 61–72.

"Suomen Osuuskauppojen Keskuskunnan toimitalo Helsingissä" [The SOK Cooperative's head office in Helsinki]. Kauno S. Kallio and Oiva Kallio. *Arkkitehti* 2 (1922): 17–23.

"Teekkarikylän kappeli, Otaniemi" [The Chapel in the College of Technology Village]. Kaija Siren and Heikki Siren. *Arkkitehti* 6–7 (1958): 87–97.

Tempel, Egon. *New Finnish Architecture.* New York and Washington: Frederick A. Praeger, 1968.

"Turun taideakatemia" [Turku art academy]. Mikko Pulkkinen. *Arkkitehti* 5–6 (1997): 30–38.

"Vapaa-ajan ateljee" [Leisure studio]. Juha Kaakko, Ilkka Laine, Kimmo Liimatainen, and Jari Tirkkonen. *Arkkitehti* 4–5 (1992): 60–63.

Vepsä, Marjo. "Mäyrämäen elämää" [Life in Badger Hill]. *Arkkitehti* 3 (2003): 78–81.

"Villa Aulikki." Erkki Kairamo. *Arkkitehti* 2–3 (1996): 66–71.

"Villa Flora." Aino Aalto. *Arkkitehti* 5 (1929): 74–75.

"Villa Silla." Kaj Englund. *Arkkitehti* 7 (1948): 104–5.

Voipio, Pentti J. *Katovuosista kumousvuosiin* [From the bad years to the years of revolution]. Helsinki: Juho Saarisen sukutoimikunta, 1996.

———. *Kirjeitä Inkerinmaalta, Pietarista ja Suomesta* [Letters from Ingria, St. Petersburg, and Finland]. Helsinki: Juho Saarisen sukutoimikunta, 1996.

Illustration Credits

All photographs by Jari Jetsonen unless otherwise noted.

p. 12 middle: Photo Kari Hakli, Museum of Finnish Architecture.
p. 16 top: Photo Patrick Degomier, Museum of Finnish Architecture.
p. 18: Map from Elisabeth Tostrup, *Norwegian Wood: The Thoughtful Architecture of Wenche Selmer*. New York: Princeton Architectural Press, 2006.
p. 19 : Drawing Sirkkaliisa Jetsonen, 2007
pp. 20, 23 top, 25 top: Drawings Margrit N. Morrow, Jesse Ian Galbraith, Megan Lubaszka, Kristyn Cosgrove, David Merlin, 2006.
p. 22 top: Photo Georg Ekholm, Museum of Finnish Architecture.
p. 22 bottom: Photo Nils Wasastjerna, Museum of Finnish Architecture.
pp. 23 bottom, 183 center, 185 left, 187 right, 188 left: Photos Museum of Finnish Architecture.
p. 30 top: Photo Einar Saarinen, 1914, Martti Saarinen family album.
p. 30 bottom left: Painting Einar Saarinen, Pulkanranta collection.
pp. 30 bottom right, 31 bottom: Drawings Museum of Finnish Architecture.
p. 31 top: Photo Helmi or Hannes Saarinen, 8 August 1903, Martti Saarinen family album.
pp. 38, 40 top: Drawings Alan Barker, Andrew Borek, Lauren Wiles, 2003.
p. 46 top: Drawing Oiva Kallio. *Arkkitehti* (Finnish Architectural Review) 5 (1930).
p. 50 bottom: Drawing Aino Aalto, Alvar Aalto Museum.
p. 50 top: Sketch Aino Aalto, 1944, Alvar Aalto Museum.
p. 51: Family album, Alvar Aalto Museum.
pp. 56, 57 bottom: Huttunen Family.
p. 57 top: Photo Kolmio, Museum of Finnish Architecture.
p. 61 top: Watercolor Erkki Huttunen, Ari Huttunen collection.

pp. 64, 66 top: Drawings Lauren Hickman, Casey Leish, Danielle Merseles, Claire Cahan, 2005.
p. 66 bottom: Siren Architects.
p. 74 middle and bottom: Photos Kaj Englund, Museum of Finnish Architecture.
pp. 72, 74 top: Drawings Brianne Culley, Teddy McCarthy, Adie Kaplan, Joel Ross, 2004.
p. 82: Alvar Aalto Museum.
p. 83: Photos Alvar Aalto Museum.
p. 85 top: Oil painting Alvar Aalto, Göran Schildt collection.
p. 94 middle left: Photo Helmi Saarnio.
pp. 92, 94 top: Drawings Bertel Saarnio.
p. 94 middle right: Photo Satu Saarnio.
p. 94 bottom, 184 center: Photo Bertel Saarnio.
p. 102: Drawing Heikki Castrén, 1980.
p. 104 top: Photos Mirja Castrén family album.
p. 108: Drawing Mikko Pulkkinen.
p. 110 bottom: Photo Mikko Pulkkinen.
pp. 118 top, 119 top: Drawings Loren Paul Stewart, Michael J. Bridges, Gavin Merlino, Matt Monahan, 2006.
pp. 124, 127 top: Drawings Laura Delaney, Emily Jane Brudenell, Mary Rose Cacchione, Tiffany Castricone, 2006.
p. 130: Drawing Pirkko and Arvi Ilonen.
p. 133: Photos Arvi Ilonen, 1970.
pp. 138, 140 top: Drawings Angela Lewandoski, Erin Hamilton, David Fruzynski, Kathryn Crepeau, 2004.
pp. 144, 148 top: Drawings Museum of Finnish Architecture: Architects Group.
p. 150: Drawings Megan Cook, Jessi Gramcko, Devon Hines, Andrew Winston Stout, 2004.
p. 158: Juhani Pallasmaa Architects.
p. 160 top: Drawings Aron Scott McKenzie, Juliana Ho, Carol Soos, Jennifer Stilley, 2007.
p. 164: Gullichsen-Vormala Architects.
p. 172: Drawing Erkki Kairamo.
pp. 174 top and middle, 175 top: Drawings by Michael Ball, Steve Plzak, Lauren Polhamus, 2005.
p. 183 left: Photo Greta Stengård, Museum of Finnish Architecture.

p. 183 right: Photo Heinrich Iffland, 1927, Museum of Finnish Architecture.
p. 184 left: Photo Alvar Aalto Museum.
p. 184 right, 186 right: Photos Siren Architects.
p. 185 center: Photo Göran Schildt, Alvar Aalto Museum.
p. 185 right: Photo Ulla Saarnio.
p. 186 left: Photo Heikki and Mirja Castrén.
p. 187 left: Photo Leif Wegström, Museum of Finnish Architecture.
p. 187 center: Photo Arvi and Pirkko Ilonen.
p. 188 right: Photo Anna-Kristiina Orterngren, 1982.
p. 189 center: Photo Matti Muoniovaara, 1986.